ALONG THE INTEGRAL MARGIN

ALONG THE INTEGRAL MARGIN

Uneven Development in a Myanmar Squatter Settlement

Stephen Campbell

ILR PRESS

AN IMPRINT OF CORNELL UNIVERSITY PRESS ITHACA AND LONDON

First published 2022 by Cornell University Press

Library of Congress Cataloging-in-Publication Data

Names: Campbell, Stephen, author.
Title: Along the integral margin: uneven development in a Myanmar squatter settlement / Stephen Campbell.
Description: Ithaca [New York]: ILR Press, an imprint of Cornell University Press, 2022. | Includes bibliographical references and index.
Identifiers: LCCN 2021047791 (print) | LCCN 2021047792 (ebook) | ISBN 9781501764882 (hardcover) | ISBN 9781501764905 (pdf) | ISBN 9781501764899 (epub)
Subjects: LCSH: Squatter settlements—Burma—Social conditions—21st century. | Squatter settlements—Burma—Economic conditions—21st century. | Precarious employment—Burma. | Capitalism—Social aspects—Burma—History—21st century. | LCGFT: Ethnographies.
Classification: LCC HD7287.96.B93 C36 2022 (print) | LCC HD7287.96.B93 (ebook) | DDC 362.83/909591—dc23
LC record available at https://lccn.loc.gov/2021047791
LC ebook record available at https://lccn.loc.gov/2021047792

Contents

Preface

In January 2021, I submitted to the publisher the final, revised manuscript for this book—a critique, in large measure, of Myanmar's so-called democratic transition. Within a month, the Myanmar military, under the direction of Commander-in-Chief Min Aung Hlaing, had arrested Aung San Suu Kyi and other senior members of the ruling National League for Democracy, annulled the results of the November 2020 election, and declared a nationwide state of emergency. The so-called transition was over.

Recognizing that a return to direct military rule posed an imminent threat to their livelihoods and their ability to organize, factory workers in the industrial zones around Yangon were among the first to strike work and take to the streets at the start of February. Convoys of workers—mostly women in their late teens and twenties, some unionized, some not—began daily trips to downtown Yangon to rally popular protests and mobilize for a general strike. Soon, the mass uprising spread to every state and region in Myanmar. Across the country, millions of ordinary people took to the streets to condemn Min Aung Hlaing and other leaders of the coup. Contempt for the military was scathing and ubiquitous, with protesters from across the country's ethnic, religious, and regional spectrum engaging with utmost determination and bravery in a diversity of creative protest tactics—from marches to musical performances to cursing ceremonies to street barricades.

The military response was merciless. Soldiers and police fired live ammunition at protesters and bystanders on the street and even into nearby vehicles and homes, killing children and adults alike. In night-time raids, police seized activists and protest organizers from their homes, taking them away to undisclosed locations. Recognizing the critical role of industrial workers in igniting the protests and mobilizing the general strike, the military leadership in late February declared illegal sixteen unions and labor rights groups, including the Yaung Chi Oo Workers Association, with which I worked closely while conducting research for this book, and among whose members I count many friends and comrades. Also declared illegal was the Solidarity Trade Union of Myanmar (STUM), a union federation at whose office I taught weekly English classes to union members throughout most of 2019. Then, on March 14, police and military forces shot and killed at least fifty-eight protesters in the working-class suburb of Hlaingtharyar. The next day, the military declared martial law across Hlaingtharyar and several other industrial townships around Yangon, including in the township where I resided while doing research for this book, and wherein the Yadana squatter settlement and its residents—the protagonists of this book—are located. As of mid-April 2021, as I write this preface, the military and police have killed over 700 civilians and seized over 3,000 activists in the postcoup crackdown. Among those abducted is my friend and comrade Daw Myo Myo Aye, director of STUM. And these numbers do not even cover the concurrent intensification of military attacks against Karen and other ethnic minority populations residing in upland areas across the country's east, west, and north. In this way, the generals have shown, yet again, that they value their own access to exorbitant wealth and to untrammeled power over the lives and livelihoods of the people of Myanmar.

But even before the coup, workers and their families in the industrial zones around Yangon were living through deep socioeconomic distress and political constraints, as I relate in this book. And amid the factory closures, job losses, constricted space for union organizing, and general economic fallout of the Covid-19 pandemic, these conditions only worsened. While the military coup and ensuing crackdown must be roundly condemned and solidarity extended to the people of Myanmar in their fight against the military's violent reassertion of direct rule, it is imperative to retain a sober critique of the so-called democratic transition that unfolded over the preceding decade. This is why I have chosen to maintain the book's existing precoup temporal vantage point; it makes clear the failures of an elitist cooption of popular demands for democratic transformation and shows consistency in proletarian aspirations for societal transformation. For in the years preceding the coup, ordinary people in Myanmar, from the industrial zones around Yangon to villages in ethnic minority upland areas, were already struggling in their everyday lives for something more than the elitist politics of bourgeois democracy. And since the February 2021 coup, the ensuing popular uprising across the country has likewise pointed towards an inclusive, egalitarian, and participatory politics that goes well beyond a mere restoration of the precoup status quo. It is in listening to the voices of ordinary people in the country and in following their day-to-day struggles that such a politics comes into view—a politics to whose realization I hope, by recording those voices and documenting those struggles, this book may contribute in some small way.

Acknowledgments

This book comes out of a collaborative research project titled *Frontlines: Class, Value, and Social Transformation in 21st Century Capitalism*, hosted by the Department of Anthropology at the University of Bergen, Norway. As a research fellow, I was engaged with the project full time from September 2018 to August 2020, after which I remained involved, but only intermittently and from a distance, as I had by then returned to Nanyang Technological University in Singapore to take up my previous faculty position in the School of Social Sciences.

As an investigative endeavor with a global focus, *Frontlines* has aimed to bring anthropological theory and ethnographic methods to bear on a critical rethinking of capitalism in the present—an analytical and political project of pressing relevance given worsening trends of gross inequality, irredeemable indebtedness, climate catastrophe, military interventions, domestic militarization, and emboldened fascist movements around the world, none of which can be adequately understood in isolation of the capitalist contexts in which they occur. In this way, *Frontlines* is situated in a long tradition of anthropological political economy, a tradition that has consistently refused economistic reductionism without shying away from broad political economic questions. Many of the ideas in this book were developed in conversation with fellow *Frontlines* participants, including Don Kalb (principal investigator), Katharina Bodirsky, Charlotte Bruckermann, Tom Cowan, Dan Hirslund, Sharryn Kasmir, Oana Mateescu, Marc Morell, Patrick Neveling, and Sarah Winkler-Reid.

For assistance in conducting field research, I am indebted to all the residents of the Yadana settlement who graciously shared their stories with me, welcomed me into their homes, and tolerated my presence at their places of work. In this respect, there are too many people to name, and in any case, I have anonymized all the settlement's inhabitants who are discussed in the book. Nonetheless, I would like to especially thank for their friendship the individuals I am calling herein Aunty Cho, Uncle Hla Soe, Brother Myo, Mister Lin, and Mrs. Sandar Oo. For further support, critical insights, encouragement, solidarity, and enduring friendship, I owe an immense debt to all my comrades at the Yaung Chi Oo Workers' Association, namely, Kyaw Zin, Naing Htay Lwin, Aye Sandar Win, Aung Thu, and Aye Myat Thazin.

During the process of writing (and rewriting) this book, I received helpful input and critical feedback on various draft chapters, and in some cases the entire manuscript, from Geoff (Soe Lin) Aung, Don Kalb, Sharryn Kasmir, Bo Bo Lansin, Gerard McCarthy, Tania Murray Li, Elliott Prasse-Freeman, Izzy Rhoads, Matt Schissler, Courtney Wittekind, and two anonymous reviewers for ILR/Cornell University Press. For parts of the book's ethnographic narrative, I received helpful input from Alexandra Shimo and fellow participants in the University of Toronto's winter 2020 creative nonfiction writing seminar. I am additionally indebted to Tania Murray Li for the mentorship she has provided over the years. And I would like to add an extra word of thanks to Geoff Aung, who, aside from commenting on an entire draft of the manuscript, has been an important interlocutor, as well as friend and comrade, for well over a decade. Many of the ideas presented in this book were developed and refined in conversation with Geoff, especially the conceptual relevance of passive revolution in understanding Myanmar's shift to electoral politics in 2010. For proofreading, I owe thanks to Hadia Akhtar Khan. If you spot any errors, I alone am at fault.

Research and writing of this book would not have been possible without financial support from the Bergen Foundation (now the Trond Mohn Foundation), delivered through the *Frontlines* project. I am also grateful to the School of Social Sciences at Nanyang Technological University, and especially Professor Teo You Yenn, Head of Sociology, for allowing me extended leave to carry out research and writing for this book. I owe thanks, as well, to Fran Benson, Ellen Labbate, and everyone else at ILR/Cornell University Press who helped push this book through to publication. And I would like to thank the editor of *Anthropology Today* for permission to include herein (as a section of chapter 3) a version of my article, "Of Squatting amid Capitalism on Yangon's Industrial Periphery," and the editor of *Social Anthropology* for permission to include (as chapter 4) a version of my article, "Debt Collection as Labor Discipline: The Work of Finance in a Myanmar Squatter Settlement." Lastly, some of the material about Myanmar's passive revolution included in chapter 1 previously appeared in the article "The Lady and the Generals," cowritten by Geoff Aung and me, which was published in *Jacobin* in January 2016.

To my parents, Anne and Bruce Campbell, I am indebted for the consistent care and support they have shown me, despite the fact that my research and travels have taken me farther afield and for far longer than they would have liked. And finally, none of this would have been possible without the support and patience of my wife and best friend, Ingyin Khaing, and our wonderful children, Oakar and Parami. To the three of them, with immeasurable love, I owe an unrepayable debt.

ALONG THE INTEGRAL MARGIN

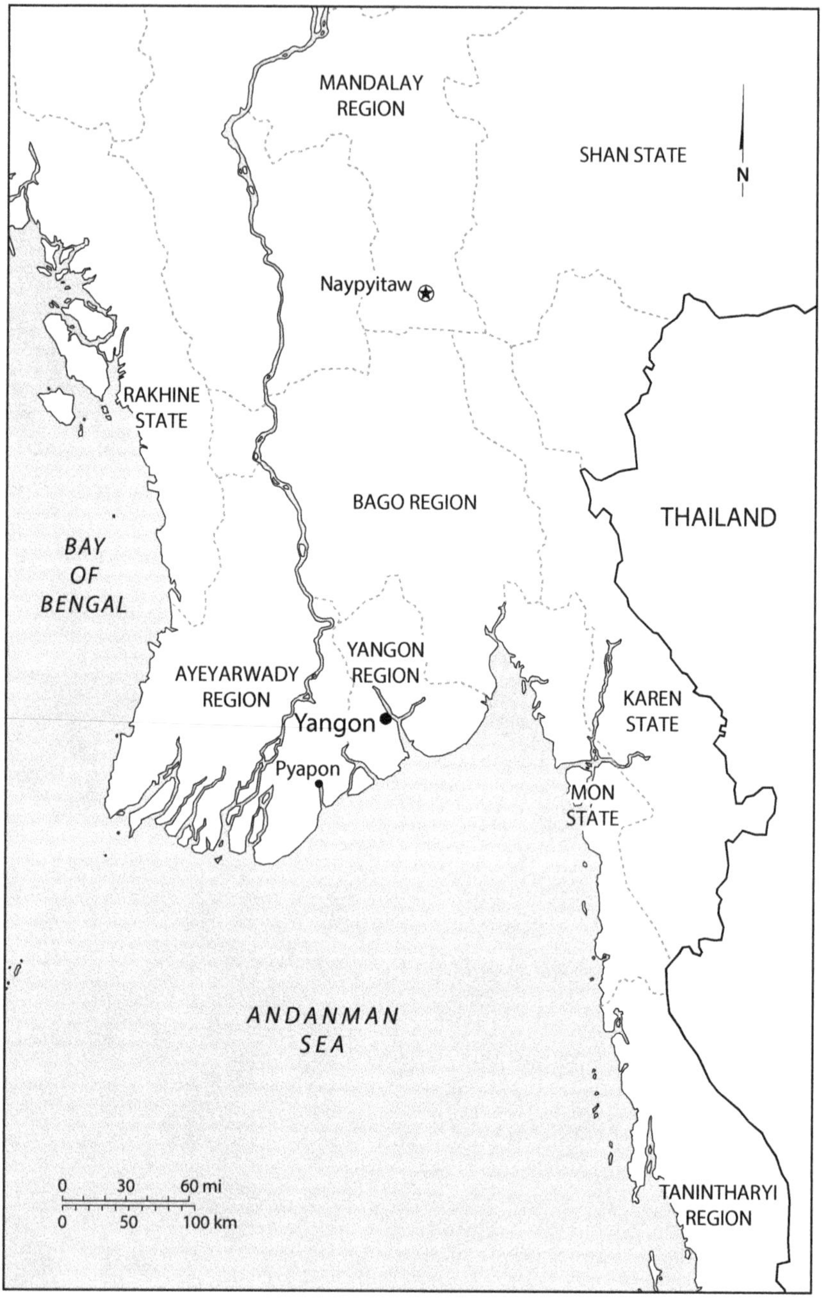

MAP 1. Myanmar

INTRODUCTION
Modernity's Integral Margins

The truth is, whatever ripples Zaw Lin Oo's death may have caused, they did not travel very far, not even in the squatter settlement where he had lived. There was Aunty Khin, of course, who said that news of the event had left her jittery (*sheinde*) such that now she dared not take discarded items lying too close to people's homes. But on this matter, she was an outlier. More common was the stoic realism of Hla Soe, likewise a waste collector, who lived at the other side of the settlement and had only heard of the incident second hand. "What can I do?" he said with a shrug. "I've got to collect plastics in order to eat."

As the proximate cause of death, the victim had suffered a punctured abdomen. But ultimately, the young man died from a loss of blood. It had obviously not helped that the ambulance took over two hours to arrive at the scene of the crime—a delay that Zaw Lin Oo's father, Mister San, recalls with no small degree of resentment. But it was the events preceding this that were more telling.[1]

Earlier that day—some eight hours before dying of exsanguination along a residential side road—Zaw Lin Oo, his eleven-year-old brother, and their father had set out from their home in Yadana, a squatter settlement sandwiched between garment factories and warehouses in an industrial zone on the outskirts of Yangon, Myanmar's former capital. As usual, the trio pushed their cart through town, collecting plastics, metals, and cardboard that others had discarded along the roadsides. Father and sons typically skipped lunch when out collecting, so afternoon arrived that day without event. Noticing an empty plastic water bottle that seemed to have been tossed aside near a small shop selling assorted packaged snacks, Zaw Lin Oo walked over and grabbed the item.

But the bottle, it turned out, had an existing claimant. The shop's proprietor—a visibly irate man in his mid-twenties—spotted Zaw Lin Oo, bottle in hand.

"Hey man! Don't take that," he shouted.

At first, Zaw Lin Oo, as though unsure, reacted hardly at all. His father, meanwhile, pushing their cart a few steps ahead, had turned to see what was happening. "Just drop it, son," he advised.

Although Zaw Lin Oo did as his father suggested, the shop owner, Mister San remembers, was persistent. "Lots of stuff has been disappearing from my store," the man asserted. "You owe me compensation."

To this, Zaw Lin Oo attempted a defense. "It's not like that, brother," he replied. "I just collect during the day. I don't take stuff at night. What do you want with us?"

It was then that the shop owner pulled out a knife—its blade so long that Mister San later spoke of it as a *ngetgyitaung*, a traditional Burmese sword. Seeing the weapon, father and sons tried to flee. But in what seemed like an instant, the shop owner had thrust his blade into Zaw Lin Oo's gut.

"He didn't even have time to beg forgiveness," Mister San recalls.

Despite his wound, Zaw Lin Oo managed to struggle free. The shop owner then reached for the younger son, but the boy slipped through the man's grasp, yelling all the while, "He's going to stab me! He's going to stab me!"

Meanwhile, Zaw Lin Oo faltered. As the young man was clearly unable to run, Mister San rushed back and offered his arm in support—grabbing, as well, the younger son by the hand. But upon making it less than a quarter of the way down the block with his father's help, Zaw Lin Oo was spent; he collapsed on the spot.

By now, the clamor had attracted the neighbors, who were filling the street, curious as to what was occurring. The assailant, having eyed the growing crowd, ran off. As for Zaw Lin Oo, lying there on the roadside, he attempted to speak. But all he could say, recounted Mister San, was "Ahrrrg, father." After that, nothing.

In due course, the police arrived, as did the ambulance, eventually.

In sober assessment, Zaw Lin Oo's father expected no justice, and there were two reasons why this was so. First, the victim was poor—a poor migrant with no political connections and but a tenuous claim to residence in a squat slated for eviction. Second, the assailant, as Mister San would subsequently discover, was the nephew of the clerk for the local ward administration, whose family enjoyed the outside benefits, it was believed, of government office. True, the assailant did have a history of violence. But in present-day Myanmar, insisted Brother Moe, a fellow squatter who sat with Mister San throughout the latter's narration, "if someone's got a lot of money, they'll prevail in a lawsuit" (*ngwe mya taya naing*).

It was an admission—and in Myanmar, spoken as a truism—to which Mister San nodded in silence. Indeed, despite questioning Mister San at the time of the incident, the police seemed to have dropped the investigation shortly thereafter; as far as Mister San was aware, the case had been closed without arrest, and rumor had it the assailant had left the township.

But why had Zaw Lin Oo been there at all, collecting discarded items—risking, it turned out, his life? His family, after all, had long been fishers. And the Ayeyarwady Delta from whence they came is renowned for its abundance of naturally occurring freshwater fish—a seasonal bounty that arrives each year with the monsoon rains and the overflowing of the estuaries.

By the time of Zaw Lin Oo's death in late 2018, it had been little more than a year since the young man had, at age twenty, quit his home village in the delta and relocated to Yangon with the aspiration of obtaining work in the city's booming construction sector. The independent fishing that had long been his family's livelihood had become increasingly unviable as consecutive elected governments, in line with a policy the country's military junta had introduced in the early 1990s, expanded privatization of inland fisheries under an auction-lease system, undoing the last of the socialist era's rural commons and dispossessing fishers across the delta.[2] "Wealthy people seized all of the freshwater ponds in the auction, so we had no more livelihood," recounted Zaw Lin Oo's mother. "We weren't permitted to fish for sale or consumption." With the mechanization of agriculture, rural wage labor, too, had declined, leading to mass outmigration of young people—to Thailand went some, but most headed to the industrial zones around Yangon. And like Zaw Lin Oo and his family, many were by then in debt.

Upon arrival in the city, Zaw Lin Oo obtained, as he had aspired, employment as a general construction laborer. But the sector's spectacular growth had not translated into a commensurate increase in formal employment; construction jobs were as a rule outsourced through intermediary labor bosses and remained casual, insecure, and in practice outside formal regulation, such that the young man could count on neither regular work nor steady remuneration.[3] On his many days off the job, Zaw Lin Oo took to collecting discarded items for resale. Before long, he left construction work, moving into informal waste collection full time, as it allowed for a more stable income. By then, Zaw Lin Oo's wife, infant son, younger brother, parents, and grandmother had all left their natal village to join the young man on the industrial outskirts of Yangon. The extended family moved into a bamboo-and-dani-palm hut in the Yadana squatter settlement, as they found the rent elsewhere unaffordable. But waste collection, too, was becoming increasingly competitive as more and more migrants to the city took it up. To obtain a sufficient income, collectors like Zaw Lin Oo and his family were compelled to push their carts farther afield while out on their daily rounds, or even, for some, to venture up close to people's homes or shops to retrieve items tossed aside, or at least seemingly so.

Unsettling the Transition Narrative

The experiences of Zaw Lin Oo and his family ill fit the narrative of transition that has come to dominate academic, government, and media accounts of Myanmar during the period of reform, which began in March 2011 with the inauguration of President Thein Sein, head of the country's first elected government in close to half a century, and ended with the military coup of February 2021. The November 2010 elections and the political reforms that followed—a relaxation of media restrictions, a release of political prisoners—led to euphoric proclamations of the country's transition from military dictatorship to liberal democracy. The World Bank, heavily invested as it was in Myanmar's political-economic restructuring, led the international chorus. Thein Sein's election, the Bank asserted, marked the start of a transition to a market-oriented economy that promised to shepherd the country's largely rural population out of "low-productivity" agrarian livelihoods and into "good, formal sector jobs" in urban manufacturing and services.[4] Going further, International Crisis Group saw an elective affinity between Myanmar's "new economy," with its more liberal investment policies, and the concurrent "political transition" to a liberal order; market-oriented economic reforms would surely challenge the monopoly privileges of the old military elite and their business cronies.[5] The "old" economy has been widely understood as one long stretch of autarkic mismanagement dating to the military's seizure of state power in March of 1962 under the banner of socialism and continuing to March 2011.[6] In this historicization, poverty in Myanmar remains but a legacy of pretransition economic mismanagement—the poor being those "untouched by the gains [of] the new economy."[7]

Several problems associated with this transition narrative deserve note. The first concerns periodization. Myanmar's military junta abandoned autarky, gave up on haphazard central economic planning, and turned to a market-oriented economy in the years after 1988, not simply since 2011. Enduring poverty is thus tied to the privatization, market liberalization, and dispossession of the "new"—that is, post-1988—economy, which has enriched a small fraction of the country's population while egregiously exacerbating economic inequality and leading in some sectors to an increase in absolute poverty.[8] The situation in Myanmar can therefore be seen as a continuation of decades-long postsocialist restructuring, thus recalling prior critical analysis of postsocialist Central and Eastern

Europe.[9] Second, the notion of political ruptures inaugurating distinct periods in the history of modern Myanmar obscures the political-economic continuities across periods and the political-economic transformations within them.[10] Finally, the transition narrative reiterates teleological assumptions drawn from Cold War modernization theory—assumptions that postcolonial histories of development have by now seriously challenged.

As a mid-twentieth century school of thought, modernization theory offered a progressive historical narrative promising broad-based livelihood gains for peoples of newly independent countries who eschewed a revolutionary redistribution of power and resources in favor of incremental capitalist growth. Capitalist industrialization, in this narrative, was to turn peasant smallholders into waged workers whose incomes and employment benefits would satisfy their social reproduction needs and allow for expanded consumption.[11] Although the strategy of import substitution industrialization that was initially associated with the theory has since been discarded, modernization theory per se has proven remarkably durable, as well as malleable—reworked as an export-oriented industrialization agenda, the global proliferation of Special Economic Zones is a prominent contemporary adaptation.[12]

Modernization theory has long been subject to detailed critique. World-systems theorists like Walter Rodney, Andre Gunder Frank, and Immanuel Wallerstein began arguing in the 1960s that modernization theory employed a methodological nationalism that treats countries as isolated units of analysis, thus neglecting their location in an unequal global order—a hierarchy of international relations that facilitates a siphoning off of value from postcolonial countries to former colonial metropoles and other neoimperialist powers.[13] In the discipline of anthropology, which informs this book, Kathleen Gough was an important early proponent of this position.[14] But modernization theory also disregards the role of inequality and social conflict within countries in shaping struggles over development processes.[15] Finally, the contemporary empirical reality of casualization, automation, and jobless growth across much of the Global South gives the lie to modernization theory's promise of something close to full employment.[16]

Modernization theory is not simply a flawed development paradigm. It is also an ideological claim deployed to oppose progressive calls for a redistribution of wealth and power.[17] It is a promise of future wellbeing demanding sacrifice in the present in return for future salvation through well-remunerated employment—an elite claim held fast amid the discrepancy between the hype and reality of unemployment and poor remuneration across much of the world.[18] In Myanmar, we see the Ministry of Labor, Employment and Social Welfare calling on workers to accept low wages and cease strikes that risk scaring away foreign investors—to make short-term livelihood sacrifices for the sake of long-term national economic development.[19] And in a prominent case of peasant protest against the dispossession of agricultural land for a copper mine, Myanmar's future state counselor, Aung San Suu Kyi, then heading a parliamentary investigation commission, rejected peasants' demands for restitution of confiscated lands. Such restitution, she argued, would likewise frighten off foreign investors, whose investments were needed to provide jobs—jobs for people like those pushed off their land to make way for foreign investments.[20]

What of Labor Outside Formal Employment?

There is a growing recognition of the limits to historicist narratives of a full transition in the postcolonial Global South from rural self-employment to well-remunerated urban wage labor.[21] In Asia, industrialization has been concentrated in spatially delimited export processing zones, whose extra-normative regulation has tended to inhibit the realization of well-paid wage labor backed by full statutory rights and employment benefits.[22] But even outside the Global South, automation, deindustrialization, and casualization continue to undermine projections of mass incorporation into the standard employment relationship, as it was once called without irony.

Arising from such developments have been searching questions concerning the relevance of prior political projects—whether liberal or radical in character—that took mass employment as a point of departure.[23] The proliferation of livelihoods outside formal wage labor has also fueled conceptual reconsiderations about what capitalism actually entails—reconsiderations that connect to earlier debates over unwaged domestic labor, self-employment, and varieties of unfree labor. Concern with the diversity of forms of labor outside formal employment has in this way become a central problematic in the contemporary rethinking of capitalism.

In this regard, the work of J. K. Gibson-Graham has informed an influential line of inquiry.[24] Starting out from poststructuralist premises, Gibson-Graham argued that anticapitalist critics had erroneously construed capitalism as an all-encompassing system—a conceptualization that made it impossible to recognize the many autonomous economic forms existing outside of capitalism. Reframing capitalism instead, and more narrowly, as coterminous with formal waged employment, Gibson-Graham proceeded to identify alternative forms of labor, such as self-employment, slavery, indentured servitude, and workers' cooperatives as noncapitalist in character, and as autonomous of capitalist logics.[25]

Gibson-Graham's work was by no means the first to attend to such nonnormative labor arrangements. The issue has long been at the heart of inquiries into capitalist development in the colonial and postcolonial world, where formal waged employment has often been marginal.[26] Arthur Lewis, for instance, writing in the early years after World War II, saw most newly independent countries as characterized by noncapitalist rural livelihoods—livelihoods that would disappear, he argued, in a transition to industrial capitalism.[27] It was along similar lines that anthropologist Keith Hart introduced the concept of the informal sector in the early 1970s.[28] For Hart, the informal sector encompassed the bric-à-brac of unregulated self-employment in the postcolonial world—a motley assortment of schemes rural-to-urban migrants adopted to support themselves until they achieved entry into formal wage labor.

It is, however, against such historicist narratives that more recent conceptual work has been positioned. Rather than undergoing mass incorporation into formal employment, rural populations dispossessed of their land—people like Zaw Lin Oo and his family—have been increasingly seen as surplus to the needs of formal capital accumulation.[29] Writing of the Indian experience, Kalyan Sanyal presented such "surplus populations" as the outcome of ongoing rural dispossession. But given a saturated formal labor market, individuals expelled from their land have, he observed, been compelled to eke out a living through precarious self-employment in the urban informal economy. This urban informal economy, argued Sanyal, while incorporated politically into a capitalist order, remains characterized by nonexploitative "classlessness" due to the predominance of informal self-employment in place of wage labor.[30] James Ferguson makes a related observation concerning individuals who, he argues, remain "functionally isolated" from capitalist production.[31] "Vast masses of poor people across the global South," he writes, "have left rural livelihoods for city living in recent decades. Yet instead of being swept up in an industrial revolution that would turn them into proletarians (as both modernization theory and Marxism might have predicted), they have more often been recruited into informal slums where they eke out a living via a complex range of livelihood strategies to which agriculture and formal-sector wage labor alike are often marginal."[32]

For Ferguson, it is not the proletarian who inhabits the urban slum or labors in the informal economy. Writing in parallel, Anna Tsing offers the case of informal collectors of wild mushrooms, foraging in the forests of the northwestern United States, whose wageless labor, subsumed though it is to a highly profitable transnational industry, remains itself noncapitalist.[33] Even Karl Marx has been read as endorsing such a circumscribed notion of capitalist labor, as being limited to the doubly free wage worker—the worker free of independent means of livelihood, but free as well to enter into contract with the employer of her choice.[34]

Heterogeneity of the Proletariat

Against such narrow framings of capitalist labor there has come to be growing analytical dissent. A large body of scholarship, much of it within global labor history, has contested the conceptual boundaries that limit capitalist labor to the doubly free wage worker.[35] Pursuing a more heterodox political economy, researchers have called attention to capitalist labor arrangements that include, along with formal and informal employment, varieties of unfree labor, unwaged domestic labor, disguised wage labor, and self-employment. Such labor arrangements have been recognized as capitalist because of a constitutive context of market compulsions, which characterizes capitalism as a mode of production.[36] These are historically particular market pressures that have emerged in consort with widespread dependence on the market and which foster a drive to accumulate capital. Amid such compulsions, owners of capital have in diverse contexts sought profit through varied relations of exploitation—at times unwaged and at times unfree. What this heterogeneity challenges is not capitalism per se but the axiomatic centrality once granted to industrial wage labor.

Crucial in pushing forward this broader conception of capitalist labor have been feminists working in the Italian autonomist tradition. Central here are Silvia Federici, Mariarosa Dalla Costa, and Selma James, who in the 1970s made critical interventions to highlight how women's unwaged labor in the home has subsidized the social reproduction of waged family members and thereby enabled profit at the workplace and the reproduction of capitalism as a whole.[37] Whereas bourgeois ideology had, they argued, framed the home as a noncapitalist sphere organized according to love and familial obligation, this ideology had in fact served to mobilize women's unwaged domestic labor while masking its exploitative character. Moreover, as Federici observed, the exploitation of unwaged workers—not only "housewives," but also slaves, colonial subjects, prisoners, and students—had been all the more effective than waged exploitation "because the lack of a wage hid it . . . where women are concerned, their labor appears to be a personal service outside of capital."[38]

Pursuing this line of inquiry further, Federici has detailed the ways extra-economic compulsions like gendered violence have been employed to regulate diverse forms of labor under capitalism.[39] Federici's position on this matter accords with that of Tithi Bhattacharya, who likewise argues that gender violence serves to discipline women's labor, notably in the expanding industrial zones of the Global South.[40] It has thus become clear that physical coercion is not truly exceptional to capitalist labor regimes. We encounter such violence in histories of slavery, where capitalist firms in Europe incorporated the slave labor of New World plantations into their global supply chains—leading, in turn, to the industrial reorganization of the labor in question.[41] Slavery, in other words, is not antithetical to capitalism. What is more, plantation slavery in the colonies subsidized and served as the organizational precedent for industrial labor regimes in the metropole, as Sidney Mintz documented in his classic study of sugar in the making of the modern world.[42] And in the present, widespread cases of human trafficking, debt bondage, and violently unfree labor persist not as exceptions but as the heterogeneous expressions of contemporary capitalism.[43]

Too often, these manifold forms of nonnormative labor have been analytically cordoned off in a distinct informal "sector" of the economy—a semantic move that maintains the conceptual purity of free wage labor as a liberal institution. However, as Jan Breman pointed out in his 1976 critique of labor market dualism, the so-called formal sector commonly relies on informal labor arrangements, such as when formally registered companies disregard legal labor protections or subcontract tasks to outworkers not covered by existing labor law.[44] Bringing Breman's critique to bear on the current anthropology of labor, Sharryn Kasmir and August Carbonella contend that the informal economy constitutes not "the 'outside' of capitalism, but, increasingly, its center."[45]

Burmese terminology is additionally helpful here in decentering the wage relation. This is because the Burmese term for proletariat, *pyitsimé lutansà*, translates into English as "propertyless class." With this conception of the proletariat, critical intellectuals in early postcolonial Burma came to understand proletarianization as referring not to entrance into industrial or other waged labor but to a wider process of dispossession.[46] Adopting this perspective, we can include as well the unemployed, the lumpenproletariat, petty peddlers, so-called surplus populations, workers in varieties of unfree labor, the incarcerated, and women engaged in unwaged domestic work—alongside industrial and other waged laborers—all within the proletariat category. It is, however, only in the twenty-first century that anglophone writers have come to fully appreciate this broader conception of the proletariat. It was thus in 2010 that Michael Denning argued, "We must insist that 'proletarian' is not a synonym for 'wage laborer' but for dispossession, expropriation, and radical dependence on the market."[47] From this perspective, it is indeed the proletarian who inhabits the postcolonial urban slum and labors in the informal economy.

Margin as Method

I proceed from the premise that the formal and informal are not distinct economic sectors, but rather mutually constitutive sides of a social whole, capitalism being in this way uneven.[48] The positing, by contrast, of an autonomous informal sector outside formal capitalism acts as ideological erasure, exculpating formal capitalist firms, state institutions, and advocates of a liberal capitalist order from the often-illiberal practices of the informal economy. This book attends to the ways such nonnormative class relations endure as the unacknowledged underbelly of formal capital accumulation. The informal margins remain, in this light, integral to capitalist modernity. This is *Along the Integral Margin*'s core thesis. Put differently, the legal-political exclusion of nonnormative labor—from employment protection laws and minimum wage rates, for example—is not merely incidental to capitalist development. In pursuing this argument, I follow longstanding feminist and anthropological critiques of dominant economic theory, which has commonly erased women's unwaged domestic labor from formal models of the capitalist economy.[49] This erasure is not solely ideological; it is grounded in the materiality of incorporated exclusion. As a term, incorporated exclusion originates in analyses of social marginalization within mixed-income neighborhoods.[50] I employ it here to label the structural incorporation of dispossessed populations into broader capitalist relations, alongside their selective exclusion from liberal labor regimes. Understood thus, illiberalism remains internal to liberalism.

Consider the so-called Standard Employment Relationship (SER), which achieved normative status under North Atlantic welfare states during the mid-twentieth century. As a concept, the SER characterized, as standard, full-time employment on an open-ended contract, performed at a designated workplace, for a single employer, with wages and employment benefits as prescribed by law. In practice, however, women, migrants, and many racialized minorities were regularly excluded from full access to these "standard" conditions of employment. The SER, with all its legal protections, was thus "never universal," writes Leah Vosko, but "nor was it meant to be."[51]

Taking a longer historical view, Lisa Lowe detailed the ways in which illiberal colonial labor regimes—African slavery and Asian indentured servitude, specifically—were intimately imbricated with the birth of liberal political orders in Europe.[52] Although slavery and coolie labor served as conditions of possibility for what eventually became liberal labor regimes elsewhere, this relationship was from the start subject to constant ideological erasure because it disrupted the universalizing claims of European liberalism. Along like lines, bourgeois political-economy has erased nonnormative forms of labor within Europe, as

Marx noted of the figure of the unemployed laborer: "The rascal, swindler, beggar, the unemployed, the starving, wretched and criminal workingman—these are figures who do not exist for political economy but only for other eyes, those of the doctor, the judge, the gravedigger, and bum-bailiff, etc.; such figures are specters outside its domain."[53]

In Myanmar, it has been the economic "transition," as a discourse and set of practices, that effected this erasure of incorporated exclusion. As the "transitional" economy fuels deagrarianization and rural dispossession, development discourse construes ex-peasants who have entered the informal economy as not yet transitioned. The role of the "transition" in producing the precarious informal economy is thereby erased. As is the crucial role of the precarious informal economy in enriching an emerging bourgeoisie and in subsidizing an emerging middle class, both of which claim privileged status grounded in the formal economy. Meanwhile, the dispossessed proletarian who inhabits the urban slum and who labors in the informal economy is told to wait for an economic transition perennially deferred.

I therefore approach the postcolonial urban "slum" not as a neglected outside, peripheral enclave, or zone of abandonment, but as a space integral to contemporary capitalism—a privileged locus from which to observe Myanmar's industrialization and, more generally, ongoing capitalist processes across much of the world. It is a methodological angle that I come to by way of Sandro Mezzadra and Brett Neilson's *Border as Method*, whereby hitherto marginal borders, border struggles, and bordering processes are engaged as centrally constitutive of capitalism's ongoing and variegated transformation—"marginal" here thus being ironic.[54] This is to say that while informal settlements like Yadana have been discursively and legally construed as external to the capitalist norm, the labor of their residents remains integral to the urban political economy. By investigating the constitutive significance of informal settlements like Yadana, I seek to shed light on the dynamic value of the labor of the site's residents—value that all too often suffers ideological erasure when the labor producing it gets construed as outside or peripheral to formal capitalist development.

A Village amid Factories

This book is an ethnographic inquiry into the lives and labor of the residents of the Yadana squatter settlement, as I am calling it here. The site, which as of 2019 comprised over 1,000 households with upward of 4,000 residents, lies between factories and warehouses in an industrial zone on the outskirts of Yangon. Covering three plots of land designated for private sale and factory construction, as well as municipal land along several adjacent roads, the settlement has been scheduled for eventual removal and relocation, although some residents remain determined to contest any such attempt at eviction.

The settlement's origins lie in Myanmar's postsocialist moment. In 1991, fifty-three households were evicted from a neighboring plot of land to make space for factory construction in what was then a newly designated industrial zone. The evicted residents relocated to the nearest of three vacant industrial plots that would come to house the Yadana settlement, whereupon they proceeded to build new bamboo-and-dani-palm homes. Over the ensuing decade, few new residents arrived, but in the mid-2000s laborers from several nearby storage and trade depots moved out of their on-site worker housing and built huts of similar fashion alongside the settlement's more established residents. The vacant factory plots on which they constructed their homes offered more spacious living than the workers' former cramped barracks, and there was at the time no significant pressure on industrial real estate—a phenomenon that would later motivate the government's planned eviction. Through what was mostly chain migration, the Yadana settlement expanded incrementally over the ensuing decade, such that by around 2016 there was little-to-no vacant land available for further construction of squatter residential units.

Almost exclusively, the settlement's residents are former rural dwellers from Ayeyarwady, Bago, and northern Yangon regions of lower Myanmar. As I expand on in chapter 2, most of these individuals left the countryside behind due to a loss of land, growing debt, declining agricultural employment, and the lingering infrastructural devastation of 2008's Cyclone Nargis. Most of Yadana's residents are ethnic Burman Buddhists (see chapter 2 for a more precise demographic breakdown). Because of the history of chain migration, as well as subsequent intermarriage, familial relations now bind many households in the settlement. These intimate kin relations, along with the rural backgrounds of the site's residents—not to mention the bamboo and dani palm construction materials, rearing of livestock, and smallholder cultivation—give the settlement a certain village character, despite the surrounding industrial context. In this way, like the blurred edge of Saigon in Erik Harms's account, Yadana violates the symbolic coherence of the city as a category of pure urbanism.[55]

As of 2016, close to half a million individuals resided at squatter settlements around the city of Yangon, with significant squatter populations also residing at other major cities in the country, notably Mandalay and Bago.[56] In English-language publications, these neighborhoods have been variously labeled slums, shanty towns, informal settlements, and squatter settlements. In Burmese, government officials and domestic media, deeming these settlements illegal, consistently refer to them as *kyu kyaw*—a term that translates into English as

FIGURE 1. The Yadana squatter settlement during the hot season, with a communal water pump in the foreground. Author's photograph.

FIGURE 2. A communal path made of sandbags in the Yadana squatter settlement. Author's photograph.

"trespasser" or "invader."[57] For the most part, *kyu kyaw* is also the go-to term among Yadana's residents in their everyday conversations, although, as I relate in subsequent chapters, this term is aggressively disputed by the settlement's more politically assertive inhabitants. Other labels that residents employ in reference to this site are *sinyetha yatkwet* (a poor people's quarter) and *palat mye yatkwet* (a quarter [built on] vacant land).

The process of rapid urbanization, with a consequent explosion of informal settlements on Yangon's industrial periphery, mirrors development patterns seen across much of the Global South. The scale of this process has been massive; by the turn of the millennium, nearly one billion people inhabited such settlements, mostly, but not exclusively, in the Global South. By 2030, this number is expected to reach two billion.[58] It was this mass urbanization, at a global scale, that led Mike Davis to speak in the early 2000s of a "planet of slums."[59] But already by the mid-twentieth century anthropologists had turned their attention to such settlements, resulting in some of the discipline's classic ethnographic studies of Brazilian favelas, South African shanty towns, and South Asian slums.[60] Since the late twentieth century, anthropological interest has largely turned away from earlier questions of political economy, which informed much prior ethnographic research on such neighborhoods.[61] This book, by contrast, builds on this rich, older tradition of political-economy-informed urban anthropology—a move to "bring capital back in," as it were, to the ethnographic study of the informal settlement.[62]

Empirically, this book is grounded in approximately ten months of ethnographic fieldwork, which began with my first visit to the township in 2016, but which was mostly conducted over an eight-month period in 2019. My initial introduction to Yadana was facilitated by a local Myanmar labor activist who invited me to the site to speak with residents regarding research I was then conducting on the restructuring of Yangon's construction sector.[63] On longer subsequent visits, I routinely traversed the settlement on foot, visiting countless homes, teashops, and places of work, at which I chatted with the site's residents about their lives and livelihoods. In some cases, I accompanied residents of Yadana to their worksites outside the settlement. And on numerous occasions, individuals I had come to know generously invited me to weddings, funerals, and annual Buddhist ceremonies held on-site. Over the course of this research, I conducted formal interviews with fifty individuals, of whom all but a handful resided within the settlement. In all but six cases, these interviews were recorded. For all interview extracts and quoted speech included in this book, I have used my own translations from the original Burmese. The names, of course, of all informants included herein are pseudonyms. As methodology, I employ in this book a mix of participant observation and oral history—the earlier account of Zaw Lin Oo's death being an example of the latter. I deviate from current anthropological convention by not writing myself into the book's ethnographic narrative; the reader can assess the merit or otherwise of that decision. Although I remain an absent presence in this book's ethnographic retelling, I have employed conventional Burmese honorifics (translated into English) that reveal my positioning by age or social distance in relation to my interlocutors. In addition, with the help of several friends in the settlement, I conducted a demographic survey of 200 households at the site, the results of which I present in chapter 2.

By focusing ethnographically on a delimited residential cluster, this book recalls the classic anthropological village studies of the mid-twentieth century. A major failing of such studies was their tendency to reify rural settlements—to assume closed corporate communities and to abstract spatially delimited units of analysis.[64] My aim here is the opposite: to engage the site in question as a space that concentrates in itself and effectively reveals broader dynamics of capitalist development in transitional Myanmar. In this way, I advance a relational anthropology, which contrasts with analyses that would construe such sites—the informal settlement, shanty town, or so-called slum—as a redundant outside, as though these spaces were detached from urban capital accumulation and the wider liberal political order.

Structure of the Book

In the chapters that follow, I investigate the socioeconomic life of the Yadana squatter settlement, not as peripheral to Myanmar's contemporary capitalist development but as constitutively integral to this development. Each chapter, following the first, ties into this overall investigative approach. Chapter 1 presents a political-economic history of state formation in Myanmar since the early twentieth century, not as the unfolding of a pregiven capitalist logic but as a series of contingent adaptations by state actors to proletarian and peasant unrest. In chapter 2, I inquire into the earlier lives of Yadana's residents, offering extended oral histories of their migration to the settlement. What these histories reveal is a relational dynamic: the dependence of Yangon's high-octane urban capitalism on processes of rural dispossession and neglect. I include as well in this chapter a demographic breakdown of the site's population. Chapter 3 then considers the ambiguity of squatting as an anticapitalist practice, whereby squatters who initially bypassed the rule of private property have gone on to profit from de facto property ownership in the settlement. Chapter 4 investigates the role of credit as a relation by which value is extracted from nonnormative arrangements of capitalist labor. Chapter 5 then considers labor arrangements that, while in principle covered by existing labor laws, have in practice remained outside such formal regulation. Along similar lines, chapter 6 investigates forms of unfree labor in Myanmar, most extensively in the offshore raft fishing industry, where many of Yadana's young men continue to seek work, despite the very real risks to their health and lives. In chapter 7, I examine several cases of squatter self-organization—cases where Yadana's residents have mobilized to address collective concerns. I then conclude the book by briefly revisiting my overall arguments and by considering some of the implications that follow from the preceding ethnography.

1

A DEEPER HISTORY OF MYANMAR'S POLITICAL TRANSFORMATION

Setting out in early 1961, the American anthropologist Manning Nash took up residence at a small dry-crop farming village in upper Burma, a short car ride from the country's one-time capital, Mandalay. It was at this site that Nash began some ten months of fieldwork for a project on the country's rural economy and politics—a project whose findings he would subsequently publish in 1965 as *The Golden Road to Modernity: Village Life in Contemporary Burma.*

Like other American anthropologists of his time, Nash's research focused on questions of agricultural development, village social organization, and local political orientations—in other words, on the challenges to, and potential for, rural capitalist modernization. All of this was done in a spirit akin to Clifford Geertz's 1963 volume, *Agricultural Involution: The Processes of Ecological Change in Indonesia.* As with Geertz's volume, Nash's ethnography drew its inspiration, albeit implicitly, from Walt Rostow's treatise, *The Stages of Economic Growth: A Non-Communist Manifesto.*

Despite the evident subsumption of Nash's project to an explicitly anticommunist agenda, it was not until 2015, in the pages of David Price's mist-clearing monograph, *Cold War Anthropology,* that it became widely known that the United States Central Intelligence Agency (CIA) had funded Nash's 1961 fieldwork, as well as Geertz's fieldwork for *Agricultural Involution.*[1] The CIA had provided these funds discreetly via the Southeast Asia Development Advisory Group (SEADAG). As a counterinsurgency strategy, the CIA had tasked SEADAG with funding social science research on socioeconomic conditions and political dynamics across Southeast Asia. The objective was to inform US economic, political, and military intervention—this in a region where the communist project remained stubbornly attractive to tens of millions of workers and peasants.

The CIA had also funded Rostow to write *The Stages of Economic Growth*, wherein the author employed his now familiar airplane metaphor to convey the economic "take off" he forecasted for newly independent countries that adopted procapitalist policies.[2] It was this book that catapulted Rostow into the role of (initially deputy) national security adviser to John F. Kennedy and then Lyndon B. Johnson. And it was in this capacity that Rostow went on to push the US government to intensify its military interventions across Southeast Asia during the 1960s.

With this abridged history of militarized academia in mind, consider the words of U Kyaw Win, former Myanmar minister for Planning and Finance, who sought, at a trade conference in the capital Naypyidaw on June 6, 2017, to reassure prospective foreign investors that Myanmar would not repeat the previous year's tepid economic performance. In an unabashedly Rostovian idiom, U Kyaw Win declared, "We see that last year the country's economy was like a plane moving on the runaway. Now this year, we will defy gravity with jet power, meaning this is the year economic development will take off."[3] Incidentally, U Kyaw Win's participation in this conference came a little over a year after Burmese media broke the news that Brooklyn Park University, the institution from which the former minister had obtained his PhD, was an online scam created by a Pakistani software company.[4] Be that as it may, soon after U Kyaw Win spoke these words, Myanmar's Ministry of Planning and Finance announced that the World Bank, which had been funding the ministry since 2013, would inject (as a loan) a further US$200 million into the national budget on condition that the government implement a comprehensive Macroeconomic Stability and Fiscal Resilience program.[5] The agenda set out a project of structural adjustment aimed at eliminating "binding constraints to private investment," the outcome of which, as part of a political and budgetary transition, was to be a proliferation of "good jobs"—an increase, that is, in well-remunerated formal employment, with rights and benefits as prescribed by law.[6]

I refer to this history of modernization discourse merely to note its persistence. As an ideology of technocratic governance and a myth of harmonious progress, modernization theory elides histories of proletarian and peasant refusal, against which it has always been a reaction. In place of such sanitized development narratives, I sketch in this chapter a different history of labor in Myanmar, as well as a different historicization of state rule—a historicization that reads state formation as a protean adaptation to proletarian unrest. In this way, I highlight a heritage of labor struggle—a heritage that endures in Myanmar in the layers of cultural sediment left by the country's tumultuous history and continues to haunt the capitalist present. But along with this chronicle of popular struggle, the deeper history that I present of Myanmar's political transformation reveals a continuity between an elitist politics of state capture in the present and that of years gone by. It has, moreover, been the struggle between these countervailing forces that has shaped the particular unevenness of Myanmar's capitalist landscape.

A Legacy of Labor Militancy

Shortly before his death in 2012, the dissident Burmese journalist Ludu U Sein Win penned a critique of Myanmar's then opposition politicians for pursuing an elitist politics distant from the struggles of ordinary people. What irked the journalist, in particular, was the practice among Myanmar's prodemocracy opposition of privileging charismatic leadership over popular participation. Pursuing this strategy, opposition politicians had, Sein Win observed, sought to identify themselves in the popular imagination with prominent anticolonial figures as a means of garnering popular consent to their otherwise elitist political projects. This strategy, argued Sein Win, demonstrated an erroneous reading of history. The reason was that "Without fully understanding the past, some assume that leaders like Churchill and Roosevelt were makers of history. And by pointing to figures such as Thakin Po Hla Gyi, General Aung San, and Saya San, they often conclude that people will follow if they are led. While it was believed that Thakin Po Hla Gyi masterminded the labor strikes of oil fields against British oil interests, it was in fact Thakin Po Hla Gyi who was born of the movement."[7]

The practice to which Sein Win referred was not new. Successive governments in Myanmar have, since independence in 1948, constructed elitist narratives of the anticolonial movement as a way to establish their continuity with the Independence struggle. The incorporation of anticolonial heroes in the foundation myths of postcolonial governments can thus be read as cynical attempts at securing popular legitimacy.[8] Maitrii Aung-Thwin, for example, showed how nationalist historians in postcolonial Burma constructed interpretations of the 1930–32 "Saya San rebellion" in ways that suggested the preindependence emergence of nationalist consciousness so as to legitimate the political claims of postcolonial elites.[9] Yet this incorporation of anticolonial martyrs into elite political narratives has ambivalent implications. As a project of rule, the celebration of popular anticolonial dissent results in an unstable unity of opposites—a claim to state authority grounded in the legitimacy of popular insubordination. This contradiction has become ever so evident amid the accelerated capitalism of Myanmar's postsocialist (post-1988) moment, for the martyrs of Burma's anticolonial struggle were so often anticapitalists as well.

Consider, in this regard, the canonization within Myanmar historiography of Thakin Po Hla Gyi—one of the three figures Ludu U Sein Win cited. As a manual laborer on the colonial oil fields, Thakin Po Hla Gyi has become iconic of proletarian participation in the anticolonial movement—a "true working-class hero of Burma's Independence struggle," as I have called him elsewhere.[10] Significantly, he was also a determinedly anticapitalist labor organizer. Amid the most momentous strike of the country's colonial period, Thakin Po Hla Gyi penned an agitational book, *The Strike War*, aimed at rallying workers across the country to join the anticapitalist, anticolonial struggle. The strike, which involved over 10,000 oil-sector workers at its peak, erupted in the town of Chauk, in January 1938, before spreading to Yenangyaung and Thanlyin (Syriam) and then ending with participants marching to Rangoon in November—facing police batons and barricades along the way. In September of that year, striking workers sold copies of Thakin Po Hla Gyi's book as a means of raising funds for the strike. The book opens with the author asserting his politics categorically: "There should be no doubt that taking hold like a great weapon of the methods included in this publication called *The Strike War* will enable the easy abolishment of the capitalist system of exploitation, oppression, and tyranny. In other words, the poor must take hold of this great weapon [the strike] that makes the capitalist robbers run for their lives trembling in fear."[11]

Here, and throughout the book, Thakin Po Hla Gyi makes two significant interventions. First, he argues that the country's independence struggle must be unambiguously anticapitalist in character. Second, he argues that it is through the direct action of the poor themselves that capitalism can and will be uprooted. The year was 1938 (1300 in the Burmese calendar) and the strike has gone down in Burmese history as the catalyst of "Revolution Year 1300," due to the ensuing protests and actions of students and peasants across the country, which amplified the significance of the oilfield workers' strike.[12]

That year has also been etched in Myanmar history for another reason: horrifically violent anti-Indian riots, which broke out in Rangoon on July 26. The riots erupted after extensive anti-Indian, anti-Muslim agitation, which several nationalist presses had carried out over the preceding months. The agitators' call to arms was a response, they claimed, to offenses against Buddhism, attributed to a local Islamic scholar. By the time the riots came to an end two months later, 240 people lay dead—181 killed by rioters, 59 killed by the colonial police.[13]

The conflictual events of 1938 occurred against a backdrop of global economic depression, which had triggered in Burma a crash in the price of rice, a major export crop, starting in 1928. The collapse of rice prices catalyzed mass dispossession of land, as farmers who had put their land up as loan collateral were compelled, on bankruptcy, to hand this property over to their creditors, a majority of whom were of the southern Indian Chettiar caste. Indian creditors obtained in this way close to 1.9 million acres of agricultural land in lower Myanmar between 1930 and 1937.[14] This rural dispossession-through-debt, and the wider economic crisis in which it played out, served as fuel to the rhetoric of chauvinistic demagogues who sought to incite Burman antipathy toward Indians of all classes; the ensuing riots were an outcome.[15]

Although the colonial oilfields employed a mix of Indian and Burmese workers, no evidence exists that the 1938 riots hurt the workers' solidarity. In fact, discussing the matter in a booklet on the riots published shortly after the event, the Burmese author Thein Pe Myint observed, "In oilfield strikes such as Yenangyaung and Syriam and some other strikes, Indian workers and Burmese workers were inseparable. And it is certain that even if the capitalist and middle-class Indians try to break their unity, they will not be divided."[16] But it was not just 1938. There had been strikes by the oilfield's multiethnic proletariat near annually over the preceding two-plus decades.[17] And it had been these multiethnic workers' strikes that had pushed the colonial government to introduce legislation legalizing trade union formation in 1926—a measure aimed at containing these otherwise disruptive actions within a procedural bureaucratic framework.

This is not to posit a spontaneous proletarian solidarity inevitably trumping ethnic division. History bellies such a claim—the history of 1930 Rangoon, not least of all. For it was in that year, at the Rangoon harbor, that an earlier episode of interethnic rioting broke out. The details of the incident, recalled by the British author and colonial judge Maurice Collis in his 1938 memoir *Trials in Burma* went like this: In May 1930, Indian stevedores struck work, demanding improved wages and working conditions from the British shipping firm that employed them. To break the strike, the firm's British managers hired Burmese workers as replacements. This move compelled the Indian strikers to call off their action, but they were nonetheless able to return to their previous jobs. Upon returning to work, the Indians displaced the Burmese who had been temporarily employed in their place. The resulting friction between the now-unemployed Burmese and the returning Indians led to verbal accusations and violent exchanges. The initially localized conflict pulled in other Burmese and Indians who were working and living in the area, leading to an expanded riot, which spread to other cities and left, in the end, over 200 people dead.[18]

The 1930 Rangoon riot highlights a pernicious structural tension in colonial capitalism—the ubiquitous racial/ethnic ordering of the economy, which J.S. Furnival, one-time Burma-based colonial administrator, would characterize as *the plural society*. Although "in all forms of society," Furnival wrote in his 1948 study of Burma's colonial administration, "the workings of economic forces make for tension between groups with competing or conflicting interests . . . in a plural society there is a corresponding cleavage along racial lines."[19] As Furnivall saw it, the tensions of plural society warranted prolonging colonial rule as a mediating and stabilizing power. But he also, contradictorily, acknowledged that this "racial" ordering of the colonial economy—involving what we would now call racialized (or ethnic) labor market segmentation—was not an inevitable result of group difference; it was the outcome, instead, of a colonial policy to "foster communal rivalry on the principle of divide and rule."[20] Colonial rule, in other words, engendered the very conflicts that it claimed in self-justification to be containing.

The outcome of racialized colonial capitalism in Burma was itself contradictory. While the ethnic ordering of the economy fueled interethnic rivalry, it also had the effect of radicalizing Burma's anticolonial movement. This was because of the economic marginalization of the Burmese. Where British, Indian, and Chinese capitalists dominated the domestic economy, this inhibited the emergence of a significant Burmese bourgeoisie.[21] There was no major indigenous capitalist or landowning class with which the mainstream anticolonial movement might enter into a coalition, a move that would have required diluting the nationalist movement's anticapitalist politics. This situation contrasts with that of colonial India, where the Congress Party was obliged to restrain its more radical anticapitalist members due to the party's reliance on Indian bourgeois and zamindari support.[22]

In Burma, from about 1930 on, the most prominent nationalist organization, the Dobama Asiyayone (We Burmese Association), was almost exclusively anticapitalist in orientation.[23] Moreover, the association's intellectual figurehead, Thakin Kodaw Hmaing, played a key role in developing a particularly Burmese form of Buddhist-Marxist syncretism, according to which socialism/communism was indigenized in the Pali compound, *lawka-neikban*, or "worldly paradise."[24] Leftist students and activists were able to push the Dobama Asiyayone to support radical worker and peasant movements, such as the 1938 oilfield workers' strike, which had among its demands, "to return to national workers the oil fields that have been in the hands of the capitalists for 50 years."[25] In addition, Dobama Asiyayone members, specifically Aung San (father of Aung San Suu Kyi), Thakin Ba Hein, Thakin Bo, Thakin Hla Pe, and Thakin Soe, were among the cofounders, in August 1939, of the Communist Party of Burma (CPB).

Crucially, however, the ethnic/racial segmentation of the colonial economy never perfectly mapped onto class hierarchy. Although Indians and Chinese comprised a significant part of the non-European bourgeoisie, they were also among the colony's many "coolie" laborers. The majority of colonial Rangoon's industrial proletariat was Indian in origin, and South Asians played important roles in Burma's anticapitalist/anticolonial movement. Such was the case with Dr. Amar Nag (Yebaw Tun Maung) and H.N. Goshal (Thakin Ba Tin), both of whom had Bengali ancestry and were among the CPB's cofounders.

This was a central contradiction of Burma's anticolonial movement: it had a strong anticapitalist orientation colored by nativist sentiment. Though anticapitalism informed domestic opposition to the colonial property regime, Burmese ideologues on the right articulated these material grievances as xenophobic anti-Indian and anti-Chinese polemics, with deleterious consequences for, especially, the South Asian proletariat. One outcome of this manipulation of grievance against foreign capital ownership was violent attacks on working-class Indians in 1930 and 1938. In rural areas, too, although Indian moneylenders had become substantial landowners through the default of peasant creditors, there were poor South Asian peasants struggling alongside their Burmese neighbors, such as the Burmese author Maung Htin portrayed in his classic 1947 novel, *Ngaba*.[26]

Both sentiments—anticapitalism and nativism—endured World War II. But the brutality of the Japanese wartime occupation of Burma contributed to strengthening domestic antifascism and bolstering the communist movement in particular. Moreover, contra elitist historical narratives, the self-organization of workers and peasants was pivotal in pushing forward the goal of independence—an objective formally achieved in January 1948. This popular participation pointed toward a radical peasant-and-proletarian democracy in place of the existing rule of property. Although subsequent elitist narratives have muddied the historical waters, the Burmese journalist, historian, and author Bhamo Tin Aung made a point, in his 1958 novel *Myaing*, of reminding the Burmese public of this important history of popular struggle. Thus, he wrote:

> [Following World War II] after the British colonialists strategically deployed their troops and annexed the whole of Myanmar, our leaders woke up with a start from their slumber. The Rakhine rebels, Leyway rebels, and Kyaukkyi rebels who raised the alarm and thus caused [the political leaders] to wake up in this way deserve our gratitude. Had our leaders not been woken up by these peasant rebels and their struggles, I can't say whether they would still be sleeping. . . . Working-class struggles, student and youth struggles, and the struggles of government employees rose up high to be recorded for posterity. Especially, it must be said that the most extraordinary thing in the history of our Myanmar national liberation struggle was the enthusiastic collaboration of the peasants with the multitude. [This collaboration] brought about the intensification of the [national liberation] struggle. The general strike of September 1946 was paramount for the post-war anti-colonial national liberation struggle of our Myanmar nationals. The huge military and the whole machinery of colonial rule that the British had established came to a halt.[27]

The Postcolonial Predicament

Burma's independence dawned over a landscape of peasant, worker, and student mobilization; widespread rejection of colonial political economy; and broad popular support for communist and socialist parties. The Anti-Fascist People's Freedom League (AFPFL)—formed as a partisan underground to resist the Japanese wartime occupation—took power as a coalition government that united CPB and Socialist Party parliamentarians. In this context, a postwar literary movement emerged that sought to focus popular attention on the lives and struggles of the country's subaltern classes.[28] It was an era in which, as the historian Robert Taylor observes, "almost every articulate politician and nationalist in the country claimed to be a socialist, Marxist, or communist."[29]

Yet the predicament of postcolonial Burma was contradictory. Even before independence, Thakin Soe and a faction under his sway had rejected the parliamentary strategy of the Thakin Than Tun-led CPB, gone underground, and adopted a strategy of armed insurrection. U Nu, Prime Minister of Burma and head of the AFPFL, became increasingly anticommunist, and in March 1948—less than three months after independence—charged the parliamentary CPB with inciting revolt. Kyaw Nyein, home minister at the time, followed by issuing orders to have the CPB leadership arrested—this for having supported a series of strikes in British-owned enterprises and for having held mass rallies against imperialism and government repression.[30] Thakin Than Tun managed to evade arrest and with him the above-ground CPB turned to a strategy of armed insurgency in the countryside. The result, in coming years, was a civil-war patchwork of communist insurgencies and armed ethnic liberation movements—a situation wherein the remaining AFPFL government became increasingly dependent on the military's support.

For U Nu, the postcolonial moment entailed overseeing a vast and largely anticommunist counterinsurgency program, while implementing at the same time his particular brand of socialist developmentalism, which sought to achieve the three goals of Burmanization, nationalization, and industrialization.[31] In this context, U Nu's development initiatives were informed by his desire to undercut popular support for the communist movement. Thus, for example, the AFPFL adopted a land reform agenda shortly after taking power in an attempt to weaken rural support for the CPB, which had long advocated land redistribution.[32] In the end, the AFPFL's land reforms—implemented piecemeal through the 1950s—remained limited and tended to benefit wealthier peasants.[33] Likewise, upon purging CPB parliamentarians from the coalition government, U Nu banned the CPB-backed All Burma Trade Union Congress and encouraged trade unions to affiliate, instead, with the Trade Union Congress (Burma), founded in 1945 by the Socialist

Party, which dominated the AFPFL coalition and held U Nu's sympathies.[34] This left, by the end of the 1950s, only a handful of independent unions, and unions affiliated with the Burma Trade Union Congress, backed by the Burma Workers and Peasants Party.[35] Meanwhile, as it endeavored to sustain a beleaguered capitalist order, U Nu's fractured and increasingly rickety government cracked down on dissent and imprisoned leftist critics like Bhamo Tin Aung.

It was because of political struggles like these that Martin Smith, in his monumental history of civil war in twentieth-century Burma, described the country like so: "Burma, since Independence, is, after all, that rarity, a country in which successive governments have been regarded as left wing, but in which the principle political opposition has come from the left."[36] The situation to which Smith referred obliged the central government, in confronting a popular communist movement, to pursue socialist policies if only to maintain some measure of legitimacy, irrespective of personal ideological commitment. It was a predicament of rule that continued even after 1962—the year the military seized state power in a coup—despite the military's restrictions on popular mobilization.

Seeking, after taking power, to remove organized opposition to its rule, the military's postcoup Revolutionary Council nullified the previously legislated role for trade unions—facilitating, thereby, their de facto prohibition. This the council did by promulgating the 1964 Law Defining the Fundamental Rights and Responsibilities of the People's Workers. Yet pursuing consent to its rule under an explicitly socialist banner, the military positioned—ideologically, at least—workers and peasants as privileged social classes pivotal to the country's prosperity. The junta may not have been sincerely committed to socialist ideals, as historian Mary Callahan suggests, but to secure its rule it nonetheless "needed strong public support from the working masses [and thus] felt it necessary to introduce new, pro-labor policies."[37] While at once rendering trade unions legally obsolete, the Revolutionary Council replaced these unions, in the 1964 law, with mass-based People's Workers' Councils, which were granted a representative role in township-level industrial dispute tribunals (*wanaikza patipekkha khonyone*). Although the law granted no legal space for workers to strike, the tribunals did provide workers with an official channel through which to pursue state-backed redress for violations of labor rights, such as are enumerated in the country's 1951 Factories Act. Officially, at least, the 1964 law aimed to establish a state of affairs in which there would "be no exploitation of the working people."[38] More instrumentally, state authorities introduced these juridical mechanisms as means to entice workers to join the government-backed Workers' Councils, and to "promote production through smooth tripartite relations between workers, the state, and employers."[39]

In this way, the military's "socialist" government pursued a project of containing proletarian and peasant discontent by embracing a limited set of popular demands, including land reform, welfare provisioning, labor protection, and increased health and education services, while rejecting democratic participation in the sense of collective self-management. Going further, the military's postcoup Burma Socialist Program Party (BSPP) pushed ahead with the nationalization of key large-scale industries, while endeavoring to remove "alien" influences in the economy, which in practice meant the expropriation of mostly Indian and Chinese-owned enterprises.[40]

It is important to keep in mind these contradictory aspects of ostensibly socialist rule in Burma when assessing the critiques of liberal historians. Economist Sean Turnell, for instance, has dismissed Burma under BSPP rule as a case of "extreme socialism."[41] BSPP ideologues, by contrast, recognized that, given the absence of worker-and-peasant democracy, their project was not truly socialist. U Chit Hlaing, the ideological architect of the Burmese Way to Socialism (the Revolutionary Council's postcoup manifesto), stated as much in his 1995 memoirs: "the Burmese Way to Socialism that existed from March 1962 to September 1988 was truly a 'state capitalism,' which was a socialist system in name, and managed by the state apparatus." Contemporary academics working outside the country reached similar conclusions. The economists Allen Fenichel and Azfar Khan, for instance, argued in a 1981 article for *World Development* that, given military-bureaucratic control over large-scale industries—namely, rice, textiles, mining, and lumber mills—amid otherwise extensive wage labor and market dependence, Burma could be said to have a centralized but not socialist economy, with military rule operating as a form of class domination.[42] Meanwhile, the prominent Bangkok-based Burma analyst Bertil Lintner, writing of the military's "socialist veneer," likewise pointed to the latter's continued ownership of capitalist enterprises following the 1962 coup.[43] It is in this regard telling that the military had, by 1970, purged the bulk of Marxists from the government (remaining ex-communists were expelled in 1977).[44] Grasped in this light, the 1962 coup can be seen as a move to uphold, rather than contest, the rule of capital.

The so-called socialist state thus came to operate as a collective capitalist. It was a fraught arrangement whose contradictions became evident in the general strike of 1974, for this was a workers' strike against a government formally committed to ending all exploitations of workers.[45] The strike began when oilfield workers gathered that year for the annual May Day rally at the Thakin Po Hla Gyi monument in Chauk, whose construction the AFPFL had sponsored in 1950.[46] While attending the rally, participants called for improved rations and wages, which inflation had eroded, and vowed not to return to work until their demands had been met. From there, the strike spread to Yangon, where workers at forty factories proceeded to walk off the job. Their action continued until June 6, when police fired on the striking factory workers, killing (officially)

FIGURE 3. Forty-five-kyat Myanmar currency note issued in 1987, bearing a portrait of colonial-era anticapitalist labor organizer Thakin Po Hla Gyi. Image by nsmm45 via Wikimedia Commons, CC BY-SA 4.0.

twenty-eight individuals, although unofficial estimates put the number of deaths at around 100.[47]

And so, proletarian subordination and exploitation persisted under the military's "socialist" state capitalism, as did growing class inequality.[48] The economy began to deteriorate significantly from the mid-1970s on. Exacerbating matters, the government implemented two consecutive currency demonetizations (in 1985 and 1987), which wiped out savings for people across the country. It was then, following the second demonetization, that the government issued two new banknotes: a 90-kyat note bearing a portrait of Saya San and a 45-kyat note displaying a portrait of Thakin Po Hla Gyi. (The curious denominations were reportedly chosen on astrological advice.)[49] Whatever the intent behind this move, it did nothing to stem widespread dissatisfaction with the military's pernicious class rule. In the end, the generals found themselves with an irremediable crisis of hegemony—they could neither deliver on promises made nor contain popular demands, as became evident in the popular uprising of 1988.

From People's Power to Postsocialist Tyranny

Adopting a practice that would come to earn Ludu U Sein Win's censure, opposition politicians in the decades after 1988 went on to construe that year's popular uprising as a foundation myth of liberal leadership. In this narrative, the Oxford-educated aristocrat Aung San Suu Kyi, who had returned to Burma to nurse her ailing mother, provided direction to the nation's otherwise inchoate protests; she claimed, it is said, her rightful place as heir to her father's legacy.[50] Subsequently, in what has become an event memorialized annually, the military, with a reconstructed junta at its helm, violently dispersed the protests—killing an estimated 3,000 or more people in the process.[51] Then, having permitted multiparty elections, the junta refused to cede power to the victorious National League for Democracy (NLD), led by Aung San Suu Kyi.

The realization of the NLD's curtailed electoral mandate thus became central to what Aung San Suu Kyi began calling the country's "second struggle for Independence."[52] A dissenting position—voiced in 1998 by the historian Michael Aung-Thwin—was that the contest between the junta and the NLD was instead an "elite struggle for the 'throne,'" reminiscent of battles over monarchical power in precolonial Burma.[53] Subsequently, scrutinizing the language that both sides had deployed in their competing struggles for legitimacy, the anthropologist Goustaff Houtman raised cautionary flags over the near-beatification of Aung San Suu Kyi and the "cult of personality" that had developed around her—phenomena that did not particularly lend themselves to participatory forms of democracy.[54]

Notwithstanding elitist accounts of 1988 and its aftermath, it is worth recalling the extensive participation and self-organization of subordinate groups amid the uprising. Fueling popular unrest that year had been the everyday frustrations that ordinary people were enduring due to economic stagnation, elite aloofness from the struggles of ordinary folk, and entrenched class inequality. The involvement of students in the protests, too, arose out of a combination of economic grievance—an increasing difficulty in paying tuition fees—and a rejection of Burma's calcifying "socialist" aristocracy. Critically, the uprising climaxed on August 8 in a nationwide general strike, wherein workers throughout the country participated in coordinated, though autonomously organized, job actions. And up until the military's violent crackdown on September 18, workers across the country hurriedly set up informal labor unions, which in their self-organization pointed toward a radical labor democracy.[55]

The reconstructed postsocialist junta reasserted control over most of the country by late September and doubled down on authoritarian rule. Amid ongoing calls for political liberalization, the generals initiated, in lieu, a series of liberalizing economic reforms, including an incremental removal of export restrictions and agricultural price controls, and of restrictions on foreign capital investment and large-scale domestic capitalist enterprise.[56] Cash-strapped and disburdened of the earlier socialist social compact, the military began selling off state assets, while reassigning ownership of still-profitable state-owned industries to military-controlled holding companies—first, the Union of Myanmar

Economic Holdings Limited (set up in 1990), and then the Myanmar Economic Corporation (established in 1997). It was, in effect, a mass conversion of public assets into private capital. In rural areas, the military began carrying out large-scale land confiscations, whereby state authorities seized "wastelands" (public forests and seasonal freshwaters, as well as untitled agricultural land), and then leased or simply handed these properties over to close associates.[57] Among the outcomes of these various regulatory changes was the emergence of a new post-socialist bourgeoisie—a class that included enterprise-owning military generals, their families, and civilian business associates like Tay Za (of Htoo Trading Co.) and Zaw Zaw (of the Max Myanmar group).[58] In Myanmar, this spider's web of nepotistic business relationships linking high-ranking military personnel and private industrialists has come to be known as crony capitalism.[59] Imbricated with these domestic transformations was increased foreign direct investment, mainly coming from Singapore, China, Hong Kong, and other East Asian countries.[60] Western investors were for the most part absent, as their respective countries had imposed economic sanctions as early as 1990.

For the bulk of wage laborers and their families, postsocialist restructuring was a decidedly painful process. The new military government shut down the socialist-era Workers' Associations (formerly Workers' Councils) and became even more draconian in restricting, often violently, workers' efforts to organize and bargain collectively.[61] Moreover, through privatization and persistent underfunding, health care, education, and social welfare were effectively outsourced to commercial elites or otherwise offloaded onto the civilian population.[62] In the expanding private sector, there was increased use of subcontractors and brokers as labor market intermediaries. And in government, there was a gradual reduction of civil servants, while many state projects, especially in construction, were outsourced to private contractors.[63] It was, in short, a moment of labor market flexibilization, particularly for those workers who had previously enjoyed privileged civil service status, or who at least had a measure of judicial protection for legislated labor rights. By the late 1990s, postsocialist restructuring and market liberalization had brought about a consolidation of rural landholdings, a heightened economic disparity, ballooning debt among the rural and urban proletariat, and an increase in urbanization and foreign labor migration due to declining rural livelihoods.[64] Meanwhile, the Myanmar army expanded militarization into ethnic minority upland areas, employing extensive forced labor on military bases and rural infrastructure.

In sum, the postsocialist military junta shifted its hegemonic aspirations from workers and peasants to an emerging domestic capitalist class, which the generals themselves cultivated through a plundering of state assets. For most of the population, however, state rule in these years was experienced as something akin to Ranajit Guha's reading of British rule in colonial India—a "dominance without hegemony."[65] Lacking popular hegemony, military rule rested on a meager base of support. It was, in part, this narrowness of support that subsequent political reforms were geared to address.

Passive Revolution

Despite the growth of domestic capitalist enterprises, the political status quo in Myanmar had by the turn of the twenty-first century become a fetter on capitalist modernization. Although foreign investment from East Asian countries was significant, ongoing economic sanctions and isolation from Western governments were keenly felt; US sanctions imposed in 2003, for instance, prohibited imports from Myanmar, which had previously exported half its garment sector output to the United States.[66] Beyond this, widespread disaffection with military rule persisted, as expressed, most visibly, in the mass street protests of 2007. The protests grew incrementally out of grievances over the increasing cost of basic goods, and culminated, after a hike in the price of fuel, in nationwide demonstrations lasting from August to October.[67]

It this context, in May of 2008, Cyclone Nargis hit the Myanmar delta—killing (officially) more than 138,000 people. The event was a moment of crisis that resulted in increased engagement with Western countries. Most visibly, international nongovernmental organizations scaled up their operations in Myanmar in response to the humanitarian emergency. And it was at this moment, eight days after the cyclone made landfall, that the military government held a national referendum on its proposed constitution. As expected, the junta announced shortly thereafter that the referendum had passed—with the approval, it was claimed, of 92.4 percent of voters. Critics decried the constitution's institutionalization of the military's role in government.[68] National elections went ahead two years later, in November 2010, with the military-backed Union Solidarity and Development Party coming out victorious; the NLD, having boycotted the elections, was sidelined.

Many foreign observers, while initially skeptical, came to see the March 2011 inauguration of President Thein Sein as marking the start of Myanmar's transition to liberal democracy. And indeed, to the surprise of many observers within the country and abroad, the new government took initial steps toward political liberalization. Six days after the elections, Aung San Suu Kyi was released from house arrest. The new government immediately relaxed restrictions on the media. And parliament passed legislation (in October 2011) legalizing trade union formation and (in March 2012) formalizing tripartite collective bargaining.

This latter legislation—drafted with support from the International Labor Organization—was explicitly aimed "to ward off strikes" by channeling workplace grievances into institutional mechanisms.[69] However, many workers found these mechanisms inadequate and thus took the opportunity provided by the new legislation to increase strikes. As a result, 2012 opened with an upsurge in worker mobilizations, leading to a wave of factory strikes across Hlaingtharyar, Shwepyithar, and Hmawbi industrial zones. By May, 36,810 workers at fifty-seven factories were out on strike, and by June, strikes had spread to over ninety factories.[70]

Notwithstanding the increase in worker strikes, the new labor legislation and broader sense of political liberalization were sufficient to assuage the concerns of Western governments, all of which proceeded to remove their sanctions on trade and investment in the years following the 2010 elections. Major international corporations, which had previously been wary of having their brands tarnished by association with the country's blatantly illiberal labor practices, likewise embraced the opportunity to invest in what was among the cheapest labor markets in Asia.[71] In this rapidly transforming context, Western financial media could not contain their enthusiasm—in one case, pronouncing investment opportunities in the country as being akin to "a gold rush."[72] Likewise, *Forbes* magazine labeled Myanmar as the "last frontier" for windfall investment payoffs.[73] Before long, international apparel brands like H&M, Zara, Adidas, and Gap were sourcing their products from Myanmar's nascent garment and footwear industry.[74] Academic appraisals, though more reserved, were expectant, seeing these changes in policy and practice as marking Myanmar's "tentative renaissance."[75]

Writing from his prison cell in southern Italy in the early 1930s, the communist political theorist Antonio Gramsci drew on the concept of *passive revolution* to grasp the political implications of Italy's fraught nineteenth-century *Risorgimento*. Passive revolution, in Gramsci's usage, referred to a top-down reformist project by which ruling elites sought to bolster their precarious political position in the face of dissent and revolt by popular masses who had rejected the dominant class's claim to govern in the general interest. Confronting such revolt from below, the Italian state had pursued, Gramsci argued, a "revolution without a revolution," a partially progressive project of modernization that would hedge against a complete bottom-up revolution in state power.[76] To maintain its dominance, Italy's old aristocracy was compelled to allow liberal political opponents and new class fractions into the ruling coalition, while granting limited concessions to popular demands as grounds for a renewed hegemony. The outcome in Italy by the early twentieth century was a new historic bloc—a reorganized ruling coalition bolstered by reformed state institutions and a refounded claim to govern in the general interest, all of which maintained bourgeois political power and the continued subordination of the subaltern masses. By adopting a limited set of liberalizing reforms as a strategy to maintain class rule, the Italian bourgeoisie had opened up a contradictory political arrangement, which was unable to deliver on its progressive promise, but which provided limited institutionalized space for new counter-hegemonic movements by subordinate classes. This is to say that Italy's passive revolution was never able to resolve the contradictions of bourgeois rule or to contain proletarian dissent.

As a project of bolstering class rule, coopting formal political opposition, and subverting popular demands for more radical political change, passive revolution as a concept offers a precise summary of Myanmar's so-called transition.[77] Simply put, the country's middle and upper classes came under the sway of bourgeois hegemony, while a neoliberal growth consensus came to reign across the formal political spectrum and in civil society. The generals and their cronies were thus able to step back from formal politics, confident that the new political order would protect their property, while reaffirming their position of moral-political leadership.

In Myanmar, too, the passive revolution was not able to resolve the contradictions of bourgeois rule or to fully contain proletarian unrest. As previously noted, the introduction of relatively liberal labor legislation was followed in early 2012 by a new wave of workers' strikes. Since then, strikes of this sort have been regular occurrences in the industrial zones around Yangon. In early 2015, for instance, approximately 5,000 workers employed at five garment factories in Shwepyithar Township staged a joint five-week-long strike. In response, township authorities dispatched civilian vigilantes and baton-wielding police to violently disperse the workers' strike camp. Dozens of the mostly women protesters were injured in the crackdown, while the police detained two journalists and fourteen striking workers, five of whom were sentenced to two-year prison terms.[78] Meanwhile, 2011 saw the eruption of antidispossession struggles by smallholder farmers in Sagaing Region—individuals who had been pushed off their land to make way for a copper mine jointly owned by the military's Union of Myanmar Economic Holdings Ltd and China's Wanbao Mining Copper Ltd. Citing draconian laws prohibiting protest, police attempted over the ensuing years to break up the entrenched strike camp, launching incendiary white phosphorus at protestors in November 2012, and firing rifles at protestors in 2014, killing a fifty-three-year-old woman involved in the ongoing demonstrations.[79] In September 2014, university students began a nationwide protest in opposition to the government's legislative tightening of control over higher education.[80] The campaign ended six months later when some 500 baton-wielding police attacked around 100 protesting students who were trying to march through Bago Region to Yangon; dozens of the students were injured and arrested. To this violence, Aung San Suu Kyi responded by warning the students against further engagement in extra-parliamentary activism.[81]

In this way, "transitional" Myanmar saw subaltern classes and urban activists rejecting the emerging institutional arrangement, which subverted the emancipatory aspirations that have long motivated popular opposition to military class rule in the country. Grounding this new arrangement was a foreign investment-driven development agenda that aimed to insert Myanmar into global commodity chains as a low-wage, low value-added export economy—an agenda unable to deliver on its promise of stable, secure livelihoods for all. Despite, for instance, an increase in cash incomes, wages in labor-intensive sectors have been unable to keep pace with the country's rising cost of living.[82]

This, then, was Myanmar's "transitional" moment—a moment of growing dissatisfaction with the emerging status quo, motivating popular struggles for a more equitable and emancipatory democracy. It was amid this dissatisfaction and dissent that a virulent Buddhist nationalist movement emerged, which fueled a series of anti-Muslim pogroms—first in Rakhine State in 2012 (leaving almost 200 people dead and close to 140,000 displaced), then in Meiktila in 2013 (leaving 40 dead and 61 wounded), followed by similar incidents that year in Okkan, Lashio, Kantbalu, and Thandwe.[83] Then, in August 2017, following attacks on police posts and a military base in northern Rakhine State by the Arakan Rohingya Salvation Army, the Myanmar military violently expelled some 725,000 mostly Muslim Rohingya across the border into Bangladesh.[84]

Aside from the brutality of the riots and of the expulsion of the Rohingya, the events served to further incite extremist Buddhist nationalism and to embolden chauvinistic demagogues demanding popular allegiance to the Myanmar military.[85] Among the latter was the vitriolic monk Ashin Wirathu, who called on Myanmar's Buddhist majority to pledge their fidelity to the military and to reject demands for constitutional reform, which would otherwise subordinate the military to civilian oversight.[86] It has been well documented that the primary financial backers of nationalist monks like Wirathu have been military elites and their business cronies.[87] Such facts unveil ethnic chauvinism as a narrow class project.

The project of foreign investment-driven capitalist modernization remains unable to deliver on its promise of good jobs for all, specifically for the millions of individuals pushed out of the rural economy. Elite appeals to Buddhist nationalism thus serve as an alternative ground for hegemony amid ongoing dispossession, abandonment of social welfare provisioning, and the basing of economic growth on the backs of precarious workers excluded, if only in practice, from legislated labor protections. Here, the rise of anti-Muslim rhetoric and violence recalls the events of 1938, when anti-Indian riots broke out during the oilfield workers' strike and the year's wider anticolonial uprising. In regard to the threat that such interethnic violence posed to proletarian emancipation, Thakin Po Hla Gyi asserted the following shortly after the events in question:

> Each time these riots have occurred they have caused the uprisings of the poor against the capitalists to fade from public attention. The capitalists' stratagem of causing dissension has been able to bring about division between those who have been close. . . . It can be seen that each time a strike uprising occurs an Indo-Burmese riot follows and covers over the strike. . . . It can be immediately seen that with the emergence of each Indo-Burmese riot, the capitalist government promulgates in reference to that riot many new laws and imposes restrictions on political activities. . . . We slaves are engaged in petty internecine fighting. There is no prestige in it at all. And we fail to get at the real issue. . . . We should understand that by stirring up religion and ethnicity the matter of the poor vanishes.[88]

What Thakin Po Hla Gyi underscores here is the contradictory character of ethnoreligious nationalism. For such a nationalism provides ideological scaffolding for the enduring subjugation of, among others, the Burman Buddhist working class, despite claiming for the latter an ambiguously privileged position in an ethnoreligious polity.[89] Although such ethnoreligious nationalism is not the focus of the present book, it informs, nonetheless, the political-ideological context of the precarious labor arrangements examined in the chapters that follow.

2

FROM RURAL DISPOSSESSION TO PRECARIOUS URBANIZATION

Ultimately, the rampaging elephants got to be too much. "One year, there was no problem," recounted twenty-five-year-old Su Mway, nearing the final month of her first pregnancy, "but the next year, elephants trampled through the village, destroying homes and killing people." "In the end," the young woman continued, "I didn't dare stay there anymore." The animals—wild elephants that lived in herds of up to fifty members—had long inhabited the forests around her native village, located at the uppermost edge of Yangon Region, where the Bago Yoma mountains encroach from the north. Yet she does not recall them ever behaving like this before. In any case, it was not something she cared to endure. Acquiring contact information for an aunt residing at the Yadana squatter settlement, who labored as a porter at a riverside gravel depot, the young woman, as yet unmarried, left her home behind and relocated to the industrial zone—holding onto hopes of a decent living, and of a life free of rampaging elephants.

In making this journey, Su Mway was not alone. Herself included, twenty-five members of her extended family—various siblings, cousins, and their sundry offspring—had left the village, albeit separately, for Yadana, which lay some eighty kilometers to the south. All sought to escape the elephants. But it was Su Mway's cousin, Ngwe Sein—now living in Yadana with her listless alcoholic husband in a one-room bamboo shack she rented a short walk down a dirt path from Su Mway's own residence—who pointed to a more enduring problem: the elephant stampedes had arrived after years of declining rural livelihoods. For the most part, machinery had displaced agricultural wage labor, leaving landless rural dwellers with little basis for an income. The trouble, Ngwe Sein stated matter-of-factly, was this: in the village, "the work and livelihood situation isn't sufficient."

In her account, these issues were connected; local villagers—mostly former agricultural wage laborers now out of work—had begun hunting elephants in what remained of the surrounding forest to satisfy an expanding market in China. The increase in elephant poaching in Myanmar has been driven, in particular, by an inflated demand for the animals' skin, which traders have marketed as having medicinal properties—able to cure, they proclaim, such ailments as eczema.[1] But to the elephants, these hunters, Ngwe Sein confided, were traitors (*thitsa phauk*), as humans and elephants had in that area long coexisted in peace. Had not the villagers traditionally, and in deference, spoken of the elephants of the forest as saintly beings (*bodaw*)? The animals were, she believed, taking their revenge for the villagers' disloyalty. But such disloyalty aside, the area had been massively deforested in the preceding decades, and forests that once offered cover for elephant herds had since been replaced by vast rubber plantations. With the terms of peaceful coexistence thus violated, neither elephant nor villager seemed able to secure dignified rural lives. Whatever the accuracy of Ngwe Sein's reading of events, the facts of agricultural mechanization, a consequent decline in agrarian employment, deforestation, a mass expansion of rubber plantations, and increased elephant poaching—to say nothing of land confiscation and other forms of rural dispossession—are well documented in Myanmar amid marketization since 1988.[2]

Government accounts of internal migration in Myanmar have, as a rule, omitted this history of post-1988 economic transformation.[3] Intergovernmental agencies and the domestic media have largely followed the government position on this, such that rural-to-urban migration is portrayed as at its root driven by the attraction of burgeoning wage labor in the city, with the push factors of internal migration understood as isolated household crises, decontextualized debt, or ostensibly apolitical natural disasters, like Cyclone Nargis. At their most structural, these narratives have portrayed rural dwellers as relocating to the city to benefit from dynamic urban capitalism while escaping preexisting rural economic stagnation.[4] Such accounts are partial at best. Aside from legitimating subordination in wage labor, they present a skewed historicization of poverty in Myanmar as but the legacy of pretransition economic mismanagement, with the "economic transition" construed as beginning with the shift to quasi-civilian rule in 2011.[5] In this way, rural poverty is rendered external to contemporary capitalist processes—the rural poor at a loss for being "untouched by the gains [of] the new economy."[6] What gets missed in such portrayals are the ways indebtedness, rural poverty, land dispossession, loss of livelihood and consequent expulsion from the countryside are very much a part of Myanmar's ongoing political-economic transformation, which began in the years following 1988, not only in 2011. We see such an omission in a 2016 World Bank report on internal migration in Myanmar, which identifies landlessness as a key factor informing rural outmigration but avoids mentioning widely documented patterns of land confiscation.[7] It has thus been left to civil society organizations to trace this relationship between outmigration and land confiscation at the hands of military and business actors—a process of violent dispossession in the countryside that underpins urban wage labor.[8]

A relational understanding of rural-urban development in Myanmar consequently demands an analytical appreciation of the ways urban capitalism is thus imbricated with and made possible by ongoing rural transformations, including state policies and practices that neglect or undermine existing rural livelihoods and the enduring violence of rural expulsion. Capitalism, it must be stressed, is not simply a matter of market opportunities, but more significantly of market compulsions.[9] In Myanmar, such market compulsions intensified under postsocialist economic restructuring, and continue to inform rural outmigration, whether to elsewhere in Myanmar, or internationally. I stress this point not to dismiss the aspirations of migrants to the city or to romanticize an earlier village life, but rather to situate migrants' desires in Myanmar's changing political economy.

Irrespective of the drivers of migration in Myanmar, the scope of internal migration in the country is profound. Using a definition of internal migration as "inter-township movement of more than 6 months," the 2014 Myanmar Population and Housing Census provided a figure of 9,391,126 internal migrants, or about 18 percent of the country's total population.[10] That figure has since grown, and it is expected to continue growing into the second quarter of the twenty-first century.[11] As the states/regions of highest outmigration, the International Labor Organization lists, based on its own surveys, Ayeyarwady and Bago.[12] These happen to be, along with Yangon Region, the states/regions of origin for the bulk of Yadana's residents. And in Ayeyarwady Region, from where most of Yadana's residents hail, 60 percent of outmigrants have chosen Yangon as their destination, with 69 percent of said individuals considering their migration permanent.[13] One implication of this mass urbanization is that the proportion of Myanmar's population residing in cities continues to expand, and is expected to double as a proportion of the country's total population, from 13 percent in 2016 to 30 percent in 2030.[14] Such urbanization accounts for the rapid expansion of informal settlements along Yangon's urban periphery, which now house close to half a million residents, or nearly 10 percent of the city of Yangon's population.[15] What these statistics suggest is that Yadana's residents—in their places of origin, their destination, and (it is fair to conjecture) their migration experiences—lie near the demographic median, or are at least well within Myanmar's urban norm.

Of Cyclone Nargis and That Which It Wrought

It is possible that Uncle Hla Soe, a most solemn man, wore the smile he presented above his wispy gray goatee as an act of politeness so as not to burden others with the emotional weight he carried. In any case, his demeanor had, years before, been otherwise. "In the past," related one of his adult daughters, "he was really bad. He would sell everything we had to buy alcohol." But Uncle Hla Soe, now fifty-five years old, had ceased such intemperance some thirteen years prior when he made a vow to that effect with an adept of the esoteric Shweyinkyaw sect, who had promised in return to instruct him in the ways of occult healing. That had been the first of Uncle Hla Soe's life-changing encounters. Cyclone Nargis, two years later, had been the second. The storm took three of his children in a single night—three dead among (officially) over 138,000 killed or left missing when the storm made landfall in the delta on May 2, 2008.[16] Uncle Hla Soe had at the time been living in a village outside of Labutta, having moved there from his natal township to the north some four years prior in search of employment in the inland fishing industry. With him were his wife Aunty Cho and three of their five children; their two eldest daughters lived elsewhere.[17]

On the day of the cyclone the wind and the rain picked up a few hours past noon; the storm surge began soon after. To escape the deluge, inhabitants of the village's hundred or so households fled to the residence of the largest local landowner—his multistoried home being grandest by far. But the inundation continued. By evening everyone had mustered on the upper floor, with some then ascending atop the roof as though to the crow's nest of a sinking schooner. Uncle Hla Soe saw to it that Aunty Cho, their four- and eight-year-old daughters and their one-and-a-half-year-old son made it into a little boat to keep out of the rising water. But it was dark, and the wind was blowing, and the water was choppy. And the wind and waves took that little boat and smashed it into a coconut tree jutting out from the water. And the boat capsized, and into the rush of water went its passengers. "At that time," narrated Aunty Cho, "I was swept away from my children. The boat sunk and there was nothing left. I could hear one of my daughters frantically calling out to me. I could hear her voice, but I couldn't see her. It was night and everything was dark. I was bobbing up and down in the water. I had been holding two of my children, but they slipped out of my grasp. I was never even able to find their corpses." Uncle Hla Soe, meanwhile—by then likewise bobbing in the water as he hugged a floating wooden plank—managed to seize hold of a branch of a siris tree as he drifted past. He held tight to that branch the whole night through, while all around him persisted that walloping gale, those gnashing waves.

It was not until afternoon the following day that the storm abated, and the waters receded. "When the water subsided," recounted Uncle Hla Soe, "there was nothing left. The entire village had been swept away. There was just me—the only person left in the whole village." Somehow, Aunty Cho had ended up alive in the next village over. Their three children, however, were gone. Dead, as well, was almost every other inhabitant of the village.

There was nothing for Uncle Hla Soe and Aunty Cho to do, it seemed, but head north—a two-day, multistage journey by boat upriver to their natal village outside Myaung Mya, where the pair had extended family residing. But as much as it had decimated the region's workforce, the cyclone had devastated the delta's infrastructure. Uncle Hla Soe and Aunty Cho sought to get by on wages from assorted casual jobs—at rice mills, for instance, and in the local fishing industry. But on most days there was no work. And in the ensuing years conditions failed to ameliorate. Thus, five years on, the couple's situation had improved little. By 2013, Uncle Hla Soe's younger brother had already quit the delta. Relocating to an industrial zone on the outskirts of Yangon, the latter had found casual but consistent employment as a porter, loading and unloading deliveries of sand, bricks, and gravel at a riverside depot, which lay but minutes down the road from the Yadana squatter settlement.

Departing by bus to join said brother, husband and wife were among hundreds of thousands of delta residents who made their way to Yangon's urban periphery during those years to escape the devastation and enduring economic malaise that Nargis had left in its wake.[18] "In my hands I had nothing left," recalled Uncle Hla Soe of the journey. "By 'nothing left' I mean we had only pots and plates with which to eat—one rice pot, one pan, and three plates. That's all that we brought with us to Yangon." Such migrants—Nargis refugees (*nagit dokhkathe*), as many continue to self-identify—were to become the largest contingent of Yadana's population. Although the storm may have been a proximate catalyst for migration, most migrants from Nargis-affected townships did not immediately leave for Yangon. It was instead the lasting economic distress tied to infrastructural devastation that prompted so many to leave in the years that followed. On this matter, critics pointed to the military government's poor handling of postcyclone assistance and recovery.[19] It was as if the junta were more concerned with pushing through, a week after the cyclone, the national referendum to ratify its new military-drafted constitution. But with the delta in ruins, military authorities were compelled to postpone the referendum in seven of Ayeyarwady's twenty-six townships.[20]

Logistical hurdles aside, observers were incredulous of the junta's claim of a 99 percent turnout for the referendum with approval of over 92 percent of ballots cast.[21] Meanwhile, the devastation endured. "Employment was scarce," recalled Aunty Cho of the delta in the years after Nargis. "And getting only 3,000 or 4,000 kyat [US$ 2.00–2.30] a day—how were we supposed to eat?," to which added Uncle Hla Soe, "There were only rice mills left. This person had no work; that person had no work. That's why we ended up in Yangon."[22]

For four years the couple labored as porters, loading and unloading sand, bricks, and gravel delivered by boat to that riverside depot, during which time they resided in on-site worker housing. Aunty Cho, meanwhile, gave birth to two more daughters. But laboring all those years, Uncle Hla Soe developed a repetitive strain injury in his foot, and a doctor he consulted advised him to cease such heavy labor altogether. When Aunty Cho, by then in her forties, was likewise unable to continue portering, the boss promptly evicted the couple and their two daughters without a single kyat in compensation paid to Uncle Hla Soe for the foot injury he had incurred on the job, or to the couple for their years of hard labor. Husband and wife then moved down the road and into a rental shack at the Yadana settlement. As a means of livelihood, they began collecting for resale waste that had been discarded along nearby roadsides.

Shortly thereafter, a man working for the Municipal Development Committee approached Uncle Hla Soe and informed him that he could make monthly payments to obtain monopoly collection rights over the neighborhood garbage dump—or, more properly, the local refuse transfer point. It was an offer that Uncle Hla Soe readily accepted, and for which he considered himself fortunate. Not once, however, did Uncle Hla Soe receive any sort of receipt for the 30,000 kyat fee that he proceeded to pay each month to get those collection rights. It was an unofficial arrangement, found only on Yangon's outskirts. Downtown, by contrast, municipal authorities employ waste collectors on fixed salaries to maintain neighborhood refuse drop-off points. In the peripheral township where Yadana is located, however, folks at the Municipal Development Committee had evidently figured out that not only could they avoid the cost of employing refuse workers, but informal waste collectors would be willing to pay them for exclusive rights to scavenge at, and thus maintain, such refuse drop-off points.

Unofficial though the arrangement may have been, there they persisted—one family among thousands who as a means of livelihood had turned to collecting discarded plastics, metals, and cardboard for resale; one family among hundreds of thousands of migrants who had relocated from the countryside into squatter housing on Yangon's urban periphery. "The truth is," reflected Uncle Hla Soe, "if Nargis hadn't happened, I wouldn't be living here."

FIGURE 4. The home of Uncle Hla Soe and Aunty Cho, behind the local refuse transfer point near the Yadana squatter settlement. Author's photograph.

The Vagaries of Debt-Driven Migration

There on her veranda, alongside baskets of betel leaves and areca nuts, but always within reach, Aunty Yu Maw, who due to a year-old back injury would be lying laterally recumbent on a mat rolled out on the floor, kept a three-foot-long bamboo slat, affixed to which was an undersized plastic basket, little wider than a hand's breadth, little longer than a hand's span. With this contrivance, Aunty Yu Maw could, without sitting up, pass to her customers their orders of betel leaves and areca nuts, their little pouches of lime powder, their selected tins of tobacco mix, or their other choice additives for inclusion in personalized betel quids. In this manner, Aunty Yu Maw labored much like hundreds of Yadana residents who sought to get by selling petty commodities from out of the front of their homes in the settlement.

Now fifty-four years old, Aunty Yu Maw had lived six years at Yadana, residing there with her husband, adult son, and two daughters. The family had upon arrival purchased a rundown shack for 250,000 kyat, which they promptly tore down and rebuilt. It was from out of that bamboo and dani palm structure that Aunty Yu Maw sold areca nuts and betel leaves—a situation quite different from her family's former life as successful rice and mung bean farmers owning twenty acres of agricultural land outside the town of Lemyethna in northern Ayeyarwady Region. Most of that land Aunty Yu Maw had inherited from her parents, and of her childhood there she recalls a comfortable peasant life, which had continued as is until the deteriorating conditions that followed 1988.

As Aunty Yu Maw recollects, the early 1990s were marked by the introduction of chemical fertilizer and pesticides, the proliferation of crop-destroying insects, increasingly erratic flooding, peasant indebtedness, and the eventual consolidation of Lemyethna's agricultural land in the hands of the township's wealthiest residents. These were all factors, believed Aunty Yu Maw, motivating the gradual outmigration of villagers from the Lemyethna countryside.[23] As she went on to explain:

> Insects were constantly eating the crops, so [farmers] had to continually apply insecticide, fungicide, fertilizer, and other chemicals from foreign countries. And after the harvest [the farmers] would have to repay those chemical sellers, who in that way got rich . . .
>
> In the BSPP era, they [insecticide and other chemicals] weren't necessary. At that time, the peasants had enough to eat. But now, ever since those chemicals appeared, insects have become more abundant. So sometimes I think it was the insecticide that caused the insects to proliferate. Is it the insecticide that has produced the insects? In my mind, I actually think that's the case.
>
> By now, that insecticide has been around for a long time. After that insecticide appeared, many cultivators became impoverished. Back then, it was rich people who had [who were able to afford] those chemicals. The peasants gradually became impoverished and one reason was those chemicals. In the end, when the harvest was done, due to the costs of insecticide and wages for laborers, there was nothing left for us. The peasants have in that way become impoverished.
>
> Some people are very lucky because they have thirty, forty, a hundred lakh to spend on insecticide and are therefore able to profit and become wealthy. As for the people who can't afford all the insecticide that's required, it's as if they cause the insects to proliferate. Eventually, all that's left is a bill for the insecticide and those various other chemicals. In the end, it's the people who are able to apply those chemicals who succeed. The people with only small fields gradually find themselves in a difficult situation and have to sell off their land to those wealthy people.
>
> For some people, it's like this: they do agriculture and, like I said, they become impoverished. They try, but they can't defeat the insects

> because they don't have enough capital, and gradually they have to sell off their land. They sell off their land and the rich people gradually get more land and are able to invest capital. Those rich people can handle the costs. And so, the people who have lots of money come to own more land and become wealthier. It's like that.

Aunty Yu Maw's observations regarding insect outbreaks following the introduction of pesticides and chemical fertilizer recall classic critiques of the Green Revolution and its aftermath across South Asia and elsewhere.[24] But more than just insects, the annual monsoon flooding in the Lemyethna area became increasingly severe beginning in the early 1990s, a phenomenon that Aunty Yu Maw connected to a changing climate, and which negatively impacted rainy season cultivation. "In the past," Aunty Yu Maw explained, "the situation was alright. What I mean by 'alright' is that the weather was regular. But later, gradually, the weather became irregular. And the flooding became really severe. Since the flooding was severe, it brought sand and debris onto our fields. As a result, the situation for the peasants was no longer alright."

Exacerbating matters, the local government responded by relocating Lemyethna town to the opposite bank of the river and constructing a riverside levee to prevent flooding into the new town. However, the levee diverted even more floodwaters to the old town and the surrounding agricultural land. For peasants like Aunty Yu Maw, who had remained behind, the effect was to further exacerbate the flooding. All told, with the insect infestations, the high costs of pesticides and chemical fertilizer, and the increased flooding, alongside more general postsocialist inflation, the result was an increase in rural indebtedness. Aunty Yu Maw continued:

> Since they've got nothing to eat, the peasants take advances from wealthy people. As soon as they harvest their crops, they have to repay that debt. So [the peasants] have nothing left to eat. Everything ends up in the hands of those rich people. We had debt of course; the reasons we came here included debt and the failure of our agriculture. Now we're in Yangon, but we're still repaying the debt that we incurred in the countryside. We couldn't have repaid it had we stayed in our village. I don't even know how the people still in the village are able to get enough to eat. As for us, since we couldn't repay our debt, we had to hand over some of our land to our creditor. It's mostly people who have debts who leave the village.

Reflecting broader patterns of chain migration in Myanmar's urbanization process, Aunty Yu Maw, her husband, and their three children relocated to Yangon, and eventually to the Yadana settlement, following a younger brother and his wife who had previously moved to the city from Lemyethna when agricultural employment in the area dissipated. Said Aunty Yu Maw:

> They [that brother and wife] had been living hand to mouth in the countryside. Gradually, agricultural employment in the countryside diminished. It was because the natural climate wasn't regular any longer. The rains destroyed [the crops]. The winds destroyed [the crops]. The insects destroyed [the crops]. As a result, the situation for peasants wasn't okay. And since the peasants' situation wasn't okay, the coolie laborers who had been living hand to mouth were out of work. So they [that brother and his wife] were the ones who initially came to Yangon. Since they arrived first, husband and wife were able to get casual jobs laboring in sand and gravel depots. As a result, they were in a decent situation. So my younger brother was here and he called me and said, "Elder sister, here in Yangon, the work situation is okay. In the countryside, it's not okay. So, come here to Yangon." So, we came and stayed with them for a day or two. Pots, cups, and plates; our mats and pillows; some clothing—that's about as much as we brought with us.

Their initial employment—casual wage labor at a cement factory—was irregular and, in turn, inadequate. And that, Aunty Yu Maw explained, was why she turned before long to market selling from out of her home in the Yadana settlement. With the contributed income of her eldest daughter's factory wage, the family managed to get by while paying off, ever so slowly, the debt that they had brought with them on their migration to Yangon from the countryside.

The Precarious Afterlives of Agricultural Wage Laborers

Uncle Tin's hut was so close to the road that every time a truck drove past, the whole place shook. And given that he lived opposite a riverside gravel depot, trucks constantly drove past. This also meant that the dust the trucks kicked up in the hot season wafted in through Uncle Tin's front door. The whole place could not have been more than 100 square feet. It was there that the sixty-five-year-old man lived with his wife and two school-aged daughters.

Uncle Tin was under no illusions. He knew where he stood in "transitional" Myanmar. And he knew, as well, the route that had brought him there. "It's like I was saying," he proceeded to explain, after an initial moment's interlude,[25]

I used to be an agricultural worker, and I came from a family of agricultural workers. In the past, one acre of agricultural land required ten people to sow it and eight people to harvest it. So during the hot season and the rainy season, the families of all those agricultural workers were able to eat. But now, with mechanization, there's no employment in agriculture. So, people who used to work in agriculture are now unemployed, and their families no longer have adequate basic necessities. They're facing difficulties. And their children's education suffers because they aren't able to attend school. It was due to that kind of situation that we fled to the city and started working in the brick, sand, and gravel industry. However, since 2016, that work has been done with a backhoe. In the past, when a ship arrived, from 40 to 70 people would have to work for three days to unload it, and we'd get enough to eat. But now we're unemployed.

So in both the countryside and the city we've got these kinds of difficulties. As a result, we're living on the side of the road on land that's deemed municipal property. It's nothing but a place to lie down. And we're living with the uncertainty of being evicted, like a crow that tries to eat while in fear of being shot. And we've got lots of difficulties paying for our children's education. We've had difficulties for a long time trying to cover the costs of our children's snacks and lunch, and the bicycle that they need to ride all the way to school. The government claims to offer free education, but that only means there's no entrance fee. It costs a lot for all the necessary books. And we have to contribute to the *waso* donation and the *kathein* donation.[26] How are we supposed to resolve these financial difficulties? We can't resolve them! And so our children can't attend school and instead have to collect plastic bottles on the side of the road so that they can eat. If they can't attend school, how are poor people like that supposed to get an education? So the government is saying one thing, but the reality is something else.

In order to investigate the reasons for these issues, our news media goes and interviews wealthy farmers, don't they? And those wealthy farmers talk about how everything is developing and transitioning. And the media takes photos of the property of those wealthy farmers and puts them in the news, don't they? Is that not the truth? Similarly, the media goes and interviews employers and takes photos of their property. But in the background behind those wealthy people are workers who can't even afford a dani palm roof to protect themselves from the rain. And these workers who are crying in the rain and living hand to mouth carrying loads on their shoulders or selling goods that they carry on their heads—there are so many of them. Is that not the case? Those are the kinds of experiences that we've had to endure in our lives. As for our children, when their parents don't have work, how are they supposed to attend school and get an education? Is that not the case? And there are monthly fees for private tuition. For tenth standard (equivalent to grade 11) students in this area, it costs 50,000 to 60,000 kyat per month for private tuition. They can only attend if they pay. At the moment, I can't afford to put my own kids in private tuition. At 7,000 to 8,000 kyat per month, how could I?[27] What work could I do that would let me afford to enroll them in private tuition? I don't have portering work. I don't have *any* work. And I don't have an enterprise of my own. Just consider our level of education.

Now, I'd like to say something that General [Aung San] said. During the revolution against the English and the Japanese, he said, "We Burmese are our own masters!" Everyone knows that statement. And like that, we Myanmar people achieved self-government. But where are Myanmar people now? They've gone to Malaysia, Singapore, and Thailand. They've been condemned to servitude in other people's countries, have they not? So, where's our liberation from servitude? And General [Aung San] likewise told us to build up our own country, our people, and our industry—to strive to build up our country. But now there's no work for us in our own country. Okay, so now there are factories being set up. But they'll only accept you for a job if you've got a National Registration Card.

Only the children of the monied class have been able to get a high level of education and continue on. As for us, we've gotten nothing from this so-called transition. Business owners, who are a minority, have become wealthy. But it's workers who are in the majority—workers who carry loads on their shoulders or sell goods that they balance on their heads. There are so many of them who have become unemployed and gone hungry. And so they're collecting plastic bottles and cups from the roadside. Is that not the case? And in, what was it, 2017 or [20]18? The police were arresting kids and charging them with stealing. But those kids weren't thieves. They had nothing to eat and they couldn't go to school. They had nothing to eat and their parents couldn't feed them. So they were collecting plastic bottles and cups from the roadside to sell. It was only when they sold those things that they were able to eat.

I saw this parliamentary representative on the news on TV who said, "Only when business owners are wealthy will the country be wealthy."

So when are those business owners going to be wealthy enough? And so long as they aren't wealthy enough, are they just going to sacrifice us poor laborers who have no property? It's like that time long ago that our parents and grandparents told us about, is it not? We've gone back to a capitalist era. I say this because we now have to beg for work and then do whatever we're ordered. That's the kind of life we've arrived at, is it not?

People are calling us invaders [*kyu kyaw*]. But what country have we invaded? We're living in our own country. We had to come here because there was no work in our native places. On an open spot on this state-owned land we built this little hut, which is just a place to lie down. And they call us invaders, don't they? If they called us migrant workers or a landless class, I could accept that. But "invader" is what General [Aung San] called Japan and other imperialist countries. We haven't invaded anything! And it's Myanmar people who are calling other Myanmar people invaders.

I've been unemployed since 2016, haven't I? And now the wild water spinach growing in ditches along the roadside doesn't even have a chance to grow back [because so many poor people are picking it to eat]. And we have to collect plastic bottles and cups—even when people discard them by their outhouses. That's what happened recently when a guy went to pick up a plastic bottle not too far from here and he got stabbed with a knife.

In the past [before 1988] we were alright.[28] There was work in agriculture for peasants and agricultural workers. At planting time, we'd plant. At replanting time, we'd replant. At plowing time, we'd plow. At harvest time, we'd harvest. And at threshing time, we'd thresh. In that way, we'd do agricultural work and our basic necessities were alright. Yes, it was alright back then.

What the Demographics Tell Us

The Yadana squatter settlement has a precise founding moment in 1991, when township authorities evicted an informal settlement from an adjacent industrial plot to make way for the construction of a new hulled sesame plant. Of the evicted households, fifty-three relocated to the nearest of three vacant industrial plots that would come to house the Yadana settlement. It had only been two years prior, in 1989, that the regional government had demarcated the industrial zone that housed these plots—a zone that lay in one of a handful of new towns that the reconstructed junta was at the time establishing around Yangon in order to house relocated public servants and downtown residents whose increasingly valuable urban property the military government was then in the process of seizing.[29] Following that initial group of squatter residents, there were few new arrivals at the settlement until the mid-2000s. It was at that time that employees of several nearby storage and shipping depots moved out of their on-site worker barracks and built bamboo-and-dani-palm homes at Yadana. Migration to the settlement then picked up, with the number of households on-site reaching around 1,000 by 2016, according to two appointed municipal representatives who resided at the settlement. That was the year in which township authorities registered Yadana's residents for the purpose of eventual relocation. There has since been a small amount of further growth, as families have subdivided their homes or sold-off land they had previously used for other purposes. However, the lack of extensive vacant land on-site has inhibited significant expansion in the number of households at the settlement since 2017.

It was in this context that, in 2019, I conducted, with assistance from several friends in the settlement, a basic demographic survey of 200 households located on-site—or about 20 percent of all of Yadana's households, representing 803 residents. The survey inquired into the number of household inhabitants, the ethnicity and religion of household members, their states/regions and townships of origin, the number of years at the settlement, and the livelihoods in which members of their household were at the time engaged. The survey data enables certain insights into the broader demographics of the settlements' inhabitants.

Of the 200 surveyed households, the mean average household size was four persons. Given the local municipal government representatives' estimates of slightly over 1,000 households on-site, the surveyed household sizes would suggest a total settlement population of slightly over 4,000 individuals. The mode and median for household size were likewise four persons, with the six largest surveyed households having eight residents. I am aware of still larger households in the settlement that have from eleven to thirteen members, but these are outliers, and no households of this size came up in the survey.

By far the most common state/region of origin for Yadana's residents is Ayeyarwady, from where 72 percent of surveyed households hail. Following this comes Yangon Region (15.5 percent), Bago Region (11 percent), Mon State (1 percent), Rakhine State (0.5 percent), and Karen State (0.5 percent). The townships of origin for Yadana residents who hail from the delta are likewise revealing. Most individuals from Ayeyarwady arrived in the years after Nargis and came from townships that were hardest hit by the cyclone, specifically Bogalay, Dedaye, Kyaiklat, Labutta, Maubin, Mawlamyinegyun, Myaung Mya, and Pyapon.

Excluding the initial group of fifty-three households who arrived at the settlement in 1991, the year of arrival for most surveyed residents was relatively recent.

Among this latter group, the mean average years at the settlement was 5.9, with mode and median similarly six years. Stated otherwise, 2013 was the year in which the largest group of residents arrived, while from 2009 to 2014, 71.6 percent of surveyed residents made it to the settlement. The site reached near capacity by the end of 2016, which is also when the government registered the settlement's residents (more on which in chapter 3). Since that time, another 22 percent of surveyed residents have arrived at the settlement. That a significant proportion of new residents has arrived since 2017 does not mean there has been a sustained increase in the number of households on-site. Although some households subdivided their plots during this time, allowing for an increase in the number of households on-site, the bulk of these more recent arrivals have purchased or rented out existing squatter homes—their former occupants moving out, in some cases to become absentee landlords. Significantly, this large group of later arrivals took up residence at the settlement after the regional government had completed squatter registration. These latter individuals therefore received no formalized basis to claim subsidized housing at a future relocation-site.

The majority of surveyed residents (97.5 percent) identified as ethnic Burman. There were other households whose members identified as ethnic Karen (2 percent) and Rakhine (0.5 percent), as well as one elderly Mon woman and a single household that identified as being of South Asian ancestry. The statistical breakdown here adds up to slightly over 100 percent because certain households identified as having plural ethnic makeup—for example, a Karen man married to a Burman woman.

Nearly all surveyed households (98.5 percent) identified as Buddhist. There were only three households among those surveyed whose residents identified as Christian. In one case, a household identified as both Buddhist and Christian; the Burman wife was Buddhist, while the Karen husband was Christian. In their home, this family had both Buddhist and Christian shrines. Finally, the single household of South Asian ancestry identified as Muslim. It is notable that, given the rise in Islamophobia and outright violence toward Muslims elsewhere in the country, this one Muslim household, which had lived at the settlement since 2013, was on amicable terms with its Buddhist and Christian neighbors.

The most commonly reported means of livelihood among surveyed households was casual portering (50.7 percent), most of which is done at various storage and trade depots along the nearby riverside. This work, called *kon tin kon kya* in Burmese, involves loading and unloading shipments of bamboo, dani palm shingles, gravel, bricks, or what have you. The labor is undertaken almost exclusively by adult men, the exception being sand, gravel, and brick depots, where women and children are also commonly employed.

Of the surveyed households, eighty-six (43 percent) stated that at least one member of their family had factory employment. Yet only twelve of these households (6 percent) had members formally employed as salaried workers in garment factories producing for export. Another twenty-five households had members with consistent but casual and unregistered employment at nongarment factories—mostly prawn, fish, potato, chili, or other food processing plants. The remaining forty-nine households had family members who took on occasional, unregistered day labor at these nongarment factories as a way to supplement income from waste collection work and casual portering.

The relatively low number of respondents reporting garment factory employment is notable. For the most part, garment and footwear factories producing for export are, notwithstanding their other labor law violations, more likely to pay the legal minimum wage, as compared with factories producing commodities for the domestic market. However, such garment and footwear factories are also stricter on the requirement that employees present valid National Registration Cards, otherwise known as National Scrutiny Cards, as proof of age. Such factories are also more selective in hiring—for the most part restricting new employment to young women between eighteen and twenty-five years of age.

When the results of Myanmar's 2014 census were revealed, the reported findings indicated that just over 28 million individuals out of a population of roughly 51.5 million held National Registration Cards.[30] The proportion is even lower than this among residents of the Yadana settlement, since many of these individuals lost their National Registration Cards as well as the documents needed to acquire new cards during Cyclone Nargis. This widespread lack of National Registration Cards has inhibited the ability of many young women residing at Yadana to obtain what is typically better paid garment factory employment.

Seventy-four households (37 percent of those surveyed) said that they engaged in informal waste collection and resale. Of these, thirty-two households engaged in such labor as their primary means of livelihood, while another forty-two said they only occasionally engaged in informal waste collection and resale. Another thirty-six households (16.7 percent) conducted petty vending (selling betel quids, packaged snacks, or home-cooked curries, for example), most often from out of the front of their homes. Finally, seven surveyed households engaged in commercial animal husbandry—the rearing of pigs, specifically—and one surveyed household engaged in the commercial cultivation of water spinach.

The statistically typical household at the Yadada settlement is therefore an ethnic Burman Buddhist family of four who migrated to Yangon from the Ayeyarwady Delta in 2013. The father has casual labor as a porter, while the mother has casual employment at a nearby food processing plant. The family's two children may attend classes at a nearby government school, but the school dropout rate is high at the settlement, and most children residing here begin working for an income by their mid-teenage years, or else accompany and assist their parents in the collection of discarded items for resale. In light of arguments that waged employment in the so-called formal sector is marginal to slum economies, it is significant that 74 percent of respondents indicated that their households were at least partly reliant on some form of waged income. This labor, as I examine in chapter 5, was for the most part within enterprises that are formally covered by employment protection legislation, even though in practice the applicable labor laws are rarely enforced.

The stories of migration presented in this chapter reveal the spatially relational character of urban-rural development in Myanmar. By this I mean that the dynamics of capitalist transformation in Yangon's industrial zones cannot be understood apart from rural experiences of dispossession and government neglect. Ultimately, it is the postsocialist and (subsequently) post-Nargis degradation and collapse of rural livelihoods that prompted mass urban migration to these industrial zones at exactly the moment when factories in these zones were proliferating and seeking large numbers of young, low-wage employees.

Attention to migrants' desires to relocate is crucial for both analytical and ethical reasons. But analysis focused exclusively so—such that migration is seen as solely motivated by the attractions of big city living and dynamic urban capitalism—risks legitimating subordination in wage labor and legitimating a development agenda that continues to push rural dwellers out of the rural economy in the name of increased productivity. Needed is a more integrated analysis that treats neither desire nor the compulsions of the market in isolation. As a precedent, we can look to Mary Beth Mills's intimate ethnography of young Thai women who migrated to Bangkok at the turn of the 1990s, for whom a desire to participate in perceived modernity and to acquire the commodified symbols of progress was inseparable from the deteriorating rural economy that they left behind in northeast Thailand.[31] However, this analytical relevance of desire notwithstanding, when government officials and domestic media go on to criticize squatters' "illegal" residency on Yangon's outskirts, these critics are engaged in blaming the victim because individuals expelled from rural areas confront, upon arrival in the city, a near-impossible urban housing market. Such antagonistic accounts of squatters' presence in the city obscure, as well, the economic value that squatters contribute through their labor to the wider industrial context in which they reside.

3

SQUATTING AMID CAPITALISM AND THE CONTRADICTIONS THEREOF

Legally, Mrs. Yin had never owned her home, but that did not stop her from selling it. And now, sitting on the floor of her new bamboo-and-plywood house, several kilometers from the Yadana squatter settlement where she had formerly resided, Mrs. Yin was quite pleased with the sale.

Like many of her fellow squatters, Mrs. Yin—hailing from Myanmar's delta region—had with her husband and children in tow fled to Yangon to escape the devastation and rural economic collapse left behind by Cyclone Nargis. Her de facto possession of the recently sold squat—legal ownership, she insisted, it was not—had begun soon after her arrival in December of 2012. It was then that she had paid 10,000 kyat (US$6.60) "tea money" to the *yaainhmu*, or "hundred house official," who oversaw day-to-day handling of the settlement for the local ward administrator. "We're in trouble," she recalls pleading, "please let us build a home here." In response, the official, not known to act out of compassion, conceded. Pocketing the money, he allowed the family, on land demarcated for factory construction, to build their dwelling—a bamboo structure with a dani palm roof, which due to the degradable materials employed demanded complete reconstruction every couple of years.

At the time she arrived, Mrs. Yin recollects, the site—covering several industrial plots and some municipal land along the adjacent roads—still had plenty of space to spare. As there were only a few hundred households on-site, new arrivals, like Mrs. Yin and her family, could without much difficulty acquire a spot on which to build a small structure, provided they paid off the relevant authorities. In the ensuing years, however, the site's population multiplied, such that bribes to the *yaainhmu* for new house construction increased to 50,000 kyat, and the number of homes on-site rose to around 1,000, leaving no open land left for further residential units—a closure of the local squatter frontier, as it were. It was then that squatter real estate and rental markets emerged, given the increased demand for affordable housing amid ongoing urban migration.

But Mrs. Yin wanted out. Her eldest daughter had recently turned seventeen, and the settlement—a rough neighborhood, she felt—began to grate on her: "When I say it's rough, what I mean is that people get drunk and fight with each other. It's disheartening. That's why we moved. I just wanted to live in peace." She added, as clarification, "those alcoholics might have done something improper with my children. My daughter has come of age, so it wasn't proper for her to be there. When my kids were young, it wasn't an issue. But now, you know, I was worried."

It was around this time that, conveniently, an acquaintance from Mrs. Yin's native village in the delta arrived in the township—her family in accompaniment and them all in need of housing. To this woman, Mrs. Yin sold her home on a verbal agreement for 600,000 kyat, to be paid in six installments over as many months. By this point, more than two years had passed since township authorities had registered the squatters and provided them with identifying "smartcards." The cards in question qualified Yadana's residents for future housing plots at an as yet unspecified relocation-site in, rumor had it, Htantabin Township—a bucolic countryside of rice fields, and quaint villages with unpaved roads lying beyond Yangon's existing urban periphery, which none of the squatters considered desirable. Whatever the eventual relocation-site—if any—the family now inhabiting Mrs. Yin's former address would have no such eligibility. What they had, at most, was an informal claim to their residence at the settlement. And it was a tenuous claim given the regional government's stated objective of removing all squatters from Yangon, and local ward authorities' recurring attempts to drive the squatters out, thereby freeing up the land for commercial sale and factory construction.

What we see at Yadana are the contradictions of long-term squatting, where an initial challenge to the existing property regime has become, over time, incorporated into manifold relations of extraction, exploitation, and rule. To be sure, squatting at Yadana has delivered tangible benefits to the individuals who have made this site their home. As such, squatting is here a classic instance of direct action, whereby participants have disregarded the existing rule of property to act, as David Graeber defined it, "as if one is already free," free of state-enforced property rights, specifically.[1] Moreover, as an ethnographic subject, squatting aligns with prominent foci in current political anthropology. This is because, as Nancy Postero and Eli Elioff observe in a recent review of the literature, "new political anthropologies" have been particularly concerned with struggles "to live otherwise," or to build "worlds organized otherwise," particularly where such struggles contest the exclusions of a liberal capitalist order.[2]

There is, however, an analytical risk. Anthropologists enthusing over seemingly progressive political alternatives may simply be abstracting their ethnographic cases from the constitutive relations in which said cases are embedded. Such is Natalia Buier's argument regarding David Graeber's idiosyncratic construal of anarchist anthropology, where an ethnographic focus on "alternative social arrangements" ends up occluding broader political questions.[3] In a similar vein, squatting has been celebrated as a project of creating autonomous spaces outside of capitalism.[4] This is a position argued by, for instance, the journal *Tiqqun*, whose editorial committee posits capitalism as dominant but porous, such that squatting operates as a practice of commoning and of establishing noncapitalist enclaves.[5] Along resonant lines, Claudio Cattaneo and Miguel Martínez argued in their study of the European squatters' movement that squatting offers a viable alternative to capitalism, an endeavor that "can escape from the capitalist logic."[6]

As with the anthropological fetishism of political alternatives, abstracting squatting in this way from its constitutive context is mystifying; it obscures the relations of power through which the squat is tied to the world around it. Amy Starecheski makes a similar argument in her ethnography of squatting on New York's Lower East Side, while advancing a dialectical analysis that allows for squatter agency. Squats, she argues, do not operate outside of capitalism—a fact that makes their potential reversion to private property an inherent potential rather than simply an external threat. Nonetheless, in seeking to defend squatted land, occupants may be able to exploit gaps and contradictions in the hegemonic property regime.[7]

Residents of the Yadana settlement did not articulate an explicitly anticapitalist politics, thus distinguishing the case at hand from the squats Starecheski studied on New York's Lower East Side, and from the political squatters' movement that Claudio Cattaneo and Miguel Martínez studied in Europe. At one level, this difference challenges analytical comparison. But I would suggest that this fact makes the present case all the more relevant for assessing squatting's anticapitalist content, which emerges here out of proletarian survival tactics, irrespective of participants' expressed political commitments.

Squatting as an ethnographic case thus offers an effective empirical entry point for rethinking recuperation in a dialectical fashion. This is a concept—recuperation, that is—which Gilles Deleuze elaborated as follows: "when we say recuperate, we mean: each time something seems to escape capitalism, seems to pass beneath its simili-codes; it reabsorbs all this, it adds one more axiom and the machine starts up again."[8] Deleuze was notoriously antagonistic to dialectical analysis.[9] Nevertheless, the ethnographic data presented herein illustrates how squatting—initially a challenge to the existing property regime—becomes dialectically imbricated with wider relations of extraction, exploitation, and rule, and with the broader capitalist context more generally. The argument here is thus against the hypostatization of squatting—against conceiving the squat as a thing in itself, autonomous of its constitutive context. Ultimately, squatting is anticapitalist only insofar as it is a moment in struggle—a refusal of relations of extraction, exploitation, and rule, where the potential reemergence of private property remains inherent. Such, at least, are the contradictory conditions of life at Yadana, as evident in the accounts that follow.

The Slow Burn of an Enduring Feud

Mrs. Sandar Oo, scrutinizing the letter, read over its words in a whisper; Brother Myint, flustered, looked on from beside her in silence. Without introduction, this man had hastened into Mrs. Sandar Oo's home less than one minute earlier, ducking, as he did so, to fit through the five-foot-tall door frame. Introductions were uncalled for. These two were not simply neighbors, but siblings and comrades, who currently served together as elected representatives in the local porter's union, which Mrs. Sandar Oo had helped establish more than six years prior.

So there on the bamboo floor sat Brother Myint, functionally illiterate, waiting for his older sister to divine meaning from the letter in question, about which Brother Myint was already, and understandably, apprehensive, given the document's origin. Straight to the point, the letter—handwritten in pen but formalized with the ward administrator's stamp—began, after naming Brother Myint as addressee, by stating its subject matter as the heading: "Trespassory construction must be terminated." To this basic premise, the body of the letter added little, though the author did, to stress his point, add the Burmese rhetorical device of doubling the adverb: "Trespassory construction must absolutely (absolutely) be discontinued."

Mrs. Sandar Oo was incredulous from the start. First, she despised the word trespass (*kyu kyaw*). Although it was the go-to term, even among her fellow squatters, she made a point of disputing it every time it was spoken. "This isn't *trespassing*," she would insist. "We're residing on vacant land [*palat mye*]!" She knew that the ward administrator lacked legal grounds to restrict Brother Myint's home repairs, as the latter was employing merely bamboo and corrugated sheet metal—materials lacking the permanence of brick and mortar, which existing laws did, it is true, restrict in the absence of the pertinent land registration. And so, knew Mrs. Sandar Oo, it was an empty threat, as were so many before. After all, dozens of households across the settlement were at that very moment similarly repairing or rebuilding their homes in anticipation of the impending monsoon.

She also knew, or at least surmised, the real impetus and individual behind the letter. It was the *yaainhmu*, a man who had profited off the sweat of his neighbors—a man who had grown wealthy, if only relatively, by extorting unofficial "fees" in the name of the ward administrator from other residents of the settlement. It was a practice against which Mrs. Sandar Oo, Brother Myint, and the union had long fought, urging fellow squatters to disregard these demands, as the yaainhmu lacked legal grounds for any such claims. "It's only out of fear that people pay," she insisted. It was this ongoing feud, believed Mrs. Sandar Oo, which lay behind present events—the letter being yet another attempt by the yaainhmu to harass the union and push its representatives out of the settlement. Just consider it: here was a man, stressed Mrs. Sandar Oo, whose own home in the squatter settlement, uniquely, had ceramic tiles but who was ordering Brother Myint, a man with only irregular employment as a porter, to cease repairs on a simple bamboo-and-sheet-metal shack in which he lived with twelve other family members.

The first order of business was to ascertain whether the letter had come from the ward administrator, given that the latter's name was not on the stamp and the signature was completely illegible. Mrs. Sandar Oo thus adopted her sweetest of voices and called the ward administrator, her handset so loud that everyone present could follow the entire conversation.

"Hello? Greetings, Ward Administrator, sir. This is Sandar Oo, sir. Ward Administrator, just now, a letter was brought to me, which orders a complete stop on repairs to a home. Did this letter come from you?"

"Yes. Yes, it did," her interlocutor replied.

"Oh, why is that?"

"It's because the house is being built too high."

"Ward Administrator, sir, if you were to come here yourself, you'd see that all of the homes are that height."

"Well, this restriction comes from the Municipal Development Committee," retorted the ward administrator.

"The Municipal Development Committee? Ward Administrator, sir, you know very well that this isn't municipal land."

"But the house is being built too high."

"Oh, it's not *that* high, sir."

"*. . . mumble, mumble, mumble . . .*"

"Okay, well, if this letter did indeed come from you, then I understand. We're just going to go ahead and continue with the repairs. My younger brother doesn't have a place to live. So, we're just going to continue. I just wanted to inform you about that."

FIGURE 5. Rebuilding a bamboo and dani palm home in the Yadana squatter settlement. Author's photograph.

"But it's too high!"

"Well, maybe it is a *little* high. But it's just high enough to keep out of the flood water and the mosquitoes. That's all."

"*. . . mumble, mumble, mumble . . .*"

"Yes, yes. He's almost finished the repairs. Okay, if that's all, then thank you very much."[10]

The letter in dispute here, believed Mrs. Sandar Oo, was but the most recent instance of a persistent effort on the part of the yaainhmu and ward administrator to evict the union from the settlement. Yet most of the squatters were not in the union. Their residence at this site was consequently more ambiguous. On the one hand, the yaainhmu accepted tea money payments in return for his "permission" (*ahkwint*) for squatters to construct homes of initially bamboo and dani palm, and to reside at the settlement forthwith. Through such transactions, the unofficial sanction that squatters obtained for continued residence remained informal and rather tenuous. There was, in such cases, no official land "grant" (*gayan*), which in Myanmar is deemed the closest thing to legal property ownership.[11]

Nonetheless, in the everyday life of the settlement, the yaainhmu regularly acted as if his permission for squatter residence had the weight of formal land ownership. Moreover, in 2016, under the then recently elected regional-level National League for Democracy government and its Chief Minister Phyo Min Thein, township officials registered squatters residing at Yadana and similar settlements, and then in January 2017 issued said individuals with smartcards, which listed the bearer's name and address, and displayed a black-and-white photo of all household members. Although government authorities issued these cards to establish squatters' eligibility for future resettlement into low-cost housing, the cards were subsequently treated as though they were quasi property ownership documents. Tellingly, a black market emerged whereby wealthy investors bought up smartcards in hopes of later cashing in on subsidized housing, while squatters pawned their cards as loan collateral.[12] The Yangon Region government proceeded to deem both practices illegal. Nonetheless, it has also become possible for registered squatters at Yadana to rent out their properties—becoming absentee landlords even—and to then request the yaainhmu's backing to evict tenants who fall into arrears. In a similar manner, squatters selling their residential units have been able to pay the yaainhmu to draw up and sign deeds of sale (*ain yaung sachok*)—though such contracts are often deemed unnecessary for transactions among friends and relatives. Many of Yadana's squatters have come to see such deeds of sale as validating their ownership of the physical structures in which they reside, if not the land on which these structures are built. Yet, in at least one case, a Yadana resident was of the belief that this document granted him "temporary legal ownership" (*yayi tayawin baingsainghmu*) over both his home and the plot on which it was built, temporary since the government could at any time disregard such ownership and forcibly evict the resident in question.

Notwithstanding such quasi-ownership arrangements, squatters both inside and outside the local porters' union faced recurring attempts on the part of the ward administrator to evict them from the land, thereby opening the site up for resale and factory construction. In the initial years of the settlement, such potential eviction was not a serious concern, as the industrial zone still had plenty of vacant factory plots available. However, with increased factory construction and ongoing migration from rural areas to the township, land prices have spiked. It is a property dynamic that mirrors broader trends across urban Yangon.[13]

It was amid such inflationary conditions that township authorities—under the government of the then president Thein Sein and his ruling Union Solidarity and Development Party—dispatched police to remove Yadana's squatters in December 2012. On the day of the planned eviction, six police trucks loaded with cops arrived on-site and announced their objective of leveling the settlement. This was before the bulk of the settlement's residents had moved in, and Yadana therefore had only a few hundred bamboo-and-dani-palm homes on-site. Still, Mrs. Sandar Oo and Mrs. Thuzar, who had in the months leading up to the attempted eviction been organizing the local porter's union, were able to rally a noisy protest of residents and then negotiate a tentative arrangement with the support of a sympathetic member of the Yangon regional parliament—an arrangement whereby township authorities agreed to hold off on further attempts to evict the squatters, for the time being. It was a relatively hopeful moment at a time when squatters across Yangon were engaged in similar antieviction struggles. The following month, for instance, squatters residing on an abandoned Ministry of Construction site in Hlaingtharyar Township seized bamboo sticks and chased off demolition workers whom the Yangon City Development Committee had hired to evict the squatters.[14]

Some two years later, in 2014, a representative of a major Burmese company arrived at the Yadana settlement, claiming his employer held existing ownership of one of the factory plots on which part of the settlement lay.[15] The representative went so far as to put up a signboard on-site claiming ownership of the plot by his employer and prohibiting trespassing. When the squatters refused to leave, the representative offered to pay compensation—below market rate—to anyone who agreed to move out. No one ceded. When the squatters then hired a lawyer to assist in the dispute, it became evident that the representative was bluffing; he had no *gayan*, the crucial land ownership document. In fact, no one seemed to have a *gayan* for the plots in question. That is why informed squatters like Mrs. Sandar Oo were adamant that they resided on vacant land, upon which squatting, consequently, did not constitute trespassing.

Given the looming threat of eviction, and notwithstanding promised relocation to subsidized housing, some of Yadana's residents sought to formalize their property ownership at the settlement. To do this, they claimed a right of ownership based on extended residence on vacant land. They also submitted to township authorities documentation of their residence at the site, which they had the township's Department of Urban and Housing Development compile at their request. To date, no conclusion has been reached on the matter of this application. In any case, most Yadana residents did not directly participate in these efforts, but rather focused on their immediate livelihood concerns, aware that they could be uprooted at any minute and dispatched forthwith to a peripheral township whose lesser land value would serve as an adequate proxy indicator for poor income opportunities.

Meanwhile, the regional National League for Democracy government carried out in June 2017 its first forced eviction of a major informal settlement—a shantytown in Yangon Region's northern Hlegu Township, which comprised an estimated 4,000 squatter homes. Having informed residents of the impending eviction the year prior, the regional government dispatched some 200 police officers accompanied by upward of 700 "hired heavies" armed with clubs, swords, axes, and chainsaws who had been instructed to demolish all squatter homes on-site.[16] Pulitzer Prize-winning journalist Wa Lone, present at the incident, reported that the squatters confronted the police, shouted at civilian demolition crews, and attempted to defend their homes from impending destruction. The police arrested at least five such individuals, and none of the evicted squatters received any compensation. Motivating the eviction, the Yangon government had partnered with an unnamed private company that was planning to develop the area into a high-end residential estate with an accompanying golf course and private hospital.[17]

All of this suggests that squatting at Yadana, as elsewhere on Yangon's urban periphery, is riven with contradictions. On the one hand, the settlement provides dense and low-cost housing to a working-class population near factories and warehouses whose employers are in need of a significant pool of cheap labor.[18] Local authorities, meanwhile, like the four yaainhmu living on-site, have incorporated squatters into quasi-official relations of rule, and have profited by extracting unofficial fees for permission—tenuous though it is—for continued residence. All of this lends itself to a functionalist analysis: the squatter settlement serving here as a mechanism for maintaining low-cost labor, along with a reserve army that suppresses wages in the surrounding industrial zone. However, by squatting at this site, residents have also challenged the existing rule of property—a fact made clear by the ever-present threat of eviction. The result of these opposing tendencies is an ambiguity with significant theoretical implications: the evident contradictions in the regulatory and extractive relations at Yadana blur a conventional formal/informal dichotomy which, when posited as mutually exclusive categories, is both misleading and analytically unhelpful. For we see here how formal state relations of rule and formal capital accumulation are intimately imbricated with informal (extra-legal) property relations, and, as I will explore further in subsequent chapters, informal labor arrangements as well.[19] It is precisely where the formal and informal blur that regulatory gaps in the existing property regime become most evident. These are contradictions that squatters have exploited to maintain their residence, however tenuous it may be, at the Yadana settlement.

From a Denial of Public Services to Privatized Infrastructure

Three fish had, until earlier that week, swum in the 1,000-liter holding tank set up on Brother Myo's roof. They were suckermouth catfish (*Hypostomus plecostomus*), an invasive species from South America with toxin-secreting spines. In the years preceding, the fish had proliferated across lower Myanmar, crowding out inland fisheries, after having been released into the wild by local aquarists.[20] Admittedly, you could barely see their silhouettes from down below, even if you stood in front of Brother Myo's teashop, staring up at the tank of translucent white plastic, squinting as needed, and mindful of passing trucks. But his customers knew the fish were there, and not all of them appreciated Brother Myo's ingenuity. Or at least they found it unappealing. After all, some of them drank that water. "I drink the water too," was Brother Myo's attempt at reassurance. But in the end, he caved, and set the fish loose in the river. The fish were inedible, and he had no wish to incur the bad merit of killing them. For most of the past half a year, Brother Myo had not needed to climb up on the roof weekly to scrub the tank himself. The fish had taken care of it for him—consuming the algae and mosquito larvae that bred in the water.

The selling of water, pumped from the ground and piped to forty homes of fellow squatters, was Brother Myo's second entrepreneurial venture—the first being a marginally profitable attempt at selling firewood. That first project had begun some five years prior, when, at age thirty-five, Brother Myo had decided to put an end to his days as a porter and warehouse hand. His body, exhausted from years of shouldering loads of bamboo poles, seemed increasingly in need of rest. But more important, he had fallen for Yin Cho, the fishmonger's daughter, at that time only fifteen years old. Twenty years her senior, Brother Myo had promptly proposed. They then got married, and he quit his job at the warehouse. Forced, as a result, to move out of the workers' barracks, he paid 250,000 kyat for a squatter home, bought at a discount from his younger brother. The residence was slotted into a row of shop-front shacks on a strip of roadside municipal land, a stone's throw from his former employer.

Five years later, Brother Myo was netting 250,000 kyat (US$167) per month from water sales alone. In comparison, among squatters employed in nearby garment factories, even the most skilled were barely able to top 200,000 kyat (US$133) per month in take-home pay, overtime included. Profiting like this, Brother Myo had been able to establish a home-front teashop and to upgrade his residence from a bamboo-and-dani-palm shack to a two-storied, corrugated-tin-and-mangrove-wood edifice. But if this was a success, Brother Myo was not one to boast. "Some people look at me and think I'm doing alright," he confided, almost apologetically, "yet I too am living hand to mouth." In either case, to his customers, it was Yin Cho, as capable of riposte as her fishmonger mother, who was truly the *bawzy*—a term adopted from the English word boss. So much was this the case that one elderly couple expressed, in private, outright disapproval that this young woman, so assertive, was able to dominate her older but taciturn husband.

Although township authorities provided no electrical, water, or plumbing infrastructure to the settlement, not everyone at Yadana bought water from private providers like Brother Myo. For those who did, it was for the convenience of water piped right to their homes. For those who did not, clusters of households had pooled their money to dig communal wells affixed with hand-operated pumps. And in 2018, visiting South Korean missionaries had donated money to install a dozen more such pumps, although some residents asserted that the yaainhmu, through whom the project funds were channeled, had profited illicitly by skimping on well depth, resulting in adulterated water. There were, in any case, by the time Brother Myo removed the suckermouth catfish from his tank, thirty or so communal wells across the settlement.

Among entrepreneurial ventures in Yadana, Brother Myo's operation was assuredly minor league. The real money was being made by the likes of Mister Shwe Sein, who operated a massive thirty-two-horsepower diesel generator, housed in a solid brick-and-cement building built on squatted land. With this behemoth, he was able to sell electricity to over 300 squatter households, at rates of 100 to 800 kyat per day, depending on the numbers and types of electrical appliances used—100 kyat per lightbulb, 300 kyat for a television—grossing him easily over three million kyat each month from a generator housed on land that he had neither purchased nor rented. These rates, it is worth noting, are at least twice as much as the metered government electricity provided to residential units in the township.

Mister Shwe Sein was but one of the more prominent cases of individuals with capital who had paid off the yaainhmu to build on a plot of squatter land, not out of duress, but as an investment whose returns the settlement's very informality—land effectively free, and a large population denied state infrastructure—had made possible. Brother Myo saw it like this: "Some people moved to the squatter settlement because you can make good money here. They came with capital [*ayin*] and invested it. . . . Actually, only about half the people in the squatter settlement live hand to mouth. The others are people who have come here to do business. The real squatters are the ones who came here because they were starving." With this claim, Brother Myo offered a stark differentiation among Yadana's residents. But in so doing, he erased significant gradients in wealth; ultimately, not starving is a poor threshold for qualifying a vernacular bourgeoisie. Even among squatters operating a business—selling betel quids out of their home, for example—most were in debt, if not insolvent, and many were barely afloat.

The mass squatting presently practiced along Yangon's urban periphery has historical precedent in Myanmar. So, too, does the government's denial of infrastructure to squatter populations. In her study of coercive urban planning in Myanmar, the legal historian Elizabeth Rhoads documents the ways in which the British colonial government employed tactical "under-equipping and under-servicing" of squatter settlements and other poor urban neighborhoods, along with forced evictions, as complementary means to acquire "strategic or valuable land" and assert control over squatter populations.[21] These were methods of dispossession—administrative and coercive—that the postindependence government of U Nu likewise embraced. In the years immediately following World War II, half a million refugees who had fled rural devastation and economic collapse wrought by the war arrived at the edges of urban Yangon, where they proceeded to establish ad hoc settlements. For U Nu, enamored as he was with the era's high modernist developmentalism, this was an urban planning nightmare. He thus employed in response a mode of urban governance that mimicked the colonial approach to urban poverty—a denial of basic infrastructure backed up by forced evictions. Although carried out with some restraint under the U Nu government, post-1962 military authorities engaged in such forced evictions even more aggressively and extensively than did their elected predecessor.

Historical parallels aside, the present government's denial of infrastructure has had certain, perhaps unintended, effects in the squatter settlements affected. Namely, this denial of government resources and services has facilitated privatization of infrastructure, which is elsewhere a more affordable public good—one whose capacity is, admittedly, severely overstretched. Privatization, consequently, has developed at the Yadana squatter settlement, not despite the challenge squatting poses to the rule of private property, but precisely because of it.

Reconstituted Peasants on an Industrial Frontier

Brother Khin's singlet was soaked through, and he was up to his belly in the water. As for the lesser part of him still above the surface, it was dwarfed by the five-meter-high cement perimeter wall to his left—an unpainted wall topped with barbed wire, as if the height had not already made scaling it impossible. But in any case, who would indulge in such a vain endeavor as to rob the warehouse on the other side, which, as it happened, held nothing but dried pulses and rice packed tight in fifty-kilogram sacks.[22]

Although it was not raining at that moment, Brother Khin had nonetheless needed to wait for the rainy season to begin, and for the plot behind his home to flood, before being able to plant his water spinach, otherwise known as water morning glory (*ipomoea aquatic*). What Brother Khin was planting—or more accurately tying to strings stretched across that flooded plot of land—were seedlings of the so-called Burmese strain of the plant. This variant, believed the thirty-six-year-old urban farmer, was more resilient than the Chinese strain that the two women in the next plot over were at that same moment planting, for the

Burmese variant could better withstand the heat. Or, as he then went on to elaborate in a moment of botanical nationalism, "the Burmese variety has more courage [*thati*] than the Chinese variety." But Brother Khin preferred eating the Burmese strain. For despite it being cheaper and taking longer to cook, it had the advantage of holding together over the long boil needed for making that watery sour curry that he so very much enjoyed.

At roughly 200 square meters, Brother Khin's agricultural plot was the smallest of seven such plots in the Yadana settlement. Now in his third year of cultivating water spinach, Brother Khin had originally laid claim to this piece of land by clearing the wild reeds and lilies growing on-site—a site that the city's urban planners had at one time designated for eventual factory construction. Although Brother Khin had no legal ownership of the plot, that initial labor of clearing the land had earned him, he believed, de facto ownership grounded in an understanding (*nalehmu*) with his neighbors. Consequently, no other squatters, he was certain, would encroach on his plot—whether to cultivate or construct a new dwelling. Although Brother Khin did not make this point explicit, his claim conveyed the principle of *dama ucha*—literally, the person "who first wields the machete" to clear land—which grounds customary tenure arrangements across much of rural Myanmar.[23] Notably, Brother Khin had, prior to his current water spinach venture, not once engaged in cultivation; his working life had been restricted to waiting tables at tea shops and restaurants in urban Yangon—a means of livelihood he had begun at the age of nine.

Given the small size of his plot, Brother Khin had no need to hire additional laborers. As neither boss nor employee Brother Khin saw his work as self-employment (*kobaing alok*). And that, he felt, had definite value. "When you work for someone else, you have to work whether you want to or not," he explained. "Whether the job is good or bad, you just have to keep working. And you have to endure harassment." And that was why his present situation, he felt, was superior to wage labor. "When you have land, you're your own boss. You don't have to follow someone else's orders." Thus laboring on his own terms, Brother Khin would in a month's time begin harvesting his water spinach to meet orders he would receive in advance from vegetable vendors in town. Such harvesting never took him more than a few hours, but he still had to begin at three o'clock in the morning, wearing a headlamp to see in the dark, for the vegetable sellers opened their stalls at six. Like this, Brother Khin earned around three-quarters of his household income. His wife, who worked at an unlicensed whisky distillery, contributed the rest.

Investigating the historical emergence of smallholder agriculture in the Caribbean, Sidney Mintz once argued that the region's peasantry had first appeared in the sixteenth and seventeenth centuries as a "mode of resistance" to colonial

FIGURE 6. Brother Khin planting water spinach in the Yadana squatter settlement. Author's photograph.

rule.[24] As Mintz proceeded to document, the Caribbean peasantry of that era comprised runaway slaves, former indentured laborers, and sundry squatters who took to smallholder cultivation as a means to stay out of slavery and other forms of colonial servitude. Having moved into smallholder cultivation, these one-time slaves and indentured laborers were, Mintz argued, as though peasants reconstituted: "Caribbean peasantries are, in this view, reconstituted peasantries, having begun other than as peasants—in slavery, as deserters or runaways, as plantation laborers, or whatever—and becoming peasants in some kind of resistant response to an externally imposed regimen."[25] It was because of this against-the-grain reading of Caribbean history that Jean Besson, in placing Mintz's analysis in a more contemporary context, writes that the latter saw peasantization as a critique of capitalism.[26]

In like ways, Brother Khin saw his cultivation of water spinach on squatted land as a means of staying out of capitalist employment, with all the restrictions and managerial harassment that such wage labor entails. It is in this respect that squatting, in transgressing the rule of property, becomes a moment in a struggle with anticapitalist content. To be sure, this particular urban farmer did not identify as a peasant (*taungthulethema*). He preferred instead the appellation cultivator (*saikbyoyethema*). His stated reasons for this terminological preference were that his agricultural plot was small, and his spouse engaged in wage labor, pooling her earnings with the household income. Notwithstanding the wider industrial context, and Brother Khin's own terminological use, his livelihood fits fine within scholarly definitions of the peasant. Eric Wolf, for instance, argued in 1955 that twentieth-century peasants not only depended on the commercial sale of their crops but were often at least partly dependent on off-farm employment.[27] And in 2012, Andrew Walker argued for retaining the term peasant in the context of northern Thailand, even though most households in that region earn a significant portion of their incomes from off-farm activities.[28] In any case, Brother Khin's cultivation grossed the bulk of his household income. Furthermore, he and his wife and their six-year-old daughter regularly consumed the fruits of their own crop. They also raised a half-dozen chickens for personal consumption.

But if urban agriculture enables squatters to avoid subordination in wage labor, why have so few squatters pursued such livelihoods? Many more would if they could, argued Brother Khin, but "most people don't own land." "At the moment," he added, "I've got a small home here, as well as this little plot of land. But the people who live over there [elsewhere in the settlement], they've only got a plot for a small home—nothing else. Next to them, there's a home. And behind them, there's a home. So they're unable to cultivate water spinach." Brother Khin's preference for smallholder cultivation over waged employment—a preference he believed to be widely shared—suggests that rural-to-urban migration does not in itself indicate an unambiguous desire among migrants for waged employment over peasant livelihoods, as the World Bank has implied in the Myanmar context.[29]

About a month after the sowing of water spinach at Yadana's seven plots, the plants were ready to harvest. Elsewhere in the settlement, and similarly up to his belly in water, was Brother Htay Win. Being half past six in the morning, the sun had risen and the forty-two-year-old agricultural worker had set aside his headlamp. Brother Htay Win and the other two workers employed for the day on that particular plot had begun harvesting at two hours past midnight. They had thus needed those headlamps to see their hands in the dark of the night as they handled the plants—pinching, pulling, and piling the leafy vegetables to one side. Like that, the three agricultural laborers were set to work for over eight hours, harvesting and tying 400 bundles of water spinach, as per the day's order. It was Mister Paing who owned, if only de facto, the plot in question, which at roughly 2,000 square meters, or nearly half an acre, was the largest of the seven plots at Yadana. It was also Mister Paing who would transport the vegetables by motorcycle to a market in town—a trip he would need to make three times that day to move the whole order. As it happens, Mister Paing was married to Brother Htay Win's younger sister. And the other two laborers out in the field were likewise his relatives—being Mister Paing's younger brother and the latter's wife. Each of these workers was to be paid at a rate of eight percent of the value of the order. But the workers would only receive their pay at the end of the day once the vendor had sold the last of the batch. At the going rate of 250 kyat per bundle, Brother Htay Win and his two coworkers were each expecting 8,000 kyat cash-in-hand for their day's labor, meaning 24,000 kyat would be paid out in wages, with Mister Paing keeping the 76,000 kyat remainder.

That Mister Paing was in the more profitable position of the employer in this arrangement was in part a matter of timing. When he had arrived at Yadana six years prior, the site had been sparsely inhabited. The newly arrived squatter had therefore been able to clear land—at the time, vacant—on which to subsequently cultivate water spinach. It had been with this land-as-capital that Mister Paing went on to profit with the use of hired labor. Brother Htay Win, meanwhile, had arrived at Yadana some three years later, at a time when there was no more vacant land available to clear for cultivation; the squatter frontier at Yadana was by then effectively closed. "Obviously it would be better," grumbled Brother Htay Win, as he stacked bundles of water spinach on the dock and pondered the counterfactual of possessing a plot of his own instead of having to labor like this for a wage. Such fantasies aside, his present harvesting job was intermittent. Although he would labor like this every day for a week, he would then need to wait at least another ten days for the plants to regrow, during which time he anticipated soliciting casual labor portering deliveries at nearby riverside depots.

A land dynamic similar to the Yadana experience played out among indigenous Lauje cultivators in upland Sulawesi, in Indonesia, as Tania Murray Li documented over the two decades spanning the turn of the twenty-first century.[30] There, the historical experience had long been one of shifting cultivation on an open land frontier. Cultivators would clear forest growth to make space for small horticultural plots but would need to move on after several years so as to allow the depleted earth to rejuvenate. So long as there was land available, prospective cultivators were able to establish their own gardens without being compelled to take on wage labor along the coast. Coastal markets were thus, in this context, an opportunity for crop sales. But upland cultivators could also consume their crops themselves if they found the market rates less than appealing. However, the expansion of plantation agriculture—the boom crop of cacao, specifically—led to a closure of the local land frontier. Individuals left landless were then compelled to seek out scarce wage labor as a means of livelihood since the cultivation of their own land was no longer an option; many also fell into debt.

In the Yadana context, such dynamics illuminate the contradictions of squatting as an anticapitalist practice. On the one hand, clearing land to cultivate

FIGURE 7. Brother Htay Win bundling water spinach, with Mister Paing gathering the bundles on the dock. Author's photograph.

water spinach enabled some squatters to avoid subordination in capitalist wage labor without requiring prior capital ownership. On the other hand, due to the limit of vacant land and the broader capitalist context, guerilla gardening as an anticapitalist practice became its opposite: a way to claim land-as-capital from which to profit by means of hired labor.

The everyday political-economic dynamics that have played out at the Yadana settlement illustrate the contradictory character of squatting within a capitalist context. To be sure, squatting at Yadana challenged the established hegemony of private property. Dispossessed ex-rural dwellers laid nonmarket claim to land that had been demarcated for private sale and eventual factory construction. Squatting at the Yadana settlement has thereby been a form of direct action, with residents under the persistent threat of eviction. In addition, at least some of Yadana's residents have argued for their "right of use," as against a "defense of absolute private property," which is a political stance that Claudio Cattaneo and Miguel Martínez attribute to the more overtly anticapitalist squatters' movement in Europe.[31] And in cases like Brother Khin's water spinach cultivation, squatting provided residents with the means to evade subordination in capitalist wage labor.

However, Yadana is neither outside nor autonomous of capitalism; the site and its residents remain embedded in capitalist relations of extraction and exploitation, and state relations of rule. It is for this reason that, notwithstanding the initial challenge squatting poses to the rule of property, a potential reversion to private ownership and state rule remains inherent from the start. Thus, with the exhaustion of vacant land on-site, real estate and rental markets emerged from among squatters themselves. And petty capitalists, such as Messrs Shwe Sein and Paing, were able to claim without cost land-as-capital for subsequent profit, exploiting hired labor to this end in the case of the latter.

Such developments are by no means unique. They recall, for example, James Holsten's research on "insurgent citizenship" in Sao Paulo, Brazil, whereby squatters contested their political exclusion by "auto-constructing" informal dwellings along the city's urban periphery—a political practice that, although initially subversive, nonetheless entangled squatters in entrenched relations property ownership and state rule.[32] In similar ways, property arrangements all across urban Yangon are marked by historically sedimented layers of informal understanding and formal-legal ownership, as Elizabeth Rhoades has documented in her research into the city's socio-legal history.[33]

This is not to dismiss the political significance of squatting as a challenge to the status quo, or to deny the practice its anticapitalist potential. But squatting is anticapitalist only insofar as it is a moment in a struggle—part of a movement to contest the present order of things, rather than a state of affairs to be established.[34] To assert otherwise would be to hypostatize the squat—to treat it, in other words, as a thing in itself, conceptually severed from the broader social context through which it is constituted.

4

DEBT COLLECTION AS LABOR DISCIPLINE

Uncle Win was not at all pleased. "This isn't meager work," the old man insisted, lugging a bucket of water back from the communal pump. The work he spoke of—the work he was now undertaking, all but naked in a threadbare sarong—was the care of three pigs he kept in a makeshift pen across from his home on the eastern edge of the Yadana squatter settlement. On top of visiting neighbors each day in search of leftover rice and curry to use as pig feed, Uncle Win had to bathe these animals at least three times a day just to keep their temperatures down. Being CP pigs—a high-value breed engineered by the Thai agro-industrial conglomerate, Charoen Pokphand—they were particularly susceptible to heat-induced illness. If Uncle Win failed to bathe them as required, they might pass out—even die.

Uncle Win's dilemma was that the largest of his three pigs was less than fifty kilograms. He had hoped to wait until the swine was at least 80 kilograms before selling. Unfortunately, Uncle Win's debt was coming due in a matter of weeks. He had somehow imagined he might get 220,000 kyat (approximately US$145) for the animal, which would have covered the arrears plus interest his absentee landlord was demanding as debt—a penalty for Uncle Win having missed his rent two months earlier. But the slaughterhouse purchasing agent who had visited the settlement the day before had offered a mere 150,000 kyat. Uncle Win was indignant, and it was not just about the labor. Having invested so much care in these pigs, he explained, as he showered them with scoopfuls of water, he now felt a sense of attachment (*thanyawzin*) to the animals. How could he go sell his largest on the cheap? What is more, Uncle Win suspected that the pur-

FIGURE 8. Uncle Win's three pigs in their bamboo pen next to the Yadana squatter settlement. Author's photograph.

chasing agent, deft at recognizing and manipulating financial duress, knew of his debt, likely having inquired into the matter with one of Uncle Win's more spiteful neighbors. Given the circumstances, Uncle Win's plan was to step up his waste collection activities, by which he could earn 4,000 to 5,000 kyat per day—not a lot, but hopefully enough to allow him and his wife to hold out for a better offer on the pig.

All planning aside, when the purchasing agent returned ten days later, Uncle Win, by now distraught over the thought of potential eviction in less than a week, dropped his price by a quarter. The agent, perhaps smelling a fire sale, lowered his own offer in turn. This was too much. Uncle Win contacted his landlord and implored her to reschedule his debt. Yes, full repayment could be deferred, she offered, but for an additional 40 percent monthly interest, either that or he sell the hog. It was not ideal, but the arrangement would allow Uncle Win to hold onto the animal for the time being. In the end, when he did sell the pig a month later, he managed to get just 195,000 kyat. Although this allowed him to pay off his debt, he had by then invested even more labor caring for the swine, and the added interest significantly eroded what remained of his profit. Perhaps if he had held out longer, the outcome would have been different. But in any case, it was now April, the hottest month of the year, and that pig might well have been dead of heatstroke within a month.

The predicament that Uncle Win confronted amid the swelter of Myanmar's hot season sheds light on the mutual imbrication of debt and labor in what is commonly known as the informal economy. Since the end of socialist rule in 1988, indebtedness has proliferated among low-income households in Myanmar—the bulk of the country's population—fueled by inflation and privatization as interrelated processes.[1] Consequently, some 85 percent of Yangon's slum dwellers, of whom Uncle Win is but one, are currently in debt to informal lenders.[2] Although these debts are overwhelmingly incurred through unregulated financial transactions, such so-called informal finance has kept pace with and remains deeply tied to more formal financialization processes at national and transnational scales.[3] As such, Myanmar's personal debt crisis echoes that of many countries globally, wherein mass financialization since the end of the last century has fueled growth of household indebtedness.[4] The role and effects of debt in relation to labor are additionally noteworthy in Uncle Win's case, given the form of labor—informal petty production—that he pursued.

Although informality simply refers to that which lies outside of state regulation, the informal economy is characterized by heterogeneous livelihoods that often diverge from normative forms of capitalist labor. Indebtedness in the informal economy thus provides a privileged vantage point from which to query the dichotomy distinguishing financial rents from labor profits, a dichotomy that anthropologists have subjected to critical scrutiny.[5] In brief, financialization alongside deindustrialization in the Global North has led some analysts to conclude that profits no longer rest on labor.[6] In what follows, I contest that claim, arguing that financialization and the multiplication of nonnormative labor arrangements are interrelated processes, whose dynamics are usefully studied together. This is to say that proliferating debt relations have enabled an effective extraction of value from nonnormative labor arrangements in the informal economy. Such is the case with Uncle Win's pig rearing, as well as with varieties of debt bondage and disguised wage labor.

On the Materiality of Fictitious Capital

That development trajectories in the postcolonial world no longer anticipate mass industrial employment, that wageless life is an enduring norm across much of the Global South, that the citizen-worker is more an ideological claim than a realistic aspiration—these are trends well documented in critical development studies.[7] Interwoven, they substantially repudiate prior developmentalist teleologies.

As means to grasp conceptually the predicament of those persisting precariously outside of regular employment, Tania Murray Li proposes Karl Marx's notion of surplus populations—surplus, that is, "relative to the needs of capital."[8] Thus, regarding rural smallholders dispossessed of their lands to make way for large-scale plantations, "their land is needed, but their labor is not."[9] Redundant to capital, such populations constitute not even a labor reserve—a jobless proletariat whose potential employment enables employers to suppress wages and break strikes.[10] Kalyan Sanyal put the argument somewhat differently. India's urban slums, he wrote, are characterized by classlessness, as ex-peasants-cum-surplus-populations pursue informal livelihoods outside of any class relations of exploitation.[11] Along resonant lines, James Ferguson rejects proletarian as a label for the inhabitants of postcolonial urban slums because of their noninvolvement in capitalist production.[12] Mike Davis, by contrast, notes that capitalist production does endure within urban slums, but he nevertheless presents such settlements, the informal sector, and surplus populations as virtually synonymous.[13] And finally, as a concrete instance of such a surplus population, Brenda Chalfin points to informal waste collectors laboring on rubbish dumps near the Ghanian city of Ashaiman.[14]

By highlighting structural unemployment across much of the Global South, these critiques effectively trouble the hubris of modernization theory. However, the analytical framing—surplus populations, in particular, when understood as individuals wholly redundant to capital—gives a misleading impression of the urban poor as a distinct group outside all relations of exploitation. The ethnographic data presented herein does not support such a characterization. Instead, I argue, the informal economy across the Global South, and in urban slums specifically, is crisscrossed by heterogeneous class relations of exploitation, with debt serving as a crucial means of discipline and value extraction. Labor, consequently, remains needed, though often outside of formal employment.

As global patterns, deindustrialization, automation, and casualization variously inform this growing awareness of the limits to employment growth. Notably, these trends overlap with financialization as a historical process since the late twentieth century. Together, these contrasting developments have led economists to posit a dichotomy between a real productive economy currently in decline, and a financial or fictitious economy on the rise. The real/fictitious binary, as Deborah James observes, has been cited most widely in countries like South Africa, where the expansion of financial markets has far surpassed labor-intensive industrial production, resulting in the phenomenon we now refer to as jobless growth.[15] But even radical political theorists, like Antonio Negri, have embraced a version of the real/fictitious binary—in Negri's case, to argue that, given the "immateriality" of contemporary finance, "profit becomes radically separated from labor."[16] Likewise, Michael Hardt writes that financialization is part of a structural shift "from profit to rent."[17]

Approaching the issue through an anthropological lens, Jane Guyer and Federico Neiburg contest the language that distinguishes a "real" productive economy from one that is "financial or fictitious."[18] Among their arguments is that the discursive construction of economic reality is not ideologically neutral; it serves to erase from consideration diverse modes of economic life, thereby legitimizing particular political-economic projects. Guyer and Neiburg are not the first to critique the real/fictitious binary. Christian Marazzi has likewise argued against analytically pitting finance, as fictitious, against production, as real.[19] Meanwhile, Carlo Vercellone insists that credit relations allow for the extraction of profit (as financial rent) from labor that operates outside the purview of direct capitalist management—a situation that has expanded with the proliferation of nonnormative labor arrangements. Under such conditions, Vercellone contends, "the very frontiers between rent and profit begin to disintegrate."[20] Veronica Gago and Sandro Mezzadra likewise argue that capitalism at present exhibits a proclivity toward extractivism—a mode of accumulation that includes literal resource extraction, as well as appropriation (through finance) of surplus from labor outside the direct wage relation. In such situations, argue Gago and Mezzadra, "we are faced with capitalist actors who do not directly organize the social cooperation that they exploit."[21] By no means unique, such conditions in contemporary urban production recall Marx's writings on the formal subsumption of home-based producers to merchant capitalists under putting-out arrangements, as well as forms of debt-based extraction long found across rural Southeast Asia's rice-growing lowlands.[22]

At first glance, contemporary use of the real/fictitious binary likewise seems consonant with Marx's arguments concerning finance as fictitious capital. For Marx, financial capital was fictitious in that it was not directly engaged in the production process. It was, however, a claim on the profits of future production, which may go unrealized or burst as a financial bubble.[23] Finance, as an anticipatory relation, in this way remains tied, though temporally displaced, to labor in production, with personal debt serving as a mechanism of value extraction.[24] Moreover, as an atomizing relation, personal debt, unlike collective employment, fragments borrowers, inhibiting collective negotiation over the terms of repayment. This fragmentary dynamic is but one way in which debt, as a technology of power, has been used historically to discipline laboring populations—from colonial peasantries to industrial working classes.[25] That debt operates in this way—as both a disciplinary and extractive mechanism—sheds light on the current proliferation of nonnormative labor arrangements, not least in the informal economies of the Global South. Such are the findings of the research I recount ethnographically in the present chapter, drawn from a selection of livelihoods among residents of the Yadana squatter settlement.

Occupations at this site are diverse, with residents engaged in varieties of wage labor, as well as otherwise independent livelihoods that are often structured by debt relations. Such was the case with Uncle Win, as it is with the other individuals considered herein.[26] In most instances, these occupations diverge from what is commonly (though misleadingly) termed the Standard Employment Relationship—that is, full-time employment for an identifiable employer at a designated worksite on an open-ended contract with rights and benefits as prescribed by law.[27] Despite this divergence from normative capitalist employment, it would be inaccurate to label these livelihoods noncapitalist, or to posit their labor as operating outside class relations of exploitation.

The Moral Economy of Disguised Wage Labor

Aunty Cho was proud of her daughters' new earrings, despite the debt. "Other children have earrings," she explained, seated cross-legged on the bamboo-slatted floor of her home. "I felt bad that my daughters had nothing to wear." True, her eldest had worn earrings in the past, but Aunty Cho had sold that pair to cover the costs of two funerals; her sister and mother-in-law died the year prior within three months of each other. And funerals are expensive. Those earrings had not been worth nearly enough. That is why she had borrowed an additional 160,000 kyat from Mister Arul, who owned the waste purchasing depot, or junkyard, where Aunty Cho sold the assorted plastics, metals, and cardboard that she and her husband collected—items that Mister Arul would resell to recycling plants, where they would be broken down and resold domestically, or exported as production materials to industrial manufacturers in China. In this way, like informal waste collectors elsewhere, Aunty Cho and her husband labored at the bottom of a global recycling industry that has been valued at over 200 billion dollars.[28]

Mister Arul, a Hindu and ethnic Tamil, was patient and good-natured, Aunty Cho remarked, her broad grin suggesting her sincerity. Not only had Mister Arul been willing to lend her the money interest free, he had not even set a repayment schedule. He merely deducted manageable repayment amounts from the total he paid to Aunty Cho and her husband each week for the items they brought to him for resale. Mister Arul's generosity notwithstanding, Aunty Cho did not seek to drag out repayment; she paid off the debt within four months. Out of debt since last year, Aunty Cho felt it appropriate to borrow once again from Mister Arul—this time 120,000 kyat for two pairs of gold earrings.

FIGURE 9. Delivering scavenged items for resale at Mister Arul's waste depot. Author's photograph.

Like this, Aunty Cho was back in debt. But it did not worry her much. The debt added to her obligation to sell to Mister Arul, even when another depot was offering a better price. But she was under this obligation anyway, since it was a condition of using the metal collection cart that Mister Arul lent her free of charge. In any case, she would not even consider selling her items elsewhere, and she had never once done so in the two-and-a-half years she had worked collecting discarded items. Since the start, she had only ever sold to Mister Arul, even though there were, according to Mister Arul, about thirty such waste purchasing depots in the township. Some collectors were disloyal, according to Aunty Cho, and despite using a cart from one depot, they would surreptitiously sell their items to another depot that was offering a higher rate. But such individuals were rare. As for Aunty Cho, her relationship with Mister Arul was based, she felt, on understanding (*nalemhu*), trust (*yongyihmu*), and loyalty (*thitsa*). It would be inappropriate to sell elsewhere. And on this matter, Mister Arul, seated at a wooden desk behind a mountain of plastic bottles at his purchasing depot some weeks later, concurred. "We've grown close," he explained, regarding his relationships with the individuals to whom he lent his fourteen collection carts. "They would never sell elsewhere."

The arrangement in place here, as both Aunty Cho and Mister Arul acknowledged, is one of monopsony—a market, that is, with but a single buyer. Relations of this sort have been similarly documented among informal waste collectors elsewhere, as they were in Kaveri Gill's Delhi study.[29] It is due to their monopsonistic character that such arrangements have come to be labeled disguised wage labor. For in such cases, seemingly self-employed producers otherwise free to sell their wares on the open market have become bound, as though employees, to a single buyer, who is able to set the price of sale.[30] Unlike formal employment, however, labor protection laws—regarding workers' compensation, social security, or the minimum wage, for example—have no purchase here.

To be sure, informal waste collectors are not everywhere bound by such obligations. And where expectations of this sort exist, collectors may decide to covertly sell their wares elsewhere, refusing the monopsonistic relationship that is being imposed. Such was the case with the migrant waste collectors I studied in the Thai border town of Mae Sot, as well as the collectors that Kathleen Millar researched at a dump outside of Rio de Janeiro.[31] Given the possibility of transgression, depot owners like Mister Arul have endeavored to cultivate committed relationships with the waste collectors on whose labor they depend. Thus, Mister Arul lent out his collection carts free of charge and offered microcredit free of interest. In response, both parties came to see their relationship as based on understanding, trust, and loyalty—a business arrangement, but one that was also inseparably an ethical relation of mutual obligation. Consequently, any attempt to account for this relationship in exclusively economistic or, alternatively, moral terms would be reductive, as well as erroneous.

It has been a standard anthropological move ever since Bronisław Malinowski's Trobriand intervention to critique economistic accounts of human social interaction.[32] In this Malinowskian spirit, anthropologists have variously framed the cultural dimension of economic life in terms (more or less synonymous) of E.P. Thompson's moral economy, Karl Polanyi's embeddedness, or Marcel Mauss's gift exchange.[33] A common anthropological understanding has seen moral economy, the embedded economy, and gift economies as operating outside, autonomous, or interstitial to the depersonalized market rationale that presumably characterizes capitalism—the household as opposed to the market, for example.[34] By contrast, subsequent theoretical interventions have critiqued this opposition that pits moral economy against political economy.[35] In this critical perspective, moral economy does not delineate an extra-capitalist realm; it instead labels, in a capitalist relation, political economy's ideological dimension—the particular value judgments and moral claims that inform everyday economic behavior.[36]

So, too, debt is never just an economic relation. Notwithstanding coercive enforcement of financial contracts, monetary debt always rests on the moral claim of an obligation to repay.[37] That is why financial markets require constant ideological work—the labor of legitimation, without which such markets would break down. In this respect, financial debts and moral obligations operate in mutually constitutive registers rather than according to their own autonomous logics.

From Filial Duty to Debt Bondage

By the age of ten, Zaw was a bonded laborer, but he does not blame his parents. Although he had not yet finished fifth grade, even he could see—"with his own eyes," his father lamented—that his parents were in dire straits. At the time, Zaw's father—Mister Lin—had intermitted work on assorted casual jobs, while his mother would pick wild water spinach from roadside ditches to sell at the market. Their household was 500,000 kyat in debt, and a doctor had recently diagnosed Mister Lin with asthma, which severely constrained his capacity to work. It was around this time that a neighbor told Zaw's parents that her own son had obtained a job at a teashop not too far away, and that Zaw could work there, too, if they so desired.

Before the week was out, Mister Lin had withdrawn his son from school, handed him over to the teashop owner, and accepted 35,000 kyat (about US$23) in return. This was a one-month advance on Zaw's future salary. Subsequently, the employer was keen to give Zaw's father regular five-month advances. The boss "was satisfied that he had a worker who wouldn't run away," Mister Lin recalls. These larger advances also meant Zaw's father only had to travel to the teashop once every five months to collect the money and to see the boy.

As far as Zaw reckoned, this was *kyayzu set*, meaning repaying a debt of gratitude to one's parents. Admittedly, there were times he wanted to run home during those first months, particularly when his boss yelled at him or smacked him on the head for a mistake he had made. But eventually, Zaw accommodated himself to teashop life. In any case, his boss was not nearly as nasty as some others of whom he had heard. Each morning, having slept about four hours, Zaw would wake at 3:00 a.m. His duties were initially limited to tidying up, washing dishes, and waiting tables, but over the years—he is now 17—he has learned additional skills, such as brewing tea and baking flatbread. He gets several hours off in the afternoon when customers are scarce, and he uses this time to catch up on sleep. Work continues from the moment he wakes until the shop closes at around 10:00 p.m. Although he does not get a regular day off, the teashop owner does let him take four days each year to visit his family.

Over the years, Zaw's salary has risen, but it has scarcely outpaced inflation. He presently gets—along with room and board—80,000 kyat (about US$53) per month, which means his father collects regular five-month advances of 400,000 kyat; no cash ever passes through Zaw's hands. Mister Lin, who no longer works, puts the money toward the household budget, or uses it to pay off recurring debts. Were Zaw to quit his job, he would have to repay or work off this advance in full before the employer would allow him to leave. In this way, Zaw remains bonded by debt to his employer—a condition he has never successfully left in over seven years.

The arrangement under which Zaw labors is not exceptional in Myanmar. Research on human trafficking in the country points to an increase in parents brokering their children's entry into labor bondage, as a response to growing poverty and debt.[38] According to the International Labor Organization, there are an estimated 1.2 million child laborers in Myanmar, between the ages of five and seventeen, who work an average of fifty-two hours per week, typically in conditions of debt bondage.[39] As Zaw saw it, the reason his boss opted to employ children was clear. Lower wages aside, the issue was one of discipline: "Adults don't concentrate on their work," he explained, "and they always want to go out. Children aren't like that. The owner just has to yell, and the children get scared and won't want to go out. The employer can control child workers, and he doesn't let them go out. When they're not on duty, he makes them sleep. And he makes them stay in the teashop."

Of course, Zaw's conditions of employment were in violation of Myanmar labor law. The 1951 Shops and Establishments Law (amended in 2016) prohibits teashops and other such establishments from employing children under the age of fourteen and requires a certificate of medical fitness (which Zaw did not possess) for child workers fourteen years old and above. This same law restricts overtime to employees sixteen years of age or older, requires that any such overtime be voluntary, and obliges employers to schedule at least one day off per week, as compared to Zaw's four days off per year. Moreover, even factoring in deductions for room and board, Zaw's monthly salary of 80,000 kyat fell well short of the legal minimum—4,800 kyat per day, as of March 2018. He received, as well, no additional pay for his many hours of overtime.

When Keith Hart introduced the concept of the informal sector in 1973, it was understood as referring to heterogeneous forms of unregulated self-employment in the postcolonial world—forms of livelihood that rural-to-urban migrants took up until they achieved entry into formal waged labor.[40] Since its introduction, critics have challenged the formal-informal dichotomy on multiple fronts, beginning with Jan Breman's classic critique of labor market dualism.[41] Central to Breman's argument was a recognition that informality denotes not a distinct sector of the economy but a condition of labor outside of state regulation; this is because of either an absence of applicable labor protection laws, or because the laws that are applicable are not being effectively enforced. It is under this latter state of affairs that Zaw has labored for so many years.

Legal issues aside, Zaw's employment challenges certain other assumptions regarding the character of capitalist labor. On the one hand, his parents and employer operated in a context of market compulsions—conditions deemed definitive of capitalism, and which have intensified in Myanmar since the end of socialist rule.[42] On the other hand, being bonded in debt, Zaw's labor was not free in the liberal sense of freedom to leave one's employer. That unfree labor is not antithetical to capitalism is by now well established.[43] Nonetheless, claims to the contrary—both liberal and Marxist—remain influential.[44] Moreover, aside from unfreedom, Zaw was also, in a certain sense, unwaged, as payment for his labor went directly to his father. In this case, the character of the capitalist labor arrangement was overdetermined by a particular cultural/ideological expectation—the extra-economic compulsion, as it were, of filial obligation.

Salvage Accumulation as Merchant Capitalism

The sack's faded lettering indicated its previous life as a bearer of rice. Today, however, it would hold nothing but worms. Repurposed gunnysack unfolded by her side, Aye Win thrust her gloveless hands deep into the mixture of mud and manure, in which, knee-deep, she stood. Each earthworm encountered, she placed on the sack, later to be wiped off and bagged. In just this way did her husband toil, working through his own section of sludge not twenty feet away. Present, as well, were her nephew and little brother, looking to earn some cash while school was out.

Like this, Aye Win and family labored to late afternoon in a vacant lot they often visited behind a commercial cattle shed. Serving as a catchment for cattle manure and urine, the site was ideal for the incubation of worms. Being hot season, however, the worms were not plentiful. Husband and wife thus ended the day with only 1.9 kilograms combined, according to the weights of the eel merchant, Ohn Pe.

Those weights—Aye Win was certain—were false. But what is a person to do? True, there was another eel merchant in town, who also paid more, but switching buyers is not easily done. For one thing, Aye Win owed Ohn Pe 60,000 kyat—a debt with no interest or expectation of immediate repayment but with an obligation for exclusive sale. And so, the debt just sat there, growing incrementally if ever Aye Win needed to cover some religious donation or unexpected consumption shortfall. This ready access to credit (albeit small-scale) was one rea-

FIGURE 10. Aye Win's husband and nephew scavenge for worms behind a commercial cattle shed. Author's photograph.

son Aye Win persisted in this work. Her debt thus grew, but slowly, serving as a bond whose repayment she could perennially defer, at least until such time as she wanted out. In any case, it had been six years—ever since her move to Yangon—that Aye Win had scavenged worms for Ohn Pe. And while she at first labeled her occupation self-employment (*kobaing alok*), she occasionally slipped into calling Ohn Pe her employer (*alokshin*).

In this way, the merchant Ohn Pe maintained a regular supply of worms, which he sold as bait to collectors of wild eels, who trapped their prey in urban pools of stagnant water. And these latter collectors were in far more debt to him than worm scavengers, like Aye Win. It was due to these larger debts—commonly hundreds of thousands of kyat invested in a motorcycle to transport the eels—that Aye Win considered eel hunting, even more so than worm collection, an employment relation. "You can't call eel catchers self-employed," she asserted. "They've borrowed so much money from the eel merchant that if they take a day or two off, the merchant will get after them. If they have a health issue, they're allowed to rest. But if they don't have a health issue, they're not allowed to rest." In this way, Ohn Pe maintained his regular supply of wild eels, which he sold to a Yangon-based export house that shipped them live to China for resale and eventual consumption.

But what about those false weights? This, Aye Win believed, was more of a problem for the eel collectors, whose catch was heavier. But either way, she declared, Ohn Pe was "stealing weight." There had been murmurs of discontent among the eel collectors, who had discussed the need to say something to Ohn Pe about the matter. But as yet, the collectors, who remained in the merchant's debt, had failed to raise the issue.

Much like Aunty Cho, Aye Win and the handful of other worm collectors at Yadana were bound by debt to a monopsonistic relationship, one whose conditions of purchase were less than ideal. Ohn Pe could theoretically have employed the worm scavengers and eel hunters directly. But such an arrangement would, for the merchant, have been unprofitable, at least in the assessment of Aye Win's sister and fellow collector Ee Phyu. And the merchant did evidently prefer to outsource this work—an arrangement that also removed whatever obligations he might otherwise bear toward these individuals as workers under Myanmar labor law.

This scavenging for worms in which Aye Win engaged, along with the hunting of eels it enabled, recalls the collection of matsutake mushrooms about which Anna Tsing has so prominently written. In both cases, the gritty work of scavenging a wild commodity is subsumed to a transnational capitalist supply chain, while the labor remains outside of the Standard Employment Relationship. It is for this reason that Tsing calls the arrangement *salvage accumulation*—"the process through which lead firms amass capital without controlling the conditions under which commodities are produced."[45] Informing her position is the work of J.K. Gibson-Graham, for whom self-employment was an economic form autonomous of capitalist logics.[46]

Similarities with the matsutake aside, the scavenging of worms and the hunting of eels by residents of the Yadana squatter settlement are not wholly outside of capitalist control. Beyond monopsonistic purchasing agreements, the merchant Ohn Pe invested the capital needed to acquire motorcycles as a crucial technology in the procurement of wild eels. And aside from the indirect discipline of debt bondage, Ohn Pe would at times directly admonish errant hunters who delayed too long in the collection of eels. The arrangement could be more precisely labeled merchant capitalism.

In ideal-typical form, the merchant capitalist merely invests in and manages commodity circulation. In practice, however, the line distinguishing the merchant and industrial capitalist is often blurred.[47] We see this ambiguity in contemporary putting-out arrangements, wherein the merchant operates as coordinator of a dispersed division of labor incorporated into factory production.[48] This conceptual blurring recalls Alexander Chayanov's early twentieth-century analysis of peasant farms that were "vertically integrated" into capitalist production networks, such that peasant agriculture became reorganized "according to capitalist principles."[49] Although the level of managerial oversight over the labor process in such cases is less than with in-house industrial manufacturing, it would be inaccurate to deem these laborers autonomous of capitalist control. In any case, the capitalist character of the labor in question derives not from its form, which may appear, like the unwaged scavenging of worms, precapitalist, but rather from the constitutive relations in which it is embedded—relations that include debt and its disciplinary enforcement.

Toward an Anthropology of Capitalist Variegation

The many critiques of modernization theory's historicist assumptions have highlighted the limits to full employment as a developmental aspiration—limits that are reinforced through automation, deindustrialization, and the casualization of labor. Despite the evident barriers to mass employment—and to stable, well-remunerated employment, in particular—the citizen-worker nexus continues to serve as a basis for allocating rights and benefits in liberal political orders.[50] Meanwhile, the privileging of employment as a capitalist norm has the added ideological implication of legitimating subordination in wage labor.[51]

At the same time, analyses that envisage all labor outside formal employment as being outside capitalism, or outside of capitalist class relations, or simply outside the circuits of capital accumulation remain in thrall of the bourgeois myth that capitalism is coterminous with the employment of free wage labor. Such is the case where the surplus population category has been taken to mean that all individuals so labeled are wholly and permanently exterior to capitalist production. It should be clarified here that what Marx spoke of were *relative* surplus populations. And he enclosed the qualifying adjectives "redundant" and "unproductive" in scare quotes to distance his own interpretation from that of bourgeois economists. His reasoning was this: aside from individuals unable to work, such as "victims of industry . . . the mutilated, the sickly," surplus populations are always potentially and often intermittently brought into capitalist production.[52] "Every worker," Marx argued, is deemed a part of the surplus population "during the time when he is only partially employed or wholly unemployed."[53] Such populations include rural dwellers pursuing peasant livelihoods who can, as needed, be enticed or compelled to seek out urban wage labor, as well as industrial workers floating in and out of factory employment according to the vagaries of the market. But populations deemed surplus by bourgeois economists (and often treated as disposable by political elites) also include, Marx observed, individuals who are in fact already engaged in capitalist production, whether by way of casual employment or as outsourced, home-based production units subsumed to capitalist enterprises. Of this ostensibly superfluous category, Marx elaborated thus: "This [group] forms a part of the active labor army, but with extremely irregular employment. Hence it offers capital an inexhaustible reservoir of disposable labor-power. Its conditions of life sink below the average normal level of the working class, and it is precisely this which makes it a broad foundation for special branches of capitalist exploitation. It is characterized by a maximum of working time and a minimum of wages. We have already become familiar with its chief form under the rubric of 'domestic industry.'"[54]

It is such so-called domestic industry, subsumed to capitalist enterprise, that has served as a livelihood for so many of Yadana's residents, including folks like Uncle Win, Aunty Cho, and Aye Win, who labor outside of direct waged employment, but who remain embedded in capitalist relations of surplus extraction, with debt facilitating their exploitation, and in some cases their bondage as well. Recognizing in this way the capitalist character of such nonnormative labor arrangements opens up for analysis the ways in which diverse forms of livelihood outside of the Standard Employment Relationship remain incorporated into circuits of capital accumulation. Put differently, in an inherently uneven political economy, such seemingly marginal labor remains integral to capital accumulation. The corollary argument here is that an individual's redundancy to capital can only ever begin as an empirical question.

The heterogeneity of capitalist relations has long been a feature of colonial and postcolonial political economy. But this multiplicity increasingly characterizes the Global North as well under deindustrialization, market liberalization, and the drive to cheapen and disorganize labor.[55] This is a trajectory of mimesis, as it were—from South to North—that Ranabir Samaddar identifies as the globalization of the postcolonial predicament.[56] And in this respect, the sorts of informal economic relations examined in this chapter are not peripheral to capital accumulation, but are instead frontiers of twenty-first-century capitalist development. Centering, in such a way, the capitalist antipodes, Jean Comaroff and John Comaroff argued that "it is the south that often is the first to feel the effects of world-historical forces, the south in which radically new assemblages of capital and labor are taking shape, thus to prefigure the future of the global north."[57] Echoing this analysis, Jan Breman and Marcel van der Linden argue that contemporary manifestations of flexible and precarious labor in the Global North follow patterns of casual and informal employment long prevalent in the South.[58] We see, for instance, the Uber Corporation extending car loans to prospective drivers who, classified as "independent contractors," enter in this way into relations of debt-bondage with the company—the drivers' loan repayments "taken straight out of their wages."[59]

Given this diversity of labor arrangements, inductive economic anthropology remains the most effective means of investigating the heterogeneity of existing capitalist relations. To be sure, anthropologists attuned to such questions of capitalist diversity have long made a case for ethnographic attention to the unevenness and combination of heterogeneous capital-labor arrangements—an approach that would align critical anthropologists with geographers' attention to variegated capitalism.[60] It has, however, been an additional argument of this chapter that attention to debt relations is critical for understanding the specifically capitalist character of labor arrangements in all of their diversity. Moving beyond scholarship, an effective political response to the challenges of contemporary capitalism requires a lucid analytical grasp of this economic variegation, in place of a formalism that would analytically delimit capitalism as coterminous with the employment of free wage labor.

5

THE INTEGRAL INFORMALITY OF MARGINALIZED WORKERS

Brother Tin Maung had that song stuck in his head again. "Oh golden princess city girl," he crooned, "the green rice fields cannot compare to your green heart." It was a cover of a classic tune by Hinthada Htun Yin, and it told of the scorned love of a country boy for a city girl who, in the end, turns her back on the countryside.[1] "When I sing that song, I recall my village life," confessed Brother Tin Maung. It was a life that the young man had left just three years prior, at a time when his adolescence was coming to an end. In other words, he was now a city resident. Or, more specifically, he was barefoot, bare-chested, and caked with sawdust, standing in the muddied lot of a lumber mill, loading sacks of sawdust onto a forty-year-old Japanese lorry that was so rusted out you could spit your betel-infused saliva through a hole in the floor of the cab and it would pass right through the chassis to the road below.

Brother Tin Maung was also at that moment one of eight in a crew of porters hired by Mister Myo, who owned that rusted-out truck, and who had bought that load of sawdust. In Burmese, the work the crew was undertaking is known as *kon tin kon kya*, the labor of "loading and unloading commodities." Where such labor occurs on riversides or at coastal wharfs workers such as these have in English been referred to as stevedores or longshoremen. In colonial India, such workers were deemed coolies, a term that was then adopted into Burmese and, although considered offensive in English, remains in circulation in Myanmar.

"Hey! We're going out again on Friday," announced Mister Myo, who in a spotless sarong and immaculate white t-shirt sat to the side on a pile of wood, observing the work.

FIGURE 11. A resident of the Yadana squatter settlement carries a sack of sawdust onto Mister Myo's truck. Author's photograph.

FIGURE 12. Loading sacks of sawdust onto Mister Myo's truck. Author's photograph.

"That's in three days. I guess I'm taking the day off tomorrow," said Brother Tin Maung to a fellow porter.

Earlier that day, a little past six in the morning, Brother Tin Maung had left his home in the Yadana squatter settlement, reached the truck parked in front of Mister Myo's residence, and scrambled atop the cab with his seven coworkers. All of them—employer and employees alike—were residents of Yadana. Seated on the roof, the workers had exchanged jokes and chewed betel as the truck traversed a neighboring industrial zone—a one-hour trip to the lumber mill through the morning traffic of public buses and factory trucks ferrying young women to garment factories for their morning shifts.

At the mill—the site where Brother Tin Maung had broken out into song—the crew loaded the truck with sawdust, for which Mister Myo paid the mill owner 250,000 kyat. The loading took about three hours and about the same for unloading. The modern, Chinese-owned box factory that bought the haul that afternoon for 500,000 kyat would employ the sawdust as boiler fuel, producing steam for use in cardboard production. In that way, explained the boiler's operator, the factory consumed two truckloads of sawdust every two days. But it was not just cardboard factories. Brother Tin Maung and his crew also shipped these loads of sawdust to garment, vermicelli, and tofu factories, and to alcohol distilleries as well. And many more crews of this sort were similarly operating across all of Yangon's industrial zones. The resulting network of intermediary sawdust trading is like this an extensive upstream industry, supplying production materials to many of the factories that dot the industrial landscape around Yangon.

When later that day the work was done, and the sale of sawdust complete, Mister Myo handed each worker their day rate of 10,000 kyat (about US$6.65) in cash. Although there was an understanding of more such jobs in the future, and while most of this crew had worked with Mister Myo on and off for the past eight years, there was no formal contractual employment arrangement. The labor was casual, meaning there was no guarantee of work on any given day. Moreover, being the rainy season, construction was slow, lumber production thus down, sawdust scarce, and loading jobs few. The crew thus worked together only two, sometimes three days per week. In the hot season, by contrast, the crew had such work almost every day. Still, as casual laborers at an enterprise of fewer than ten employees, the workers were not included under the Social Security Law's obligatory enrollment; they could not file for compensation if the boss decided not to rehire them for subsequent jobs; and they were not covered by existing legislation requiring paid time off. In this way, the wage labor of Brother Tin Maung and his coworkers remained informal—

that is, outside legal labor regulation. Yet their labor was, through the registered factories that acted as buyers, incorporated into the industrial zone's more formal—that is, legally registered—circuits of capital accumulation, and in some cases (as with garment factories producing for export) into global supply chains as well.

The trading of sawdust in which Brother Tin Maung and his crew labored thus challenges certain prominent claims regarding the informal economy, and regarding the informal economy of the postcolonial urban slum in particular. Recall James Ferguson's contention concerning former peasants throughout the global South. Such individuals, he writes, "have left rural livelihoods for city living in recent decades. Yet instead of being swept up in an industrial revolution that would turn them into proletarians . . . they have more often been recruited into informal slums where they eke out a living via a complex range of livelihood strategies to which agriculture and formal-sector wage labor alike are often marginal."[2] It was along resonant lines that Kalyan Sanyal earlier argued—regarding the informal economies of India's urban slums, in particular—that such economies operate outside the circuits of formal capital accumulation and are characterized, furthermore, by classlessness, due to the prevalence of self-employment rather than capitalist wage relations.[3]

What we see at Yadana, by contrast, is extensive wage labor, further instances of which this chapter considers in depth. Although much of this labor is informal, it is often integrated into wider circuits of formal (legally registered) capital accumulation. But this insight is not new. Much of the classic anthropological work on Brazilian favelas, South African shantytowns, and South Asian slums documented similar class relations.[4] It was for such reasons that Jan Breman, in his critique of labor market dualism, argued against the concept of an informal sector, as it gave the misleading impression of a rigid dichotomy between autonomous economic spheres, whereas the so-called formal sector is often dependent on, and subsidized by, informal labor arrangements—in other words, arrangements not covered by legal labor protections, or where the applicable labor protection laws are not being effectively enforced.

This latter state of affairs informs Dae-Oup Chang's distinction between labor that is not covered by existing labor protection laws, and is thus de jure informal, and wage labor that is covered by such laws but where in practice the relevant laws are not being effectively enforced, leaving the wage labor in question de facto informal.[5] It is this last category that orients the present chapter—the cases that follow offering instances of labor that remains informal in fact, though not always in law.

The Home-Factory as Locus of Informal Employment

The-one-who-confronts-danger, as Mrs. Pwint had named her dog, appeared disinclined to raise its head despite all the chopping, frying, and grating. And so there on the bamboo floor the mottled mutt remained unmoved among cross-legged women slicing coconuts as one stage of production in Mrs. Pwint's home-factory, which lay along the road at the west end of the Yadana settlement. As for Mrs. Pwint's beige cats, all three were asleep, lying like weathered coconut husks discarded upon a mat unrolled below the household Buddha shrine. Production floor by day, this space would by evening become the living-room-cum-bedroom of Mrs. Pwint and her family. By then, exactly 450 coconuts were to be chopped, sliced, fried, weighed, and dispatched by truck to the wholesale vegetable market downtown—there to be resold as a fragrant additive for use in betel quids.

The term betel quid is somewhat misleading, as the key ingredient is areca nut, which along with slaked lime is wrapped in a betel leaf, to which the vendor will add a customer's preferred supplements—tobacco, for instance, or fried coconut shavings. The chewing of areca is ubiquitous in Myanmar—practiced by over 62 percent of men and over 24 percent of women—while the sale of the carcinogenic betel quids is dominated by equally ubiquitous independent roadside vendors.[6] As an addictive stimulant, betel quids are something of a staple of working-class life in Myanmar, such that domestic capitalist production is itself dependent, as it were, on betel consumption. Thus confessed one Burmese journalist regarding his dependency: "I worked late nights so to keep me awake and alert, I would chew betel the whole night."[7]

As for Mrs. Pwint, she had just finished bathing and was wearing a long Burmese skirt pulled up high across her chest as she sat grinding sandalwood into a paste to apply to her cheeks. With her in that section of the two-room home-factory were the five women shaving coconuts into slices, and another two women who were bagging said shavings once fried. Among the former was Sister Mon, who was managing with notable skill the dual tasks of slicing coconuts while breastfeeding her eight-month-old infant boy. Concerning these women, Mrs. Pwint felt obliged to clarify: "They can't get jobs in [garment] factories because they're too old," by which she meant the women had reached or passed their late twenties. Twenty-three-year-old Sister Mon would have been eligible for factory employment, but she would not have been able to keep her child by her side had she been working in garment production. She also lacked the requisite National Registration Card. Meanwhile, seventeen-year-old Cho Cho—likewise seated on the floor and repetitively slicing a segment of coconut—was below the age of legal factory employment.

FIGURE 13. Chopping coconuts in Mrs. Pwint's home factory. Author's photograph.

FIGURE 14. Frying coconut shavings in Mrs. Pwint's home factory. Author's photograph.

Chopping coconuts at that moment in the front room, which was little more than a bamboo-and-dani-palm vestibule over a dirt floor littered with spent husks, were thirteen-year-old Khin Zaw and twenty-four-year-old Brother Aung. Brother Aung had, for the moment, paused his chopping and put aside his machete because his four-year-old son had wandered in to ask for money to buy a snack. Behind the visiting boy stood forty-year-old Brother Kyaw—shirtless, silent, and sweating while stirring coconut shavings in a massive pan of boiling oil, using to do so a three-foot-long wooden paddle.

All ten individuals laboring for Mrs. Pwint were her neighbors and fellow squatters. While Brother Kyaw earned 9,000 kyat for a 7:00 a.m. to 6:00 p.m. shift as a fryer, the men chopping coconuts earned but 7,000 kyat for a similar period; the women doing the slicing and bagging got only 4,500 kyat. Given overtime hours, wages for everyone but Brother Kyaw were below the legal minimum of 4,800 kyat for an eight-hour shift, with a stipulated 1,200 kyat per hour of overtime. The workers also had no written contracts, got neither the legislated weekly day off nor paid holiday leave, and had not been registered with the Social Security Broad, which meant that they had no access to subsidized medical coverage at the township's Social Security Hospital. This last exclusion was particularly significant, since as Brother Kyaw proceeded to exclaim, "Of course there are injuries!," by which he meant the near-monthly accidents of men missing their coconuts and landing their machetes on their fingers and hands; Brother Kyaw held up his own scarred limbs as evidence. Finally, employment of a thirteen-year-old and seventeen-year-old violated the 2016 amendment to the 1951 Factories Act, which restricts factory employment to individuals fourteen years of age and older, limits factory employment of fourteen- and fifteen-year-olds to four hours per day, and requires a doctor's signed statement of medical fitness for the employment of children between the ages of fourteen to seventeen. In short, waged labor in Mrs. Pwint's fried coconut factory was in practice informal, despite the existence of applicable labor protection laws.

Given its small workforce, this enterprise was of the sort that is often called petty capitalist.[8] In much of the global South, enterprises of small size have been deemed informal based on their low employee numbers. In India, a government commission on informal employment deemed private enterprises employing less than ten workers to be constitutive of an unorganized sector, by which was meant a sector whose employees are legally excluded from social security benefits, and whose employment is, in that respect, informal.[9] In Myanmar, the 2012 Social Security Law similarly requires only enterprises employing ten or more workers to register their workforces with the Social Security Board. Consequently, enterprises employing fewer workers are, in regard to social security, de jure informal, in that they are not mandatorily covered by the relevant labor legislation. For this reason, some researchers engaged in Myanmar persist in speaking of an informal sector encompassing all enterprises of fewer than ten employees.[10]

In any case, with ten employees, Mrs. Pwint's fried coconut enterprise made it just over the threshold for obligatory social security registration—a requirement with which she did not comply. But even if the number of employees had been fewer, the 2013 Minimum Wages Act would have remained applicable. Consequently, as their wages were below the legal minimum, Mrs. Pwint's employees were informal in this respect as well, to say nothing of their lack of a weekly day off, in violation of the "Leave and Holiday Rules" that the Ministry of Labor, Immigration and Population had promulgated in 2018. Thus, even if the enterprise had been excluded from social security coverage due to a low number of employees, these employees would have remained de facto informal, because the Minimum Wages Act and other relevant labor laws were not being effectively enforced.

Matters of legality aside, the labor arrangements at this factory were clearly wage relations. The workers were thus proletarians in the broad sense of dispossessed individuals radically dependent on the market, as well as in the narrow sense of waged laborers employed in capitalist production—a working class, in the latter case, as it is more conventionally understood. In other words, we see here the proletariat's persistence, and wage labor specifically, within the postcolonial urban slum.

Now it so happens that Mrs. Pwint had for several years been head of the women's section of the local porters' union. Executive members of the union, when pressed on the matter, did not find this fact—an employer's membership in a workers' union—contradictory or even problematic. Since the union administration was only tangentially involved in workers' collective bargaining, Mrs. Pwint's role had been limited to following up and attempting to intervene in isolated cases of child rights violations in the township. She also donated to the annual May Day rally. Moreover, Brother Kyaw felt that as neighbors he and his employer had been close since before he had started his job. Indeed, as all these workers were neighbors, they had known each other and Mrs. Pwint since before the latter had opened her home-factory two years prior. Consequently, as Brother Kyaw saw it, the atmosphere at the home-factory was relaxed. Or as he subsequently elaborated: "There are few rules, and our family members can come and go as they please; that's a plus." Mrs. Pwint also provided ad hoc financial contributions toward the medical expenses of her employees' children. And since the enterprise was unregistered, she did not demand that workers possess a National Registration Card. This also meant that Mrs. Pwint was willing to employ workers below the legal age for factory employment. And although the workers got no scheduled rest days, they could, if requested in advance, take an unpaid day off, or so claimed Brother Kyaw, who also asserted that Mrs. Pwint had not once fired a worker since the enterprise opened.

The informal character of this enterprise thus facilitated opposing tendencies. On the one hand, the employer paid her employees below the legal minimum; employed child labor; did not provide legislated employment benefits, like statutory paid leave or compensatory income for such leave not taken; and she had not registered her employees with the Social Security Board. On the other hand, the informal relations at this enterprise blurred the conventional workplace-household distinction, such that workers as neighbors could impose social obligations on Mrs. Pwint. The latter had, in turn, acceded to a comparably relaxed workplace free of strict rules, where parents could care for their children at work.

As an informal home-factory, Mrs. Pwint's fried coconut enterprise also challenges certain dichotomies associated with social reproduction. In the 1970s, social reproduction theory emerged as an effective means of grasping analytically the ways in which women's unwaged domestic work was imbricated with, rather than autonomous of, capitalist production. Specifically, under a gendered division of labor, social reproduction was understood as critical to the reproduction of capitalism as a whole, such that women labored without wages in the home to reproduce the wage laborers (especially male family members) on whom continued capitalist exploitation depended.[11] The tendency has been to conceptualize an opposition between unwaged social reproduction in the "private sphere" of the home and waged production in the workplace.[12] This is a dichotomy that the evidence does not always support.

We see in Mrs. Pwint's home-factory such a blurring of categories, which troubles the analogy whereby the household is to social reproduction as the workplace is to production. The reason is that in Mrs. Pwint's fried coconut enterprise capitalist production occurred in the home, while unwaged social reproduction—Sister Mon's nursing of her child, for instance—took place on the factory floor. Moreover, the production and consumption of betel quids, which along with their various ingredients are a staple of working-class life, is itself part of Myanmar's culturally specific social reproduction process, much as Karl Marx observed in the reliance of British workers on beer and of French workers on wine.[13]

Varieties of Irregular Employment

Unlike everyone else, Brother Min lacked a satchel. What he did not lack was a bottle on a string. The bottle, empty of water, was plastic, while the string, tied around his waist, was like a belt worn threadbare. In the bottle were two faded dowels, some ten inches long, as though over-thick chopsticks in need of a bowl of Shan noodles. Those dowels were Brother Min's counters, and it was the fact that he had only two which lay at the root of his present consternation.

Employed as a stevedore, Brother Min was paid by the sack—100 kyat for each fifty-kilogram gunny of dried corn that he carried from the ship at the dock to the truck in the lot. But hardly five minutes into the job, and the labor boss had instructed them all to wait—the cause of the delay being the seemingly inexplicable fact that the truck currently being loaded was not, in fact, the correct recipient of the corn. The driver was thus on the phone with his boss trying to figure out how he could have possibly ended up at the wrong pier. By this point, Brother Min, who was killing time oscillating between jocular banter and indignant complaint, had carried exactly two sacks—thus two dowels. And thus exactly 200 kyat in earnings, enough for a single cup of instant coffee or two sticky-rice fritters, such as his mother, Aunty San, was selling to the idle stevedores lounging around her bamboo tray in the shade of another truck parked in the lot. Then all of a sudden, Brother Min went off: "I've got a son to feed!," the twenty-four-year-old father yelled, in a moment of indignation, as if to no one in particular.

When Brother Min had woken up that morning, lying on a mat rolled out on the floor of his home in the Yadana squatter settlement, next to his wife of three years and their eighteen-month-old son, he had not known he would later be loading sacks of dried corn onto a twenty-two-wheeled tractor-trailer parked at Mister Khin's riverside depot. He had not even known whether he would be working at all that day. That is because Brother Min was the type of employee whom Mister Khin referred to as an outside worker—the type who showed up looking for work in the morning, got paid cash-in-hand when the job was done and left with no commitment on the part of the employer for any subsequent employment. True, Brother Min had worked for Mister Khin on and off over the preceding four-plus months. But then again, he had also worked for several other depot owners up and down the riverside, loading and unloading sacks of gravel, rice, dried corn, or what have you. Like this, Brother Min's employment under Mister Khin had been long term but casual—intermittent, in other words, as opposed to permanent.[14] As such, the work in question was not covered by various labor laws. Brother Min received no guaranteed minimum wage, for instance, nor could he claim legislated compensation for arbitrary dismissal or seek subsidized medical coverage at the township's social security hospital. In this respect, his employment was de jure informal.

At the very moment that Brother Min was idling in frustration amid the confusion of the erroneous corn load, Brother Naing was unloading sacks of rice from a truck at a factory elsewhere in the industrial zone. Yet this man too was

FIGURE 15. Brother Min and fellow stevedores unloading sacks of corn at Mister Khin's depot. Author's photograph.

FIGURE 16. Aunty San (sitting) selling fritters to stevedores waiting around at Mister Khin's depot. Author's photograph.

employed by Mister Khin, who had dispatched the delivery truck in question. Brother Naing, however, had worked at the depot for the past nine years, ever since he was fifteen years old. He was also, significantly, an inside worker—the type who resided in on-site worker housing; the type who needed to request permission to take a day off; the type who had responsibility for transferring from truck to ship the near-daily deliveries of putrid slurry discharged as a by-product of rice-based alcohol production from distilleries in the zone, which someone had figured out could be used as a cheap fish-food substitute in the delta's many aquaculture ponds. Being a slurry, however, this distillery-waste-cum-fish-food tended to leak through the seams of the sacks in which it was stored—a phenomenon that lent the depot its persistently rank smell.

Mister Khin, the depot owner, was an enlightened sort of fellow. Critical of military rule, he argued that the prevalence of alcoholism in Myanmar was connected to the country's postsocialist transition and the military government's eagerness to profit off the sale of liquor licenses. He deplored the constrictive socioeconomic conditions in Myanmar, which had obliged most of his employees to drop out of school as children. He spoke of running a democratic workplace, which meant, he explained, that he permitted stevedores living on-site to take on additional piece-rate work at depots elsewhere on the riverside. And he made a point of emphasizing that he helped workers injured on the job by contributing out of his own goodwill (*sedana*) to their medical expenses. Here, *sedana* is a colloquial usage of Pali Buddhist terminology, which marks the subject's virtuous character. For *sedana* is used in Myanmar to index the selfless volition underlying charity (*dana*), the latter being one of ten Theravada Buddhist *paramis* (virtues), whose cultivation moves the agent that much closer to *naikban* (nirvana), the final and ultimate goal.[15] In any case, at least some employees at the depot considered Mister Khin good-natured (*seik gaungde*) and confirmed that their boss did indeed contribute to the medical expenses of inside workers injured on the job.

Putting aside Mister Khin's perceived generosity, workers employed inside remained informal, if only in practice. Crucially, their employer provided them with no written employment contract. They were paid out on a piece rate at the end of each day but were not guaranteed the legal daily minimum wage—a fact that left them with little or no earnings on days when deliveries were scarce. Their employer had also not registered them with the Social Security Board (as is required by the 2012 Social Security Law). Such registration would have obliged Mister Khin to contribute the additional value of 3 percent of each workers' monthly earnings to the government's social security fund. In addition, although inside workers had in the past been dismissed for inconsistent work practices, none of these individuals had ever received severance pay, as is legally required by the 2013 Employment and Skills Development Law and the Notification of Severance Payment (No. 84/2015). And finally, although Mister Khin construed his contributions to workers' medical expenses as acts of generosity, he was legally obligated under the 1923 Workmen's Compensation Act (amended in 2005) to compensate workers for on-the-job injuries—a legal requirement that Mister Khin never acknowledged. In practice, it was the workers' themselves who covered the bulk of their medical expenses, using to do so a collective fund to which inside workers regularly contributed. The employer's contribution was never more than a quarter of total medical costs.

But what about Mister Khin's claim of running a democratic workplace? "That's nonsense" (*alakar*), rebutted Mister San, with a dismissive wave of his hand. The incredulous respondent here was a resident of the depot's on-site accommodations, where he lived with his son, a stevedore in Mister Khin's employ. "If a worker isn't present when a ship arrives," explained Mister San, "the boss would just fire him, and then kick him out of the worker housing."

What we see among stevedores employed at Mister Khin's riverside depot are two types of employment arrangements. Workers here are segmented between those living on-site and those living off-site, the latter residing almost exclusively in the neighboring Yadana squatter settlement. The literature on informal labor has often highlighted such employment segmentation, where casual workers excluded from legal labor protections are intermittently employed to flexibly complement a relatively stable, formally employed workforce.[16] That inside workers had more employment security than outside workers was a fact that Mister Khin readily acknowledged. Yet it was not formal from informal workers that labor segmentation in this case bifurcated, for all these workers were in practice informal. Segmentation instead divided outside workers with unambiguously casual employment from inside workers with relative job security, but whose employment conditions remained de facto informal and in certain respects casual as well, or at least irregular, since their piece-rate labor was inconsistent, while dismissal without compensation was an ever-present possibility.

Overlaid on this informal employment arrangement was a local variant, in a Buddhist idiom, of what in recent years has become a globally prominent ideology of ethical capitalism. For the nonunionized workforce at Mister Khin's depot, marginal employment security and partial financial support to treat on-the-job injuries were construed as conditional on the arbitrary generosity of a capitalist patron instead of on the judicial enforcement of existing labor legislation. In this respect, Mister Khin's depot was not unique. Political scientist Gerard McCarthy has convincingly argued that Myanmar's post-1988 military government encouraged Buddhist notions of *sedana* and *dana*, while underscoring the meritorious implications ensuing therefrom, as means of domestically legitimizing crony capitalism while funding infrastructure development through well-publicized private donations in the absence of an effective system of formal taxation.[17] Along similar lines, the anthropologist Sohini Kar argues in her study of financial lending in the slums of northern Kolkata that the Indian government promoted microcredit within a discourse of ethical capitalism and financial inclusion while simultaneously slashing budgets for public services.[18] The effect has been to offload the burden of structural poverty onto the shoulders of the newly financialized poor. More globally, capitalist institutions and financial elites have, in the face of surging economic inequality and popular demands for redistributive taxation, instead advocated philanthropy and ethical capitalism, which would render redistribution an arbitrary expression of elite generosity rather than a political obligation grounded in the popular will.

In a more theoretical vein, anthropologists have often celebrated moral economies and gift economies as humanizing alternatives to the "calculating and self-serving materialism" commonly associated with market calculus.[19] And at Mister Khin's riverside depot, there was indeed a moral economy of sorts, as expressed in the ethical idiom through which the latter construed his relations with his employees. This moral economy, however, was the legitimizing pretense for employment outside existing labor protection laws—that is, ethical life as bourgeois self-rationalization. The workers here remained precarious, while their employer—however amicable a fellow—pursued a fraught micro-hegemony over his workforce.

The Trajectory of an Underage Factory Daughter

Su Su and her cousin, baskets in hand, were off to work. The murky floodwater, colorless but for discarded plastic food wrappers and broken flip-flops floating therein, was well above their ankles, as the pair made their way down narrow paths winding through the Yadana squatter settlement. "The Municipal Development Committee won't do anything about it," deplored Su Su's neighbor on the matter of the flooding when the two cousins had stepped out of their bamboo-and-corrugated-tin home several minutes earlier. It was not raining, but because of the settlement's poor drainage the floodwaters from last night's storm had nowhere to go. But at least two-year-old Bo Bo appreciated the opportunity for play the flooding afforded—until the boy's mother, another of Su Su's neighbors, projecting her voice from the back of their home, threatened the child corporally were he to not exit that filthy water immediately.

Stepping out from those flooded footpaths shortly thereafter, the turbid water ran easily off Su Su's feet and sandals, revealing toenails painted pink with polish.

FIGURE 17. A mother and her two children (not Su Su) wade through flooded footpaths in the Yadana squatter settlement during the rainy season. Author's photograph.

And while the water had almost reached her calves, her purple dress was sufficiently short to have stayed clean and dry throughout. Her hair, meanwhile, tied back, left visible ears bedecked with little gold studs, while her cheeks she had adorned with sandalwood paste (*thanaka*), a distinctively Burmese cosmetic. Before long, the cousins were strolling the streets of the industrial zone, appearing much like the thousands of other young women whose presence they had joined, all of whom were heading to jobs at mostly garment factories in the area, seeking to make it on time for the morning shift. Thousands there may have been, but these women were a tiny fraction of the close to one million workers employed in Myanmar's garment, footwear, and accessories sectors as of 2019, of whom 94 percent were women, and 84 percent were between the ages of sixteen and twenty-seven.[20]

Had Su Su not left school at the age of nine, she might have now, at sixteen, been entering tenth standard. The girl's mother, persistently in debt and working piece rate in a shrimp processing plant, had felt it necessary to bring Su Su along to help increase her output and thus her wages. As a child laborer, nine-year-old Su Su had not been alone; there were other children her age and older laboring alongside their mothers in the shrimp plant's casual workforce, though none among the plant's hundred-or-so formally registered employees. Tasked with peeling and beheading prawns as an unregistered helper, Su Su's output was incorporated with that of her mother; the girl received no separate wage. Her mother, Mrs. Phyu, used their combined income to support the family. Several years later, Mrs. Phyu was able to leverage her good relations with the factory administration to get, as an exception, her by then thirteen-year-old daughter Su Su hired as an official employee, or *wundan* in Burmese.[21] It was by then 2016, and the boss paid formally employed (meaning registered) workers the legal minimum wage of 3,600 kyat per day—an amount the government had set the year prior. This was a wage that Su Su, upon receiving her pay each month, diligently handed over in full to her mother.

Although Su Su often worked until seven or eight o'clock in the evening, the employer did not pay her or anyone else at the shrimp factory additional wages for overtime, as is legally required by the 2013 Minimum Wages Act. "He held onto those overtime wages for us," recounted Su Su. Then, once a year, the boss would in lieu of overtime pay take all registered employees on a pagoda pilgrimage. They had gone to Mandalay one year, to Dawei another. Su Su and her mother felt that in this way the employer obtained *kutho* (Buddhist merit). It is, however, difficult to conceive how such trips could have cost anywhere near the total value of all unpaid overtime wages for the plant's registered employees for the year.

It then so happened that at age fifteen, Su Su quit her job and left those prawns behind. "She quit the shrimp factory," her mother explained, "because she was getting older, and I had no inheritance for her, and I wasn't able to give her an education. Had she continued at the shrimp factory, in the end she wouldn't have had a decent livelihood." The garment sector, by contrast, offered what Su Su and her mother believed to be the most realistic prospect of upward mobility: from helper, to sewer, to (someday perhaps) supervisor, with transferable skills to boot.

Su Su applied to work at a garment factory within walking distance from Yadana. She was at first hired as an unregistered helper, and despite her youthful appearance, the manager who interviewed her did not request proof of age. From the start, Su Su earned the legal minimum of 4,800 kyat for an eight-hour shift, but her overtime pay of 600 kyat per hour was half the legally stipulated amount. Moreover, being casually employed, Su Su had no guarantee of work from one day to the next. Among the one thousand or so employees at her factory, there were, she estimated, some fifty to sixty casual workers like herself, many of whom, she believed, were under eighteen—the minimum age legally stipulated for factory employment in Myanmar without a signed statement of medical fitness, which Su Su did not possess.

Within three months, the manager invited Su Su to apply to become a formally registered employee—in other words, eligible for employment rights and benefits as stipulated by law. This required Su Su to present a National Registration Card as proof of age. Fifteen-year-old Su Su borrowed such a card from an older cousin, interviewed for the position, and got the job. Although the manager was firm on the requirement that the applicant present evidence of her age, Su Su believed the manager may have nonetheless suspected that the card she presented was not her own, and that she was thus below the legal age of factory employment.

In any case, Su Su appreciated the job. By then, her mother had stopped working, her little brother and cousin for whom her mother was caring were still too young to work, their household was mired in recurring debt, and her father had been dead for two years, having been killed while laboring at sea in the raft fishing industry off the coast of Pyapon in the Ayeyarwady Delta. Under these conditions, Su Su continued to hand over to her mother her wages in full—a filial obligation, she felt, and a contribution to the household more generally.

Monetary and ethical compulsions aside, Su Su contrasted garment factory work positively to the limited income opportunities that were otherwise available to her—in particular, to informal waste collection, the livelihood of many of her neighbors. Although waste collectors could earn more, reasoned Su Su, garment factory workers—or at least those employees who were registered—received regular salaries and (ideally) legislated employment rights and benefits. And whereas the labor of waste collection was dirty, exhausting, and exposed to the elements, "one positive aspect of factory work," Su Su pointed out, "is that you can make yourself beautiful and dress nicely, and you don't get dirty. There's dignity (*gon theikhka*)." Echoing, it seemed, Su Su's positive valuation, garment factory employment was the livelihood of choice for hundreds of young women in the Yadana settlement. Given her personal preference for such garment factory work, Su Su reckoned that the main reason so many people instead collected discarded items for resale was that "they're old; they're over thirty," by which she meant such individuals were beyond the eligible age of garment factory employment. That may be true. But some of Yadana's waste collectors offered divergent views—specifically, that waste collection, as a plus, allows the laborers involved some measure of control over the time and pace of their work, as well as freedom from the managerial harassment often encountered in factory employment.[22] It was due to similar appraisals that Kathleen Millar, in her ethnography of informal waste collectors outside Rio de Janeiro, argued that her informants took up informal waste collection as a refusal of the workplace discipline encountered in normative forms of capitalist labor.[23] Minh Nguyen likewise underscores, in her ethnography of Vietnam's recycling industry, the role of desire in motivating the waste traders whom she studied.[24]

In any case, evident within Su Su's stated motivations are multiple factors at play—market pressures, to be sure, but also the felt obligations of a daughter to her widowed mother, aspirations for upward mobility, and the desires of a young woman who values the dignity she feels dressing up and making herself beautiful. As with those of informal waste collectors, the values and desires of factory workers are of definite ethnographic interest. Still, as a relatively new employee, Su Su's positive appraisal of garment factory employment was at odds with the critical evaluations of her more experienced coworkers. Sister Aye's experiences are telling. The latter had only recently, after two years on the job, quit the very garment factory at which Su Su obtained her employment.

Sister Aye had entered that factory after a previous employer had fired her due to her involvement in mobilizing a month-long strike.[25] Sister Aye thus brought to her new job a critical view of employment, as well as practical organizing experience. These were strengths that this woman, by then in her mid-twenties, immediately put to use when her new supervisor ordered her and her coworkers to work unpaid overtime, handing out papaya slices and instant noodles in lieu of overtime wages. At the new factory, recounted Sister Aye, her supervisor, "would say that there was going to be overtime until twelve o'clock at night, but that there wasn't going to be any overtime pay. So, I said, if there's no overtime pay, I'm not working. I went to organize some other workers. I said, 'We should get overtime pay.' And I told them the [legal] overtime rate. . . . Some workers thought that they should get overtime pay, but they were afraid to complain."

Despite her coworkers' initial trepidation, Sister Aye was able to get enough people on board to make a collective demand for overtime wages, backed by a collective refusal to work any further unpaid overtime. In the end, the manager capitulated without the workers having to negotiate through the bureaucratic process of the Township Conciliation Body. Consequently, by the time fifteen-year-old Su Su entered that same factory, registered workers were receiving the legally stipulated overtime pay rate of 1,200 kyat per hour. It is, as this case shows, not a given that formal sector factories follow formal (legally stipulated) labor standards. It often depends on collective struggles by the workers employed. Absent such struggle, the so-called formal sector is quite often informal in practice—that is, in violation of legislated labor standards.

This particular win notwithstanding, Sister Aye quit that factory after two years, at the age of twenty-six. The work, she felt, was impacting her health. The factory was excessively hot, her eyes had begun to ache from focused needlework under fluorescent light, she had lost considerable weight, and by the end she had begun shedding her hair—all this aside from the fact that the wage was so low she could not afford to pay off her debts. "Before entering garment factory employment," concluded Sister Aye, "people had told me that garment factories were better [than other means of livelihood], and that's what I had imagined—that they'd be really good. But once I started working and saw for myself, I realized that they weren't so great."

Sister Aye's experiences are widely shared. Although garment, footwear, and accessories factories producing for export in Myanmar are more likely to pay the stipulated minimum wage for an 8-hour workday (4,800 kyat as of May 2018), these factories are nonetheless often in violation of various other labor laws. Many such violations pertain to clauses in the 1951 Factories Act, as amended in 2016, which remains the primary legal statute covering employment conditions at factories in Myanmar.[26] For example, during the period of my fieldwork, common labor law violations at factories in Myanmar included forced overtime and forced work on holidays; nonpayment (or payment below the legally stipulated amount) of overtime wages; not granting the legislated ten days of annual paid leave (*lok thek kwint*) and not paying compensatory income for such leave not taken; arbitrary dismissal of pregnant workers; arbitrary dismissal of worker organizers (in violation of the 2012 Settlement of Labor Disputes Law); and deducting workers' pay beyond legally permissible amounts for minor infractions, like late arrivals. In addition, widespread violations existed of the Occupational Health and Safety Law (promulgated in March 2019) and of various Labor Department directives updating the 1951 Factories Act. Such violations included not having adequate fire exits, having an insufficient number of toilets, not having separate toilet facilities for women, lacking clean drinking water, and not providing an appropriate canteen for workers. There have also been frequent cases of outright wage theft, such as in 2019, when the South Korean owner of World Jin Garment Co. Ltd. deducted social security payments from hundreds of her employees' monthly wages but did not then transfer this money to the Social Security Board, thus leaving the affected workers not only short of wages but also without medical coverage at the government's social security hospital.[27] Meanwhile, officials of the Yangon regional government's Labor Laws Inspection Department rarely visit factories to assess compliance with existing labor laws. Despite all this, many women (and some men) in Yangon's industrial zones continue to seek employment at such factories. And of those who obtain such employment, most seek to retain their jobs, despite the less-than-ideal wages and working conditions that they encounter.

In seeking to understand precarious labor—informal waste collection, specifically—as a livelihood decision, Kathleen Millar argues for a focus on desire in place of scarcity. For as a paradigm for understanding life amid precarity, scarcity leaves "little room to ask why this work is taken up by those who pursue it, how it emerges from and fashions particular social and political relations, and how it expresses different visions of what life is for."[28] In advancing this argument, Millar pushes anthropological analysis beyond a narrowly economistic reading of people's entry into particular forms of informal labor, precarious though such labor may be. In this regard, Su Su's stated views offer support, despite the latter's preference for garment factory employment over informal waste collection. But Su Su's appraisal of her limited livelihood options also illuminates the ways in which desire, on the one hand, and a historically particular manifestation of scarcity, on the other, are inextricably entwined. Su Su understood her own livelihood decisions through culturally informed tropes of dignity and filial obligation. But the young woman's motivations to work and her desire to hand her wages over in full to her widowed mother were also informed by her household's debt and market dependence, and indeed, by a wider context of scarcity.

We see a similar intertwining of scarcity and desire in Susanna Rosenbaum's ethnography of immigrant Mexican and Central American domestic workers in Los Angeles. Many such women, Rosenbaum observes, have come to hope for, or to embrace the ideology of, upward mobility—the "immigrant version of the American Dream."[29] It is, in part, this dream that motivates these women to endure low-waged domestic work. At the same time, conditions of want—specifically, "poverty, a narrow labor market, and an individual's need to provide for their families"—further inform this willingness to persist in Los Angeles.[30] Together, these intertwined factors have motivated many immigrant women to continue in low-paying jobs with "less-than-ideal employers."[31] Underpinning all such precarious labor, we could add, is a radical dependence on the market, behind which lies a historical moment of dispossession, whatever the subsequent desires of the individuals involved.

The cases of informal wage labor presented in this chapter challenge certain claims concerning the informal economy, and the informal economy of the postcolonial urban slum, in particular. The inhabitants of the Yadana squatter settlement were almost exclusively former rural dwellers who had left behind the agrarian or otherwise rural economies of their natal villages, the very types of individuals whom the World Bank has argued will move into "good, formal-sector jobs" as a result of Myanmar's political-economic restructuring.[32] And indeed, as projected by the World Bank, many of these former rural dwellers have obtained employment in the so-called formal sector—within, that is, enterprises large enough to be covered by the 2012 Social Security Law, as well as various other labor legislation. Yet, as the examples in this chapter reveal, for many such individuals these are not good jobs in the limited sense of employment that meets the bare legal minimum in wages and working conditions.

The individuals considered herein are, moreover, contra Ferguson, very much proletarians, both in the narrow sense of wage laborers engaged in capitalist production, as well as in the broader sense of being propertyless individuals radically dependent on the market. And contra Sanyal, many of these individuals remain incorporated into formal circuits of capital accumulation, despite the informality of their employment.

Notwithstanding the critique of informality presented herein—as being effectively a violation of legislated labor protections—situations exist where individuals may value the autonomy and relative flexibility that informal labor arrangements allow. This was the case with the individuals employed at Mrs. Pwint's home factory who were able to care for their children at their workplace, and with the informal waste collectors who are able to set the time and pace of their work. But such positive valuations of informality aside, employment outside legal labor protections also includes, in Myanmar, forms of labor that are not only highly exploitative but brutally violent as well, as the cases in the following chapter will attest.

6

UNFREEDOMS OF CAPITALISM

The hut behind the neighborhood refuse drop-off point was but a temporary accommodation. Sister Myat, that is, was not to be long at Yadana. She had come up from the delta simply to visit her parents, who had built the hut in question so as to be nearer their place of work—the refuse drop-off point at which they collected discarded items for resale. At twenty-eight years old, Sister Myat had not attended a day of school in her life. Although illiterate, this woman had experienced much and felt confident enough to get by. Her marriage was not a troubled one, and she now had a baby daughter whom she dearly loved, whose childhood, Sister Myat aspired, would be different from her own.

That childhood, or rather that part of her childhood, had begun when Sister Myat, then living with her parents at a village in the delta, had been nine. It had been the first year of the new millennium, a time of heightened rural inequality alongside the consolidation of agricultural land and inland fisheries in the delta.[1] "We were living hand-to-mouth," recalled her mother, Aunty Cho, who with her at-the-time-heavy-drinking husband had been endeavoring to earn a living at sundry casual jobs in fishing and agriculture. Amid rampant inflation, their household had been mired in cyclical debt. It had been under these conditions that, one day, nine-year-old Myat's grandmother took her away. Informing the girl that she was to be employed as a domestic helper, grandma deposited her with a household across the river, took a three-month advance on the child's wages, and left. "I'd never been apart from my mother," recounted Sister Myat, "so I cried when she took me away. I didn't have any clothes or sandals with me. Grandma took me away, and I cried as I went along with her. Grandma said to me, 'Your family is in a difficult situation, so don't cry. You have to do this for them.'" It had likewise been grandma who, from then on, went to collect regular advances on the girl's wages; mother stayed away. "Had I gone," explained Aunty Cho, "she would've wanted to return with me."

As a domestic servant, Sister Myat had been responsible for cooking, cleaning, and taking care of her employer's children—in other words, the labor of social reproduction. "The employer wouldn't let me go out," Sister Myat recalled of that first household, "I was in someone else's home, so for the most part I didn't have freedom." Further, "As a nine-year-old daughter, I was just a child; there was so much I didn't know. So of course I got beaten. I got yelled at. I was a child, so I might break a pot, and for that I'd get beaten." After two years, Sister Myat's employer, a part-owner in a rice milling enterprise, fell into economic distress of his own and could no longer afford to retain the child. The girl's grandmother took her to a new employer—a middle-aged woman who ran an alcohol parlor in a neighboring village. As the proprietor of this establishment, the woman made Sister Myat—eleven years old at the time—labor as a waitress in the alcohol parlor on top of her domestic duties. But regarding the hours she had worked or the money she had earned, Sister Myat could not say. "Back then, I didn't really understand money matters," she explained. "Since I couldn't read, I never knew what day it was. And I didn't know how to read a clock." Like that, Sister Myat went on to change employers every few years, working as a domestic servant until she got married at twenty-four years of age to a young man from her natal village. By then, she had worked for eight households—her grandmother having collected her wages in advance up to the end, leaving the young woman perennially debt-bound to each consecutive employer.

Tragic though her case may have been, Sister Myat's childhood as a physically abused and debt-bound domestic servant, pressed into employment by her family, was in no way exceptional in Myanmar. In research carried out by the International Labor Organization, 26 percent of internal labor migrants surveyed in Myanmar were found to be in situations of bonded or otherwise unfree labor, with 14 percent of said individuals having been trafficked into these labor arrangements.[2] Overlapping with these statistics, there were as of 2018 1.2 million child laborers in the country, between the ages of five and seventeen, who worked an average of fifty-two hours per week, typically in conditions of debt bondage.[3] In this context, Myanmar investigative journalists have brought to light horrific cases of domestic worker abuse, specifically cases of employers beating, burning, scalding, and cutting their underage domestic servants with knives.[4] And across Southeast Asia, accounts of indebted parents brokering their children's entry into paid labor have become commonplace, as Nicolas Lainez, for example, has documented in the case of sex work in Vietnam.[5]

To be sure, waged domestic service as a labor form is not particular to capitalism. However, such labor acquires a capitalist content amid a constitutive context of market compulsions. Within this context, young women employed as domestic servants in Myanmar have regularly been put to work as servers or retail workers in their employer's shops and establishments, much like Sister Myat had been in her employer's alcohol parlor. But even laboring exclusively in the home, domestic servants perform, through their socially reproductive labor, a crucial role in the reproduction of capitalism, whether by enabling members of their employer's household to work as higher-earning wage laborers outside the home or by otherwise subsidizing the class privilege of Myanmar's nouveau riche. It is along such lines that Susanna Rosenbaum argues in her ethnography of immigrant Mexican and Central American domestic workers in Los Angeles—specifically, that the socially reproductive labor of underpaid and overworked domestic servants has made possible the class privilege and hierarchically ordered class society that these women's bourgeois employers have gone on to trumpet as the fruit of independently earned success.[6]

Going further, contemporary forms of labor that involve debt-bondage, physical abuse, and other extra-economic compulsions challenge narrowly economistic conceptions of capitalist labor. In such conceptions, capitalist labor gets limited to the contractually free wage worker, who is otherwise free to enter into (or break) contract with the employer of her choice. Such a circumscribed notion of capitalist labor endures among liberals, of course, but also among Marxists of a certain stripe. As illustrative of the latter, Benno Teschke puts the argument like this: "Once a capitalist property regime is established . . . direct producers are no longer coerced by extra-economic means to . . . work for a lord—since workers are politically free."[7] For this reason, Teschke continues, capitalist labor arrangements are to be understood as but "civil contracts among politically (though not economically) free and equal citizens subject to civil law . . . [operating in] a non-coercive 'economic economy.'"[8] It is this exclusively economistic conception of capitalist labor—as being limited to the free wage worker—that has gone on to inform the liberal conceit that capitalism equates to freedom. David Graeber, among others, has rightly critiqued such a narrow characterization of capitalism, according to which "all those millions of slaves and serfs and coolies and debt peons disappear, or if we must speak of them, we write them off as temporary bumps along the road."[9]

Unfree labor, in short, is not an aberration to capitalism. It endures as the unacknowledged underbelly of any liberal order. Ultimately, it is this relation that scandalizes liberalism: privileged enjoyment of rights and freedoms in capitalist societies remains grounded in exclusion of the poor, the enslaved, the bonded, the noncitizen, the incarcerated, the colonized. The liberal order is thus exposed as a narrow hegemonic appeal ever in denial of the exclusions it engenders, exclusions on which any existing liberal order inevitably depends. Such is the case with the offshore raft fishing industry that operates in Myanmar's Bay of Martaban, where each August tens of thousands of young men enter into bonded, and often violent, labor arrangements, but which also provides staple seafood for Myanmar cuisine. It is an industry that I will discuss at length in this chapter.

Unfreedom and the Liberal Order

When John Stuart Mill wrote that freedom of contract was the most efficient and equitable basis for organizing capitalist labor relations, he was authoring what would become a classic treatise of British liberalism.[10] Yet this was a man with some thirty-five years of service to the British East India Company, a veteran colonial administrator who remained to the end an unapologetic advocate of despotism in the colonies.[11] Here was Mill the liberal—a man who downplayed "the horror of the workhouses," where English paupers were subjected to corporal discipline under a regime of coerced labor.[12] As a deterrent, the workhouse, Mill argued, admirably served its purpose in goading free workers to labor diligently in British factories.

Given such seemingly incongruent positions—a liberal defense of empire, in particular—contemporary critics have charged Mill with a racist double standard: liberalism for the European, illiberalism for all others.[13] But what Mill's position reveals, I suggest, is more than a moral failure to include colonized peoples within an otherwise universal liberal ethic. At the base are the constitutive relations grounding European liberalism in a necessary exclusion of non-European colonies. Such was the argument of Sidney Mintz regarding plantation slavery in the Caribbean, as it is with Lisa Lowe in her historical study of African slavery and Asian indentured servitude. Both scholars have traced the connections through which these coercive forms of exploitation served as conditions of possibility for the emergence of liberal labor regimes in Europe.[14] And it was this sort of relational understanding that led Immanuel Wallerstein to likewise argue, at an earlier moment, that "slavery and so-called 'second serfdom' are not to be regarded as anomalies in a capitalist system."[15]

It was, however, scholars working in what came to be known as the Black Radical Tradition who, following Marx, most effectively blazed the analytical trail for our current understanding of chattel slavery's operation in a capitalist order. Pivotal texts in this regard were W.E.B. Du Bois's *Black Reconstruction in America*, C.L.R. James's *Black Jacobins*, and Eric Williams's *Capitalism and Slavery*.[16] While showing how investors and plantation owners incorporated industrially regimented slave labor into capitalist production networks, these authors also made clear that New World slave revolts were forward-looking movements pointing towards a radically egalitarian future, not the mere spontaneity of primitive rebels condemned to a backward-looking nostalgia.

With a different focus, but likewise interrogating a form of unwaged labor, feminists in the 1970s—activists like Mariarosa Dalla Costa, Selma James, and Sylvia Federici—foregrounded the ways women had historically exhausted themselves without pay in the home in order to reproduce the proletarian body, and in this way the capitalist order writ large.[17] Moreover, when carried out under conditions of gender violence, such labor has been unfree in the physically coerced sense as well.[18] In this way, capitalism has been parasitical on a noncommodified and often coerced form of domestic labor, which serves as a condition of possibility for free wage labor in the workplace.

It was, however, a central insight of Marx that the distinction between free and unfree labor is, in a capitalist context, mystifying. The proletarian, after all, being propertyless, is forever compelled "by the silent compulsion of economic relations" to sell her labor power to a capitalist.[19] She is thus, as a corollary, denied the freedom to opt out of such a transaction without penalty. Under such conditions, the labor contract expresses not the worker's freedom of choice but rather "the anodyne fictions of consent," in the words of Jairus Banaji.[20]

Amid high-profile accounts of human trafficking in Southeast Asia, the preceding argument gains regional relevance. Peter Vandergeest and Melissa Marschke, for example, warn against the "modern slavery" framing that anti-trafficking activists have employed to spur action in response to reports of bondage and violence in the Thai fishery sector. Notwithstanding the success of such terminology in mobilizing action, the "slavery framing," argue Vandergeest and Marschke, "re-affirms liberal and capitalist understandings of freedom and exploitation, in how it situates modern slavery as outside of capitalism and as ideologically incompatible with capitalist freedoms."[21] Taking a longer historical view, Tania Murray Li finds that Indonesian plantation employers have responded to workers' struggles and labor market fluctuations by oscillating between more-or-less free and more-or-less bonded labor regimes, the aim always being to "secure well-disciplined labor at the lowest possible price."[22] Such dynamics blur the apparent boundary between free and unfree labor.

Given this blurring of categories, many critical analysts have argued that free and bound forms of labor are best understood as lying on a continuum, the difference being a matter of degree.[23] Situating such labor on a continuum, however, while usefully challenging a rigid dichotomy, risks downplaying significant political disparities and the unequal privileges they afford. This can be "politically dangerous," writes Marcel van der Linden, as the logic of a continuum obscures the specificity of the most extreme forms of bound labor (equating wage slavery with chattel slavery, for example) and the fact that slaves and other bonded laborers have often struggled to escape their particular forms of subjugation. Disagreements, such as these, over a continuum's usefulness as an analytical tool rest in a conventional logic that opposes quantitative and qualitative forms of difference.[24] Logic of this sort is unable to adequately grasp the internal relations connecting forms of labor that, while on one level distinct, are never wholly so. It is in such cases useful, I suggest, to see a constitutive relationship between the free and the unfree. This analytical move avoids either treating these labor forms as wholly distinct or flattening their differences by construing their respective unfreedoms as equivalent. Seen in this light, Myanmar's raft fishing industry, with its bonded and often violent labor arrangements, is part of the unfree ground subsidizing liberal freedoms elsewhere.

Of an Industry That Devours Its Workforce

Brother Hein's roof was not yet repaired. And that was a problem, given the impending monsoon. He might have bought new dani-palm shingles and fixed the roof up himself had he not been swindled of all of his earnings by the broker—Brother Hein was sure the guy was a cop—who had sold him into the tiger raft industry based at the coastal town of Ye, in Myanmar's southeastern Mon State. But he had indeed been swindled of that money. And now he was broke. And his roof had holes in it. And in a matter of days the sky would disgorge that ocean of water it was holding onto until what seemed the last possible minute, dragging the hot season on far longer than was proper, folks said. But at least Brother Hein was alive. His coworkers, at least five of them, were not, and Brother Hein claimed to have personally witnessed their murders. And that was the reason he was sure he would never again seek work in the offshore raft fishing industry.

Perhaps Brother Hein could have quit the industry a year prior, after a different broker had similarly swindled him of his earnings, albeit not that time in full. That first broker, said Brother Hein, recounting events at his home in the Yadana settlement, "told me the salary was good, and stuff like that. But when I got there and started working, it wasn't what I'd been expecting. And the salary wasn't what he'd told me." The job to which the young man referred was as a general laborer on an ocean-going raft made of nothing but bamboo poles, anchored some eighty miles out in the Bay of Martaban for eight months straight, from August to April—eight months at sea with no shore leave on a motorless craft with but two other men, facing winds of up to fifty miles per hour, often short of food and drinking water, and tasked with lowering and drawing every six hours a twenty-to-thirty foot long "tiger mouth" net, and then sorting, boiling, and drying on board the catch of mostly prawns.[25] Given pervasive malnutrition—thiamine deficiency, specifically—beriberi among these workers is common, leaving many fishers debilitated in their lower limbs.[26] And given the threat of storms, the industry has been decimated twice in recent years. Thousands of workers stuck out on the rafts were killed during Cyclone Nargis.[27] And a subsequent storm in 2011 left almost 700 more raft workers dead—drowned, evidently, at sea.[28]

Despite such disasters, the industry at present operates from 5,000 to 10,000 rafts, employs as fishers on rafts and carrier boats close to 50,000 men—mostly internal migrants—and harvests 10,000 tons of seafood annually, which is sold domestically or exported to China, Singapore, or Thailand.[29] On each raft is stationed one raft supervisor (*paung usi*) along with two or three general laborers (*nauk laik*). The rafts, in turn, are anchored in clusters of eight, which are managed by a skipper (*usichok*) who patrols between these bamboo crafts in a motorboat.

In Myanmar, the raft fishing industry began in the 1970s, first off the coast of Pyapon in the delta and then expanding to the waters off Mawlamyine in the 1990s.[30] Up until 2017, little had been published about the industry in either Burmese or English. That year, investigative journalist Khin Myat Myat Wai, working for the Burmese-language newspaper, *The Voice*, published an exposé of the industry based on her own field research in the delta. The article went on to win the Myanmar Journalists Association award for best feature. Also in 2017, policy analysts Yin Nyein and Sebastian Mathew published an English-language account of the industry, albeit with little mention of the violence and human trafficking that Khin Myat Myat Wai highlighted.[31] Since then, other domestic and Myanmar-focused media outlets, including Radio Free Asia, BBC Burmese, *Frontier Myanmar*, and *The Irrawaddy*, have reported on the industry, emphasizing, in particular, the widespread abuses uncovered therein.[32] Overall, these exposés do much to corroborate Brother Hein's account of his own experiences in the raft fishing industry, which he retold only days after making it back to his home in the Yadana settlement following his ordeal.

By the time the young man returned from that second stint at sea, he was nineteen years old. At Yadana, by then, he had lived for close to a decade, having migrated from the delta with his family amid the Nargis aftermath. Upon arrival, the nine-year-old boy had taken up assorted casual jobs, most often, by his teenage years, portering loads on a piece rate at gravel depots along the riverside. Brother Hein's financial contribution notwithstanding, his family was unable to stay out of debt. Such were the conditions that made attractive a neighbor's offer of fishing employment with a 600,000 kyat (US$400) cash advance—more money than most squatters can save in a year. Such motivations Brother Hein believed to be widespread. "For some people," he explained, "it's convenient for their families if they can get an advance of 500,000 or 600,000 kyat. With that money, they can repay their debts," adding as clarification, "it's because their families have debts that most people do this work." The dynamic to which this young survivor of human trafficking referred—debt-driven migration—has in recent years been documented with increased frequency across Southeast Asia.[33] Moreover, by taking this advance, Brother Hein had entered into a relation of debt bondage. Other restrictions aside, he would not have been able to leave his job without repaying his employer in full—a move that was, for Brother Hein and most other raft fishers, a practical impossibility.

That first year, Brother Hein did get his advance—minus a 100,000 kyat fee that the broker took. It was rather the promised post-season bonus that the raft owner refused to hand over. Despite this wage theft and the beatings Brother Hein occasionally received at the hands of the raft supervisor, the young man accepted a similar offer the following year—a promise of 600,000 kyat cash in advance for raft fishing work off the Pyapon coast. It was a neighbor and fellow Yadana squatter who informed Brother Hein of the offer and who took him to a dormitory in Hlaingtharyar Township where the broker—the guy whom Brother Hein believed to be a cop—was gathering prospective workers before transporting them by truck to the coast.

When the workers eventually arrived at the coast, Brother Hein realized that he had not in fact been taken to Pyapon, as he had previously been promised, but instead to the town of Ye—or just outside of it—in southern Mon State. Upon arrival, the workers were corralled into a holding pen and not permitted to leave. "It wasn't possible to run away," Brother Hein explained, "and it wasn't possible to return. The guys guarding the compound had sticks and knives. In the fenced compound there were twenty people in my group, and there were over 100 others. We had to wait five days in that compound."

In their survey of the raft fishing industry, Yin Nyein and Sebastian Mathew confirm the use of such enclosures to confine laborers, especially women shelling prawns on shore. "In some yards," the authors write, "additional fortifications are made to prevent women workers from running away."[34] The practice of forcibly corralling laborers derives its logic from growing rates of desertion alongside a scaling-up of production and a fall in the number of individuals willing to accept such work.[35] Tellingly, most raft owners are obliged to find a new batch of workers each fishing season.[36] After being taken from the pen on shore to a raft at sea, Brother Hein found himself similarly constrained. The workers "couldn't run away," he pointed out, "because we were in the ocean."

One resident of Yadana who was able to offer some insight on the increased use of brokers in the offshore raft fishing industry was Brother Thiha. This forty-two-year-old native of the delta had labored for over a decade in the raft fishing industry until the day he was blinded in one eye by a tiger net cable that snapped and whipped back as he was reeling it in. Half-blind, the at-the-time-thirty-one-year-old quit the delta and relocated to Yangon where he took on piece-rate labor as a stevedore in a depot adjacent to the Yadana settlement. As Brother Thiha saw it, conditions in the tiger raft industry had at one time been more favorable. (He had entered the industry in the late 1990s.) But over the preceding decade, working conditions worsened to the point where delta inhabitants familiar with the industry have been unwilling to accept this employment. Raft owners have therefore turned increasingly to brokers to secure the needed number of workers at the start of each fishing season. It is this increased use of brokers, argued Brother Thiha, which underpins so much of the fraud in the industry:

> At present, brokers are ever more crooked and deceitful [*kalain kakyit*]. This is because, at present, these brokers—based on my experience, what I've seen—they come in order to gather workers. These workers' families are facing livelihood difficulties. The broker says to the worker, "You'll get a 500,000 kyat advance. You'll get a 700,000 kyat advance." And the worker goes along. But in the end, the broker doesn't hand over the money in full. The type of worker who goes along with the broker doesn't have experience, has never done this work, and doesn't understand.

Adding support to Brother Thiha's account, Yin Nyein and Sebastian Mathew report that brokers have had to travel farther afield to obtain laborers for the rafts, going as far as Sagaing, Mandalay, and Magway regions in the dry zone of upper Myanmar.[37] To this broad pattern, Khin Myat Myat Wai provides more detail. "The majority of tiger raft workers," she writes, "are individuals who have been sold into this industry by brokers and are even unaware of the very low salary and other allowances that they will receive."[38] More evocatively, Khin Myat Myat Wai quotes a certain Zin Maung Maung Latt, a native of Amar Village in the delta, who spoke of the human trafficking that he witnessed in the raft fishing industry off the coast of Pyapon. "In this area during the fishery season," recounted Zin Maung Maung Latt, "sometimes groups of five people are brought from unknown places and handed over at the houses of the tiger raft owners. For each worker, the broker gets a 50,000 kyat commission. I've seen some cases where brokers have gotten these people drunk and forcibly brought them here. And there are cases of people whose relatives have brought them here and sold them at an employer's house."[39]

As for Brother Hein, it was during his second stint at sea in the raft fishing industry that he witnessed the torture and murder of his coworkers, the trauma of which remained with him on his return to the Yadana settlement. Of a particularly memorable incident, Brother Hein recounted the following: "The supervisor was standing guard with a bamboo pole. There was a pot of boiling water in which to put shrimp. The raft supervisor dumped the pot of boiling water over a worker and then beat him with a piece of firewood. Then the guy vomited and made this gurgling sound. That guy had been in front sorting shrimp. And while he was sorting the shrimp, the raft supervisor just came up from behind and dumped the pot of boiling water over him."

It was the fleet's hard-drinking and frequently intoxicated skipper (*usichok*), who was most prone to outbursts of gratuitous violence. It was to this man that Brother Hein attributed the killing of five of his coworkers. The *usichok*, irritated and often drunk, would find cause to punish a worker. "And if, in the end, the guy died," recounted Brother Hein, "they'd put his corpse in a plastic bag and sink it." Brother Hein offered the following case as illustrative:

> Another person was killed when the *usichok* drove the boat and the guy drowned. It was like this: They tied the guy's hands and dragged him behind the boat. They just dragged him like that behind the boat. Actually, that guy hadn't done anything wrong. But he just couldn't work anymore. It was the *usichok* who did it. It wasn't an accident. The guy was killed. . . . Whenever I saw [a worker killed], I felt out of sorts. I wanted to do the same thing to him [the *usichok*]. I wanted to kill him. He killed those people as though they were just little chickens. I had a desire to stab that *usichok*.

Horrific to the extreme this case may be, but it is worth noting that similar incidents have been documented in the fishing industry off the coast of neighboring Thailand, which also employs primarily migrant workers from Myanmar. Beginning in 2014, the *Guardian*, *Associated Press*, and several nongovernmental organizations began publishing exposés on human trafficking, violence, and murder in that industry.[40] The *Guardian*, for instance, gave accounts of migrant fishermen who had witnessed the execution-style killings of their coworkers. Among the survivors with whom the *Guardian* spoke was Ei Ei Lwin, a migrant fisherman from Myanmar who claimed to have witnessed the murder of between eighteen and twenty fellow workers—specifying that "some were shot, others were tied up with stones and thrown into the sea, and one was ripped apart." Regarding this last case, Ei Ei Lwin explained that the fisherman in question "hated his captain and tried to beat him to death. But the captain escaped by jumping into the sea. The other captains came and pinned [the fisherman] down. Then they tied up his hands and legs to four separate boats and pulled him apart."[41]

For Brother Hein, an ever-present threat of violence there was, but the young man managed to survive his second season at sea. And together with the other workers remaining in his crew, the young man was able to return to shore the following April, as dark clouds were filling the sky, anticipating the coming monsoon. The onset of the monsoon is a time of year that raft workers dread, the weather being a major reason why so many of them drown each year at sea. The problem is that raft owners often push the limit, keeping the men out hauling loads into the early monsoon when anyone with enough sense and the freedom to act on it would be back on shore. Fishermen are in this way sacrificed to the sea, a testament to the raft owner's greed.

Even though Brother Hein was able to reach the shore, the owner would not allow him and his fellow fishers to return home. Instead, the owner had his men put the workers back into the corral—there to remain under guard for the duration of the off-season. In the end, Brother Hein managed to get out by phoning an uncle, who caught a bus to the coastal town of Ye, located the encampment, and bought his nephew out of bondage. The young man was therefore able to return home—alive and grateful for it—but with no wages to speak of for his eight months of labor at sea.

Accounts such as this of trafficking and violence in the raft fishing industry are in regular circulation among Yadana's residents. Yet each year inhabitants of the settlement accept offers of what seem like large wage advances. Or they get deceived or otherwise trafficked into the raft fishing industry. Wage theft, malnutrition, physical abuse, and death are common—so common, in fact, that victims include family members of individuals who have already made ethnographic appearances in this book. Just two doors down from Brother Hein's home, for instance, had lived Brother Aung, twenty-nine at the time of his death in February 2017. Having gone with a broker to labor on a raft off the coast of Pyapon, Brother Aung was subsequently beaten to near an inch of his life by a supervisor wielding a metal rod. The victim, in this case, was a brother of Yin Cho, brother-in-law of Brother Myo, and son of the fishmonger, Mrs. Khaing, individuals whose stories appeared in chapter 3.

Slowly dying from his wounds at a hospital in the coastal town of Daw Nyein, near Pyapon, Brother Aung sent word of his condition to his mother by way of a fellow patient. Although Mrs. Khaing was able to bring her son back for hospital treatment in Yangon, the young man succumbed in the end to his injuries. Two years later, sitting on the bamboo floor of her home in the Yadana settlement, the deceased's mother leafed through photos of her son's bruised body, x-rays of his broken bones, a medical report indicating "nutritional deficiency," and a signed witness statement from the Pyapon District Court. Handling these documents, Mrs. Khaing, as though retreading a well-worn path, told what she knew of the incident. "The raft supervisor did it," she said, "because he [her son] couldn't work—because he was sick and exhausted and had sat down. That's why the supervisor beat him. It was like this: He was sitting and looking up and [the supervisor] just stomped [*hsaung kanda*] on him." After the victim died, about a month following the beating, his mother made several trips to Daw Nyein in pursuit of some sort of justice—efforts that culminated, she recounted, like this:

> There was a guy named ———. He said he'd handle the case for me. He kept coming to my home. I didn't know anything about him, but he said he'd handle the case for me and stuff like that. My son-in-law believed him and said, "Mother, you should get him to handle the case." So, I got him to handle the case. Once, twice, three times I went along with him [to Daw Nyein]. After that he went on his own without taking me. Then when he got back, he told me, "They've put the guy who beat your son in jail. So, you don't need to keep going." . . . But since they had jailed the guy, I wasn't going to get anything [in financial compensation]. Surely [the raft owner] had already spoon fed someone [*hkunlaikpyi*; paid a bribe]. So I was at a loss. He [the man handling the case] said, "The guy who beat your son has been jailed. So you can stop going."
>
> Then one last time he told me to go along with him to the police station [in Daw Nyein]. So I went. I went and they asked me questions about what'd happened and I answered. Then the police showed me some young guy in handcuffs. Whether or not this kid had done it, I don't know. I'd never seen this person before. But I don't think he was the one. It seemed like they were putting on a show [*hanyepyade*] and were later going to release the guy.

In this case, the victim's mother received no financial compensation. In other cases of raft fisher deaths, however, the standard compensation, if obtained, has been 600,000 kyat (US$400) paid to a relative of the deceased. Commenting on this meager amount, a resident of a coastal village interviewed by Khin Myat Myat Wai said, "The life of such a person is worth just as much as little chickens or birds."[42]

In addition to Brother Aung, there was another victim, the father of Su Su, the young woman discussed in chapter 5 who had begun her working life laboring alongside her mother in a seafood processing plant at nine years of age. All grief aside, her father's death added to her household's financial insecurity, and to the pressure Su Su faced to obtain an income, despite her young age. The victim in this case may have died of natural causes; that, at least, is what his widow had been told. However, Khin Myat Myat Wai documented dozens of deaths on the rafts due to malnutrition caused by an insufficient provision of nutritional food to the workers. Moreover, under conditions of debt-bondage on a raft out at sea, malnourished or otherwise ill fishery workers cannot simply leave their post or quit their jobs to seek medical treatment or more adequate sustenance on shore.

Whatever the ultimate cause, the victim's widow in the case at hand remained in doubt over the true nature of her husband's death. The latter had taken an offer of bonded fishing work on a raft off the coast of Pyapon shortly after the couple had moved to the Yadana settlement in 2015. Several years later, his widow recounted as follows the moment she learned of her husband's death:

> The raft owner had agreed to pay something like 600,000 or 700,000 kyat once my husband arrived out on the ocean. He [her husband] had instructed his brother to send the money to me. He had said, "My wife's renting a home, so make sure she gets this money." His brother phoned from Pyapon and told me he'd received only 510,000 kyat [from the raft owner]. With that money, I bought this little house. And with the little that was left I paid off some debts. Then, eight months later I heard that he had died.
>
> During the waning moon of the month of Tagu [mid-April] they pack up all the rafts because that's when it starts to rain—because of the storms. At that time, the rafts get really damaged because they're out in the storm all day. [Subsequently] they told me that it was close to that time that he had died from an illness. [But at the time] I didn't know. I still thought that he'd be returning here alive. That's what I was expecting. But he didn't come back. I didn't believe he had died. He was only 44 years old. To tell the truth, I didn't have the money to go down [to Pyapon]. If I'd gone to look for him, my children would have starved. That's the reason I couldn't go to find out the truth. I had to accept what they told me.
>
> At that time, I thought it was impossible that he'd died of an illness, because he'd been portly.[43] When I saw him after two days had passed, he was rotting. And he stank. He had died out on the ocean. And when he died, they rolled his corpse up in a mat. At the coast they have those rough bamboo mats. It was one of those. They rolled up the body and wrapped it in a coarse cloth and then tied it up with string—just like they tie up *kaokhnyinhtok* [a sticky-rice snack]. That's how his body arrived here [in Yangon]. The raft owner sent the body to Kyunkatwin police station, and it was then transferred to Kyunkatwin hospital.[44] His family—there are a lot of family members on his side—they came to determine what the illness had been. Had it been an intracranial aneurysm? Had it been some kind of intestinal gas? Actually, they couldn't determine what the illness had been. . . .
>
> The raft owners have their own doctors. And the police and the hospital are on the raft owners' land. I'm just a poor, propertyless person

> and not even from that area. So there was nothing I could do. Even if the raft owners have actually done something wrong, it's not a big problem for them. They don't have to answer a lot of questions. They've got money, right? I'm telling you their ways. Did my husband die from an illness? Or did he die due to some injury at work? I haven't been able to find out the truth because I don't have money.
>
> I got a 600,000 kyat indemnity [*yawkye*]. But they said, no, it's not an indemnity, it's a compensation for your loss [*nitnakye*].[45] At that time, I was really hurting emotionally. When I accepted the 600,000 kyat, they made me sign [a document]. Is the life of a person worth only 600,000 kyat? I can't answer that. But I want to know the real reason he died. I haven't been able to get the answer because I don't have money.

Adding support to the cases discussed here are Khin Myat Myat Wai's initial exposé, along with further investigative reports by BBC Burmese, Radio Free Asia, *Frontier Myanmar,* and *The Irrawaddy,* all of which have documented instances of trafficking, violence, and other abuses in the raft fishing industry.[46] *The Irrawaddy* cites, based on witness interviews, cases of raft workers who died when their skippers refused to promptly return them to shore for medical treatment; cases of workers who, after enduring repeated physical abuse by their supervisor, committed suicide by jumping into the sea; and still other cases of fishers who grabbed a floatation device and tried to escape by swimming to shore—a distance of roughly 80 miles.[47] It is significant that *The Irrawaddy* also cites cases of raft workers who, unwilling to endure further abuse, went on to kill their supervisors, acting on a desire that Brother Hein similarly expressed in regards to the violent skipper who murdered five of the former's coworkers.

To get a sense of the scale of death in this industry—whether due to violence, malnutrition, or otherwise—consider the statistics Khin Myat Myat Wai obtained from Amar and Daw Nyein townships, the two centers of the raft fishing industry in the delta. In Amar Township, the 2016 police death registry listed twenty-five raft workers who died from malnutrition and nine raft workers who were killed (whether by a skipper, supervisor, or fellow worker is not indicated). This same registry then lists, for just the first two months of 2017, 30 raft workers who died from malnutrition, and four workers who died due to fights on the rafts. Meanwhile, the Daw Nyein administrative unit hospital provided the following details. In March 2017, up to 30 raft workers died as a result of malnutrition or other illness, while six raft workers died from injuries. And over the preceding year, fifty-five raft workers died from malnutrition, while ten raft workers died from injuries, according to Daw Nyein administrative unit hospital records.[48] To these figures, *The Irrawaddy*, in a two-part article from 2019, added that in 2018, 81 raft workers died (of which fourteen were killed) on rafts based out of Daw Nyein village tract, while 120 raft workers went missing and were, as a result, recorded as "cases of disappeared persons" (*lupyaukhmu*).[49]

The magnitude of death in this industry—due to injuries, fights, malnutrition, illness, or drowning—is self-evidently egregious. But the high number of raft fishers listed as disappeared persons has additional financial implications that need to be made explicit. Myanmar journalist Hein Thar, reporting for *Frontier Myanmar*, quotes the following dialogue from a conversation he observed between the widow of a deceased raft fisher and a government labor officer in Pyapon Township:

> "It clearly states in the 1923 [Workmen's Compensation] law that you cannot get compensation unless you have a death certificate," the labor officer said. "How can I believe your husband is dead unless you can produce the death certificate?"
>
> "But officer, my husband died at sea and his body has not been found," Myint Myint San replied. "How can I show you a death certificate?"

Recall here what Brother Hein recounted about the bodies of his murdered coworkers: "And if, in the end, the guy died, they'd put his corpse in a plastic bag and sink it." Adding supportive detail on this practice, Khin Myat Myat Wai offers a quote by Zin Maung Maung Thant of Amar Village: "Whenever an unclaimed corpse of a fishery worker is discovered on shore having floated in from the sea, we just put it in a plastic bag and four people take it away and bury it in the Amar cemetery."[50] To spell out what is going on here, disposing at sea of the corpses of deceased raft fishers—whatever the cause of their death—enables raft owners to avoid paying compensation to the deceased's relatives and to evade potential criminal charges, however unlikely the latter may be.

As relatively affordable sources of meat protein, fish paste (*ngapi*) and dried prawns are staple foods across Myanmar. And it is from the raft fishing industry operating out of Pyapon Township that, according to the Myanmar Fisheries Federation, 80 percent of the prawns and fish for these commodities derive.[51] That these foods are at the core of social reproduction in Myanmar heightens the politics of the matter. Thus observed U Soe Win Naing, chairman of the Association of Fish Paste, Dried Fish, and Fish Sauce Entrepreneurs, in an interview with *Frontier Myanmar*: "You can say that *ngapi* [fish paste] is political because if the cost of *ngapi* goes up, people throughout the country will complain."[52] Stated otherwise, the unfree labor of Myanmar's offshore raft fishing industry subsidizes everyday social reproduction across the country.

Following Khin Myat Myat's Way's 2017 exposé, domestic media and Myanmar-focused media abroad have gone on to publish numerous accounts of trafficking and violence in the raft fishing industry. In most cases, raft workers in this industry have not simply been unfree in the sense of having been physically coerced into these labor arrangements. Instead, most of these workers have, whatever the fraud and violence they may subsequently face, accepted initial offers of eight months' debt-bondage in return for a promised wage advance. This is a "choice" on the part of raft workers, but one they have made against a historical backdrop of rural dispossession, a decline of agricultural wage labor, inflation in the cost of living, and increased household debt—in other words, an exacerbated market dependence.

Foregrounding this political-economic context helps render comprehensible a remark that Brother Hein made following his own traumatic experiences at sea: "I have no thought of going back to that work for another year. I don't have that plan anymore. And I'm going to tell other people not to go [to do that work]. But if it's for their family, then they'll go regardless of what I say." At root here is the fact that unfree labor in the offshore raft fishing industry has been constituted by its specifically capitalist context. That is why suppressing the industry in the name of anti-trafficking would fail to address the market compulsions that each year pressure so many young men in Myanmar to "freely" enter such a notoriously dangerous form of bonded labor. And that is also why struggles against the sorts of bonded arrangements considered in this chapter are inseparable from squatters' collective struggles over other livelihood matters—fighting eviction, for example, or workplace organizing. It is to these latter struggles that I turn in the following chapter.

7

SQUATTER SELF-ORGANIZATION AND COLLECTIVE STRUGGLE

It was only a matter of hours until the authorities were due to arrive, officials of the Township Municipal Development Committee. The intent, as announced in advance, was to enforce an order to dismantle shopfronts encroaching onto the roadside, and to evict a dozen or so squatters operating food stalls—micro-stalls, really—on a narrow strip of land pinched between the laneway to the west and the fence of the hulled sesame plant to the east.

The reason given was that the squatter shopfronts and food stalls were obstructing vehicular traffic along the roadway. Yet stall operators spoke of a conspiracy; the owner of the hulled sesame plant surely had a hand in the matter, they surmised. "That tycoon [*thuhte*] doesn't want to see these stalls," decried Brother Lwin as he pulled dani palm shingles off his hut. "He's mean spirited" (*seik pokde*) denounced Aunty Cho, who had been told she could no longer store her waste collection cart on the roadside opposite her home. For almost everyone else at the settlement, however, the matter was more banal. "Those stall operators keep moving further onto the road, so cars can't pass," reasoned Mrs. Yin, seated at a teashop overlooking events. "They [the stall operators] are without discipline" (*sikan mè*).

Fully aware at this time of the imminent eviction, and the yaainhmu's instructions that stall operators were to dismantle their huts by noon, Aunty San was still there, seated on the discarded wooden pallet that served as ad hoc floor of her stall, chain-smoking her cheroots, and furiously frying her fritters of sticky rice and beans—the kind she carried each day on a bamboo tray balanced on her head as she made her rounds from factory gates to riverside depots, selling her snacks to workers at 100 kyat a piece.

FIGURE 18. Brother Lwin pulls down dani palm shingles from his roadside stall. Author's photograph.

FIGURE 19. Aunty San frying fritters despite orders to dismantle her stall. Author's photograph.

This is not to say she was unconcerned. Indeed, Aunty San had been distraught ever since she had heard rumors of the impending eviction earlier that week. And just two days prior, she had been near tears as she walked down the road on the settlement's south side, balancing that ever-present tray of fritters on her head. "What can I do?" she had queried at the time, as if the question were at once sincere and rhetorical. "If they make me dismantle my stall, I'll just have to dismantle it."

For the moment, however, Aunty San, a fifty-six-year-old single mother with a teenage daughter as her dependent, was still at it. "I've got to keep frying so that we can eat today," she said. "I'll dismantle the stall this evening. If I don't fry now, we'll go hungry today." She also harbored a hope that negotiations with the Municipal Development Committee might yet achieve a conciliatory settlement whereby stalls would be moved back from the roadside but be allowed to continue operating. It was to such negotiations that her fellow squatter, Mrs. Thuzar, was imminently headed, with as many stall operators as the latter could muster. "Are you coming?" asked Mrs. Thuzar, who, not coincidentally, was a prominent organizer in the settlement and a co-founder of the local porter's union. But Aunty San could not leave her fritters. And so, only five stall operators ended up going—five plus Mrs. Thuzar. Together, these six women hopped on a single motorcycle sidecar and sped off.

As it turns out, negotiations failed. But perhaps there had been nothing the union could really do. That evening, the yaainhmu took Aunty San and several other recalcitrant stall operators to the ward office and made them give their thumbprint on a written agreement to not rebuild their dismantled stalls. The next day, not one stall remained.

Yet within three days there appeared along that very roadside a single stall, rebuilt—a betel vendor's table next to the motorcycle taxi stand, right where it had been before its recent removal. And as everyone knew full well, the proprietor of said establishment was none other than Mrs. Than, the yaainhmu's wife. The reconstruction of her stall did not go unnoticed; in time, further stalls reappeared. They were leaner than before and now had tarpaulin roofs, which could be pulled down in a hurry, if need be. And there, too, not three weeks since her eviction, was Aunty San, squatting before a pan of boiling oil, chain-smoking her cheroots, and furiously frying her fritters in a makeshift hut on the side of the road.

Looking back on these events, there are several features that can be read as instances of more general patterns in the organizing endeavors of squatters at Yadana and other such settlements on Yangon's periphery. There was the prominence of women organizers, for example. There was the challenge of mobilizing individuals facing dire and immediate livelihood concerns—Aunty San's unwillingness to leave her fritters, in particular. There was the central role (and thus relevance) of a local union organizer in a community-based struggle outside of the workplace. There was an effort (unsuccessful in the end) among residents of the settlement to achieve a negotiated compromise, even if such a tentative resolution would not have been in line with legal stipulations or with the municipal regulatory code—an effort that recalls the informal negotiating tactics that Partha Chatterjee terms the politics of the governed.[1] And finally, there was a persistent and subtle reclaiming of land by those evicted, despite the intransigence that the squatters encountered when they directly engaged officials of the Municipal Development Committee. Such surreptitious forms of everyday struggle recall the sorts of tactics that James Scott has termed weapons of the weak.[2]

Most broadly, this event underscores the enduring relevance of self-organization and collective struggle among squatters on Yangon's industrial frontier. What we see here is a contemporary proletarian politics that reveals deep contradictions. On the one hand, there is a radically democratic and egalitarian potential, which emerges "from below" out of the very conditions of dispossession and political marginalization that otherwise constrain the individuals involved. On the other hand, there is a yearning for benevolent state intervention, despite the frustrations and disappointments so often encountered when petitioning those "who speak in the state's name."[3]

It is to such contradictions that this chapter attends. In contrast to liberal narratives that erase the proletarian as a political actor in the present moment, I call attention to the endurance of proletarian struggle, with proletarian understood here in the local idiom of a propertyless class inclusive of petty peddlers like Aunty San—a dispossessed class radically dependent on the market, as Michael Denning put it.[4] We thus encounter proletarian struggle in this space as collective self-organization by dispossessed individuals learning and adapting as they go. Such struggles are not to be romanticized as an autonomous expression of subaltern desire. Yet they deserve to be recognized as a class politics with an emancipatory potential that must necessarily emerge from out of the contradictory emplacement of the individuals involved.

Proletarian Self-Organization as Pathway to Nirvana

There was no need for Sister Myat to call further attention to the mid-morning's swelter. But convention being what it is, Sister Myat proceeded to do just that: "Sure is hot, isn't it?" At least the heat and lack of rain over the preceding two days had managed to dry up some of the settlement's floodwaters, which made reconstruction of the paths and footbridges on the site's westernmost side that

FIGURE 20. Residents of the Yadana squatter settlement engaging in collective labor to rebuild paths and footbridges. Author's photograph.

FIGURE 21. Residents of the Yadana squatter settlement laying bags of sand for a new path. Author's photograph.

much simpler. And then there were the dozens of Yadana residents now volunteering on that reconstruction—they did not need to labor that day in the rain, only in the sun and the heat.

"Where's that pouch of betel?" asked a barefoot woman with a sarong wrapped around her head like a turban while searching the bench where she had earlier tucked her stash. "It's all gone," answered her friend, with a smile—the last of that stash being by then in the latter's mouth. The two women were among the fifty or so Yadana residents laboring at that moment to rebuild the paths and footbridges in the settlement's northeast corner. From a mound of sand dumped on the roadside—brought in by truck earlier that day—participants filled large sacks bearing labels of Thai fertilizer and cement companies. The sand-filled-sacks they hoisted upon their shoulders, carried to where the path was being constructed and dropped aside for other volunteers to more properly lay in place. The path being three-to-four sacks wide, the whole operation required a fair amount of sand and sacks, to say nothing of volunteer labor, which had begun that morning and would continue past mid-day. Meanwhile, barefoot children clenching opened bags of potato chips had climbed the mountainous sandpile, on which they pounced up and down, giggling as though there were nothing more pleasurable in the world. As the sacks holding the sand would eventually wear out, reconstruction of these paths was an annual endeavor—one carried out with the arrival of every rainy season.

The-tall-one, as his friends and neighbors called him, held responsibility for collecting donations toward the purchase of sand and sacks. Although the suggested contribution had been 3,000 kyat (US$2), some households—notably those headed by single mothers—had been unable to afford that sum, whereas other households had offered more. Yet even families lacking such funds could join in on the communal labor. The-tall-one spoke of it all in religious terms, such that contributions of money or labor were based on *sedena* (goodwill) and garnered *kutho* (karmic merit; a Burmanization of the Pali Buddhist term *kusala*). Sister Nandar, whose home lay along the path under construction, likewise stressed the karmic merit that volunteers earned for their efforts: "They obtain *kutho* because it's for the benefit of the whole neighborhood." The project, meanwhile, was deemed *lokapay*—a customary form of voluntary communal labor common in rural Myanmar, which is often contributed to a monastery or to maintaining village infrastructure. "Everyone's happy," observed The-tall-one regarding this collaborative activity. "It's a donation festival [*ahlu pwe*], and it's alive with a teeming crowd."

Notwithstanding The-tall-one's positive appraisal of the labor that day as *lokapay*, the latter term has a notorious history in Myanmar. In the years after 1988, the reconstituted military junta initiated mass infrastructure construction and rural militarization in ethnic minority upland areas. To implement these projects, the military imposed widespread forced labor, which military commanders would refer to in the legitimizing language of *lokapay*.[5] For villagers subject to such demands, the term *lokapay* took on a cruelly ironic meaning. It was in contrast to such coerced forms of labor, and in contrast to wage labor more generally, that The-tall-one asserted the democratically egalitarian character of the communal labor being volunteered that day to reconstruct the paths in the settlement: "We organize ourselves," he stressed. "The people who live here organize each other. . . . Everyone is equal [*tantu*]."

Underway that day among Yadana's residents, in their collective effort to rebuild the settlement's footbridges and paths, was an instantiation of mutual aid—self-organized and articulated in a local Buddhist idiom. For the nineteenth-century Russian anarchist Peter Kropotkin, mutual aid was a revolutionary expression of proletarian autonomy and solidary.[6] Along similar lines, Maurice Brinton and the British libertarian socialist group Solidarity argued in the mid-twentieth century that meaningful revolutionary action is "whatever increases the confidence, the autonomy, the initiative, the participation, the solidarity, the equalitarian tendencies, and the self-activity of the masses."[7]

In collectively reconstructing the settlement's footbridges and paths, Yadana's proletarian population pursued an explicitly egalitarian endeavor—one that emerged from out of their immediate material concerns, their sense of collective obligation, and the vernacular spiritual idiom through which they understood their actions. This was not an elitist intervention aimed at establishing mere formal equality grounded in liberal freedoms—the type of project favored by international nongovernmental organizations. It was, moreover, because of the government's denial of infrastructure to the Yadana squatter settlement that the site's residents felt compelled to collectively organize in this manner. And it was due to their slender means that they were obliged to continually—annually, in this case—engage in such self-organized initiatives. To the extent that this solidarity has endured and spilled over into other areas of social life, Yadana's residents have through such collaborative activity bolstered the social grounding needed for more confrontational forms of collective struggle, such as their efforts to oppose eviction or to assert collective demands at their places of work.

The Fire of Mrs. Sandar Oo

"Take a look at my shoulder," insisted Mrs. Sandar Oo, as she peeled back the collar of her blouse to reveal a fleshy lump underneath. "It's callused—unlike the other one." That which the fifty-five-year-old woman was there exhibiting was a mark she bore with self-assured dignity, the embodied credentials of her proletarian life. Through years of hard labor at riverside trade depots, hauling on that shoulder loads of mostly sand and gravel, Mrs. Sandar Oo had earned that callus. If nothing else, it garnered respect.

Laboring those long years at those riverside depots, Mrs. Sandar Oo had repeatedly fought against underpayment, wage theft, overwork, and hazardous working conditions. Doing so, she and her fellow porters had regularly engaged in wildcat strikes as means to press their demands. As Mrs. Sandar Oo went on to describe, "The workers would just stop working. They would calmly [*nyein nyein hsein hsein*] go on strike—just discontinue their labor."

That had been the climate when, in October 2011, the Thein Sein government introduced its new Labor Organization Law. "I heard from someone that it had become legal to form labor unions," recollected Mrs. Sandar Oo. "I didn't know [about the unionization process] so I went to ask some political activists what I could do. They gave me some suggestions. They said, 'There's now a law that gives workers the right to organize. You should form a workers' organization.' So the workers and I began to form our organization." In that way, Mrs. Sandar Oo became one of four coworkers who led the organizing drive that brought together over a hundred porters in a new local union. Together they built with their own hands a union hall of bamboo and dani palm in the very squatter settlement where most of them resided. "It wasn't easy," admitted Mrs. Sandar Oo, recalling those initial efforts to build up the union.

Among the challenges that the workers confronted, local authorities immediately sought to evict the fledgling union from the settlement. "The Municipal Development Committee personally came to drive us out," recounted Mrs. Sandar Oo.

> After we built our union hall out of bamboo, the Municipal Development Committee came with police trucks to drive us out. They claimed that they were expelling us because we had trespassed on government land. At that time, I confronted them, saying, "We're not trespassing. No one has ownership here. It's vacant land. We're Myanmar nationals and we've got nowhere else to live."
>
> They took the four of us [organizers] to the Housing Department office. They took us by truck. They said, "We'll give each of the four of you a plot of land with a brick home." They made us that offer so that we'd lose interest in the others [at the settlement]. But I told them, "I don't want that. No matter what you offer me, what I want is land for everyone [at the settlement]." I wasn't willing to compromise about that.

In the end, Mrs. Sandar Oo and her fellow squatters managed, through their protest and the intervention of a sympathetic member of the Yangon regional parliament, to prevent the eviction, although the union's presence in the settlement has remained tenuous. In any case, the union was still there eight years later, as was the union hall, with Mrs. Sandar Oo holding an elected position in the union's seven-member executive committee. Although underpayment, outright wage theft, and excessive working hours remained regular grievances among union members, Mrs. Sandar Oo had become increasingly engaged in supporting cases involving non-members. She would accompany survivors of sexual assault, for instance, who sought to pursue legal cases against their assailants. And she supported fellow squatters who fell victim to wage theft and human trafficking in the offshore raft fishing industry, or the families of individuals killed while laboring out at sea. And she continued to struggle against the municipal government's attempts to evict the squatters. Simply put, Mrs. Sandar Oo had come to understand the union's mandate broadly—a social role that she articulated like this: "For the most part, we help migrants who have fallen into distress [*doukkha*]."

Throughout her organizing endeavors, her activism, and her working life more generally, Mrs. Sandar Oo had come to develop a critical perspective on employers. She thus treated with skepticism the claim that employers—such as the individuals who owned the riverside trade depots near Yadana—were motivated by goodwill toward the workers they employed. "The only reason an employer pays any compensation [for workplace injuries]," reasoned Mrs. Sandar Oo, "is that they're scared of the law. Employers don't have a sense of goodwill [*sedena*] toward workers. . . . They might claim to have goodwill, but they don't have goodwill. And they don't pay as much compensation as they're legally obligated. . . . If an employer were to adhere to the law [by paying compensation in full], they'd incur a loss. So instead, they give the [injured] worker a small amount and say it's out of goodwill. In that way, the worker suffers, while the boss gets off easy."

Mrs. Sandar Oo traced her sense of justice and activist drive to her father, who had worked as an unpaid rural administrator in a township just outside of Yangon during the socialist period. "You could say that my father was politically involved," explained Mrs. Sandar Oo.

> He was head of our village tract and he did many humanitarian [*parahita*] activities. But he didn't get any salary. At that time [during the 1970s], the Communists were active. The police would come to our home while on patrol, but my father wouldn't allow them to enter our house. The police would arrive and ask for help; they'd ask for gasoline.

> It was an era when the police would regularly patrol. My father didn't grant the military government any priority . . .
>
> To tell the truth, my father—how should I say it? He cooperated with the Communists. He'd cooperate with them when what they were doing was proper. But if what they were doing wasn't proper, then he'd staunchly oppose them. . . . Some Communists were good. They had a good ideology [*wada*]. And my father would cooperate with them for the benefit of the neighborhood. For example, there was one case I know. It was a case of murder in our neighborhood. Some robbers had killed a husband and wife and stolen their gold. My father cooperated with the Communists to solve that case. The Communists had the courage to confront the robbers.

The lesson Mrs. Sandar Oo took from all this—from her struggles and experiences in life—was that workers had to fight for themselves. "We have to take action for ourselves if we want a labor movement to emerge," she asserted. "The government isn't giving us any support. So, for us to take action for ourselves—that's my objective."

Confronting the Limits of Industrial Relations

With Nway Oo back at home, it brought the total up to eleven family members under one roof, but in two rooms if the partition sheet hanging by a wire counted as a wall. "It's a lot," Nway Oo acknowledged, but with a smile. The young woman's mother, seated nearby, had a hoarse voice like a lifelong smoker, but it was in fact due to a recent illness. After jettisoning the betel-marinade that was her spittle through a gap between two bamboo floor slats, Mother admitted she was happy her daughter was back helping out at home. But when eighteen-year-old Nway Oo had a few weeks prior been fired together with twenty-seven co-workers from the vermicelli (*kyahsan*) factory where she had been employed, Mother had been sorely disappointed. Nway Oo had been more ambivalent.

True, the young woman had been overworked and underpaid, with the factory in egregious violation of numerous labor laws, such that Nway Oo and her husband each got only 4,000 kyat (US$2.66) for their entire twelve-hour shifts—well under half what they were legally due. But as Nway Oo's mother saw it, those wages when pooled were sufficient to keep the couple fed. What is more, the workplace had been close to home, only minutes by foot from the Yadana squatter settlement where Nway Oo had lived since birth, and where nine of her coworkers resided. This proximity put the young woman's mother at ease, for Nway Oo had what might be called a minor cognitive disability. Her mother put it bluntly: "The child's not complete in her head." The issue, among others, was that Nway Oo often lost her way. So with the factory close by, her mother explained, "I could drop her off at six o'clock at night, and go pick her up at six o'clock the next morning." That had been the situation before Nway Oo got married at the age of seventeen, which is when the young woman had joined her coworker-husband in the factory dormitory. That was also when Nway Oo had ceased handing her wages over in full to her mother and began submitting them instead to her mother-in-law.

Her mother's positive appraisal notwithstanding, Nway Oo had been less than thrilled with the employment arrangement. Although the factory supervisor harassed all the workers, she seemed to have taken a special interest in cognitively impaired Nway Oo. "While we were working," the young woman recounted with scorn, "the supervisor would yell and swear at us; she tormented me in particular." After consecutive days on shifts of twelve hours or more, with the workers exhausted and disinclined to get out of bed, "the supervisor," Nway Oo narrated, "would come into our rooms to get us. She'd swear and hit us like we were children. I'd never seen anything like that before. She'd hit us with a bamboo stick. Once I was lying on my mat, and she came and hit me two, three times. That happened whenever we didn't want to work." The targets of such abuse were inevitably the young women at the factory, even though the men, too, were often sluggish with exhaustion.

At this point, it is worth recalling the arguments of Sylvia Federici and Tithi Bhattacharya on the matter of corporal discipline and gender violence within capitalist contexts. In no way an aberration, both writers argue that such violence serves crucial disciplinary purposes in the mobilization of labor. Bhattacharya has for this reason termed export processing zones "theaters of discipline and punishment."[8] It is notable, however, that Nway Oo and her coworkers were not unfree in the coercively restricted sense of slave labor or even in the debt-bound way of workers employed in Myanmar's offshore raft fishing industry. Instead, disciplinary violence in the present case served to complement an otherwise free wage labor regime. Violence within such labor arrangements thus breaks down the dichotomy distinguishing physically coerced labor, on the one hand, from free wage labor, on the other—the ostensible opposition in capitalism between extra-economic coercion located outside the wage relation and economic compulsion located within.[9]

Despite Nway Oo's low wages and excessive unpaid overtime—both of which were in violation of existing labor laws—there were other workers at the vermicelli factory who labored longer (often eighteen hours per day and up to twenty hours in some cases) and earned wages even lower (as low as 2,500 kyat [US$1.66] per day for workers on piece rate). The employer granted no paid statutory holidays or weekly day off; provided no paid sick or other leave, or compensatory income for such leave not taken; did not pay legally-stipulated compensation to workers who were arbitrarily dismissed; and was, as of mid-2019, employing ten workers below the legal age of factory employment, the youngest being thirteen years old.[10]

All told, the factory was in violation of a slew of clauses in the 2016 Payment of Wages Law, the 2013 Minimum Wages Act, the 2012 Social Security Law, the 1959 Employment Restriction Act, the 1951 Factories Act (with its 2016 amendment), the 1951 Leave and Holiday Act (with its 2014 amendment), and the 1923 Workmans' Compensation Act (with its 2005 amendment).

This had been the situation at the vermicelli factory when, at the end of June 2019, Brother Aung—employed for over a year in the factory's boiler department—had reached out to Nway Oo and invited her to join a collective demand for back pay, and henceforth for full overtime pay and daily wages in line with the legal minimum. Involved in the organizing drive from the start, Brother Aung was keen to share the backstory. It began in the early part of June 2019, when the Burmese owner had relocated the factory to elsewhere in the township. Thus recounted Brother Aung:

> The situation got worse and more constraining, and the eating and living situation got worse. It got to the point where the workers were going hungry. . . . One day, after we got paid, I went outside. I went to a teashop to drink tea with my brother-in-law [who also worked at the factory]. I said to him, "Brother, what do you want to do? I can't endure it anymore." . . . He said he wanted to organize—adding, "There are at least 60 workers in the factory. If we can get 40, or at least half, then we'll be in an alright situation to make demands." [Then, in an intimate group of five workers, they asked each other,] "Who are you close with? You go get them on board." We went ahead with that plan. Each person was to go recruit the workers for whom they were responsible. . . . We started by organizing workers in the teashop. We'd drink tea and discuss demands. We'd call a worker and talk to them one-on-one. . . . In the end, we got 34 people. Once we got that many, we contacted Yaung Chi Oo.

With paralegal assistance from the Yaung Chi Oo Workers' Association, an organization of mostly ex-factory workers that supports workplace struggles, the thirty-four vermicelli factory employees drafted a list of fourteen demands in line with existing labor laws. Then, on July 1, the employees involved struck work and took their list to the Township Conciliation Body where they met with a relevant government official. Thus began a series of visits to the Township General Administration Department and to the respective township offices of the Department of Labor, Department of Labor Relations, Labor Laws Inspection Department, and Social Security Board, each of which held jurisdiction over different matters related to the case at hand. Three days after first submitting their grievances, however, the employer enforced—illegally—an unpaid lockout of the employees involved in the case from July 4 to 22. The move, as the workers saw it, was an attempt to compel them to drop their demands. Then, on August 14, the employer fired eight of the ten underage workers at the factory, and on August 25, fired the nineteen remaining adult workers who had thus far refused to relinquish their demands; of the initial thirty-four employees involved, seven had already accepted minor compensation in return for abandoning their legal claims.

Throughout the industrial dispute resolution process, the officials at the various township offices demonstrated what the workers involved felt was a consistent reluctance to act against the employer or even to officially acknowledge that the employer was in violation of the law. Officials handling the case at the Labor Laws Inspection Department and the Social Security Board, for example, claimed an inability to adjudicate on the submitted labor law violations because the workers were unable to provide written documentation as to the alleged abuses. Officials at both offices instead urged the workers to negotiate with the employer to reach an understanding that would resolve (*hpyeleaung*) the dispute. At this point, the officials involved neither requested the relevant documentary evidence from the employer nor dispatched (as both of these offices are by law entitled) a labor inspector to the workplace to acquire the relevant documentation or to otherwise ascertain the facts of the matter. It also needs to be stressed that the employees involved in this case were demanding nothing more than the legal minimum in wages and working conditions. Any compromise on their part would thus, by definition, have been an agreement for the employer to remain in violation of the applicable labor laws. Speaking of the Conciliation Body, in particular, Brother Aung maintained an informed cynicism: "The official at the Township Conciliation Body would say just a little on the side of the workers, and would say a lot on the side of the employer. I don't think that he was trying to achieve justice . . . I think that the employer and the official were working together."

This lack of action prompted the workers, with Yaung Chi Oo assistance, to file grievances on two matters (back pay for the period of the illegal lockout, and reinstatement of, or at least severance pay for, all twenty-seven workers fired for their organizing activities) with the Yangon Region Arbitration Body, which has a juridical power that the Township Conciliation Body lacks. In response, the Arbitration Body passed judgments on both matters. But once again, the workers involved in the case felt that these region-level officials, like their township counterparts, were reluctant to use their full authority to ensure the employer's compliance with existing labor laws.

The Arbitration Body's ruling concerning back pay for the illegal lockout is illustrative. The workers had demanded, in line with the 2013 Minimum Wages Act, back pay to the value of the minimum wage for the nineteen days of the lockout.[11] The employer, however, denied that any such lockout had occurred, and that it had instead been the workers themselves who had chosen not to work during the period in question. In such situations, Article 44 of the 2012 Settlement of Labor Disputes Law requires parties to a dispute to provide any requested evidence concerning the case at hand, and to facilitate inspection of the workplace in question in order to determine employment conditions or relevant facts concerning the case. On the matter of the factory lockout, however, the employer denied possession of any documentation concerning the attendance or otherwise of the twenty-seven workers over the period of July 4 to 22. Instead of then dispatching a labor inspector to the factory to determine the facts of the matter, the Arbitration Body went ahead and issued its ruling on August 25. In its written decision, the Arbitration Body stated that, as neither the workers nor employer were able to provide written evidence to support their respective positions—specifically, "as both parties have fallen short on the matter of whether it was possible for [the workers] to enter the factory"—the employer would only be obliged to disburse back pay for ten of the lockout's nineteen days.

By late October, the case was ongoing. The workers were still waiting for decisions by the township-level Labor Department concerning their demand for back pay to make up for payment below the minimum wage over the preceding year, and by the Labor Laws Inspection Department concerning their demands for back pay covering paid leave not taken over the preceding year and unpaid overtime over the preceding six months, and for reinstatement of the underage workers involved in the collective action who had been fired without cause. When the workers expressed a desire to take the employer to civil court to sue for full back pay and reinstatement in their former positions, the official of the township-level Labor Department pressed the workers to instead accept a negotiated settlement without reinstatement. Or more precisely, the official stated the following, as one of the workers recorded during an October 22 meeting: "If you pursue this case to court, I can't say how many days it'll take. But it'll take a long time. You'll have to submit evidence and hire a lawyer. And then, what will happen? In the present era, if someone has a lot of money, they'll prevail in a lawsuit [*ngwe mya taya naing*], isn't that right? . . . From my perspective, I want this case to be resolved. Wouldn't it be best if you calmly accepted [the employer's offer] and left [the factory]?"

This appeal notwithstanding, the Arbitration Body went on to rule that the nineteen adult workers fired for organizing activities were to be reinstated in their former positions. The employer, however, refused to allow the fired workers back into the factory and appealed the Arbitration Body's ruling with the national-level Arbitration Council. Then, on October 29, the Arbitration Council ruled that the workers did not merit reinstatement—this on the grounds of the employer's (newly procured and submitted) time sheets (which the workers disputed), according to which the fired workers had consistently skipped work throughout the preceding year. Despite claiming, however, that the dismissal of these workers warranted no legal indemnity, the employer offered to pay 45,000 kyat (about US$30) to each of the fired adult workers as a "compassion payment" (*kayuna kye*), which was listed as such in the October 29 Arbitration Council ruling.

The disparity between this amount and the severance that the workers should have received under the 2005 amendment to the 1923 Workmen's Compensation Act (0.5 to 13 months' salary according to the duration of employment) was significant, especially for employees with many years of experience at the factory. Explaining this lesser payment, an official from the Arbitration Council told the workers that this compassion payment was based on the employer's goodwill (*sedana*) and did not in any way indicate a legal obligation on the part of the employer. The workers were left baffled. After all, the employer had initially denied possessing any documentation concerning the workers' employment history. Then, all of a sudden, the employer had produced this dubious documentation once the case reached the Arbitration Council.

Notwithstanding the Arbitration Council's decision on severance pay, the township-level Labor Department ruled that the employer was legally obligated to compensate the workers for unpaid overtime wages for the duration of their employment and for unpaid compensatory pay for annual leave not taken. On these matters, the employer complied. Each of the 19 adult workers therefore received slightly over 500,000 kyat (about US$333) cash in hand. But unable to return to their former employment, the fired workers were compelled to procure other means of livelihood. Nway Oo, for instance, having moved back in with her mother, took up intermittent casual day labor beheading prawns on a piece rate at a seafood processing plant near the Yadana settlement.

Given the outcome, many of the workers held mixed feelings concerning their struggle—they had obtained, it seemed, about half, financially, of what they were legally due. The employer, meanwhile, had managed to purge the workforce of its most militant organizers. Nonetheless, aside from the obstacles the workers encountered in taking their claims through the official industrial relations process and the eventual shortfall in legal redress, Brother Aung remained positive throughout the experience. "We've been in this fight for almost three months now," he reflected at the end of September. "We made a decision to struggle until we get our rights. And no matter how exhausted I feel, so long as I know that there are other workers standing with me, I'm happy."

A crucial aspect of this case, and most cases of workers' collective action in the industrial zones around Yangon, is that the workers involved were demanding nothing more than the legal minimum in wages and working conditions. It was, in other words, left to the workers themselves to push for legal compliance—a responsibility with which specific state actors have officially been tasked. What is more, the workers encountered inaction and disingenuous appeals for compromise from officials at government offices that are entrusted with upholding the country's labor standards—this on top of excessive delays by township-level authorities in moving forward on the case, delays that benefitted the employer while being detrimental to the fired workers.

To contextualize this case, it is worth recalling the historical backdrop to the new industrial relations framework that the Myanmar government introduced with the 2011 Labor Organization Law and the 2012 Settlement of Labor Disputes Law. As detailed in chapter 1, when the newly elected Thein Sein government took office in early 2011, it sought to have economic sanctions by Western governments repealed and to attract foreign investment by, among other sources, Western apparel companies that had until then been wary of having their brands tarnished by association with the unabashedly illiberal labor conditions long prevalent in Myanmar under military rule. In addition, in the years preceding the new Labor Disputes Settlement Law, even though trade unions were effectively prohibited, a wave of wildcat strikes erupted in the industrial zones around Yangon between November 2009 and March 2010, with one day seeing an estimated 10,000 workers taking part.[12]

It was in this context that the International Labor Organization (ILO) supported the Thein Sein government in drafting the 2012 law that established Myanmar's tripartite industrial relations mechanisms. As a Yangon-based ILO adviser subsequently elaborated, Myanmar's new industrial relations mechanisms had been designed to "ward off strikes," and in their principal objectives this ILO adviser had by 2015 found these mechanisms to have been "remarkably successful."[13] It is for this very reason that Myanmar labor activist Ye Yint Khant Maung argued, "Existing trade union legislation is ostensibly intended to ensure workers' right to organize. But in fact, these laws aim to achieve industrial tranquility and workers' acquiescence in order to promote Foreign Direct Investment and stable capital accumulation."[14]

There is a pertinent anthropological precedent here. In Myanmar, as elsewhere, the institutionalization of workers' struggles within a bureaucratic industrial relations framework has sought to turn what were at first subversive struggles into that which Max Gluckman called *rituals of rebellion*—ritualized hostility to centers of power that, counterintuitively, serves to stabilize and reproduce the status quo. Gluckman's argument (made in his 1952 Frazer lecture) was that the "instituted protest" often seen in seemingly transgressive rituals expresses real social tensions. However, by providing a managed release for built-up antagonism, such rituals serve to redirect the disruptive power of these tensions into a renewal of the overall system of hierarchical relations.[15]

I note that—though this should by now be an obvious point—even as Myanmar's current industrial relations mechanisms have sought to "ward off strikes," these instruments have not been "remarkably successful," as the ILO adviser suggested. Factory strikes remain common occurrences across Yangon's industrial zones. What is more, workers in these zones have often pursued their struggles outside of the formal tripartite framework. And Myanmar workers have, based on their own direct experiences, developed scathing critiques of the country's official industrial relations mechanisms and of the officials who manage them—as seen, for example, in Brother Aung's comments regarding the behavior of the officials he encountered in the Township Conciliation Body.

Given the limits of the instituted process, workers employed in the industrial zones around Yangon have often chosen to pursue their struggles outside of the institutional framework—to throw off the straitjacket, as it were, of the official dispute resolution mechanisms. This has, for instance, been the explicit strategy of the All Burma Federation of Trade Unions (ABFTU), which has opted not to register as a formal union federation due to the restrictions such registration entails. At the level of the factory, ABFTU workplace unions have instead pursued a strategy of negotiating directly with employers and then striking when necessary without working through the tripartite mechanism.[16] More dramatically, workers in Myanmar have, in some cases, set up barricades around their factories, blockaded managers within factory offices, and destroyed production equipment in protest over their employers' recalcitrance in negotiations.[17] And in early 2015, over 5,000 workers from five garment factories in Shwepyithar Township carried out a joint five-week-long extra-legal strike. After nearly a month, township authorities dispatched squadrons of baton-wielding police to disperse the striking workers, injuring dozens of the mostly women strikers in the process. Then, close to two weeks later, police directed deputized vigilantes to remove—again, violently—the last of the workers' strike camp. In the end, the police apprehended fourteen striking workers and activists, along with two journalists.[18] Then in February 2017, hundreds of workers infuriated over their employer's determined refusal to negotiate over unpaid wages at the Chinese-owned Hangzhou Hundred-Tex Garment factory in Hlaingtharyar Township stormed the workplace, "damaging factory vehicles, breaking windows, wrecking machinery, attacking the Chinese manager, and taking seven Chinese supervisors hostage."[19] Finally, in August 2018, workers from the Fu Yuen Garment Factory aggrieved over unpaid wages and disillusioned over the biases and failures of the official tripartite industrial resolution mechanism struck work outside the legal framework. A month and a half into the strike, hired thugs attacked the workers' encampment, beat the striking workers with metal bars—injuring twenty-eight, of whom all but one were women—and demolished the workers' strike camp.[20]

Evidently, the tripartite industrial relations mechanisms of "transition-era" Myanmar have managed neither to ensure employers' compliance with existing labor protection laws nor—even when backed by directly violent means—to contain workers' insubordinate fury. In short, collective proletarian struggle remains widespread and vibrant across Myanmar's expanding industrial zones.

CONCLUSION

The Margins at the Heart of Modernity

This book has been an inquiry into disparate arrangements of precarious labor in transitional Myanmar. By investigating the diversity of livelihoods pursued by residents of the Yadana squatter settlement, I have sought to raise some critical questions concerning the narrative of transition that has dominated academic, government, and media accounts of Myanmar during the period of reform that began with the shift to quasi-civilian rule in March 2011 and ended with the military coup of February 2021. Undergirding this narrative has been an assumption, which the World Bank has made explicit, that by eradicating "constraints" on private investment, the ensuing dynamism of capital would shepherd the country's largely rural population out of "low-productivity" agrarian livelihoods and into "good, formal sector jobs" in urban manufacturing and services.[1] The development agenda derived from this premise has consequently privileged owners of capital over the country's proletarian and peasant majority, with the aim being to insert Myanmar into global commodity chains as a low-wage, low value-added export economy.

But this agenda is not new. Rather than beginning with the inauguration of President Thein Sein in 2011, we see the continuation of a program of structural adjustment that Myanmar's reconstituted military junta introduced after 1988. It was at that moment, in a shift toward a more market-oriented economy, that rural dispossession, declining agricultural employment, inflation in the cost of living, and rising debt fueled a mass outmigration of rural dwellers in search of substitute incomes elsewhere. It was an outmigration that has continued to the present. Many such migrants headed to Thailand, Malaysia, and other countries in the region, while others left in search of employment at mines, plantations, and aquaculture farms elsewhere in Myanmar. Others departed for industrial zones newly established around urban centers like Yangon.

This political-economic restructuring has not delivered on the promise of stable, well-remunerated livelihoods for all. In other words, the majority of ex-rural dwellers have not been absorbed into good jobs, defined in the narrow sense of secure employment that meets the bare legal minimum in wages and working conditions. This has been the case where individuals have remained unemployed or where they have taken up forms of informal self-employment, the latter often subsumed to capitalist enterprises. But it is also true among those who have obtained employment in the so-called formal sector, as many such jobs remain in practice informal—that is, in violation of manifold labor protection laws. Such is even the case for migrants working abroad, as employment conditions in host countries often fall short of their own minimum legal standards.[2] Meanwhile, within Myanmar, employment in the so-called formal sector remains, for so many ex-rural dwellers, out of reach, as is the case with garment factories producing for export, which as a rule restrict hiring to young women in their late teens and early twenties. The capitalist landscape of contemporary Myanmar remains, in this way, persistently uneven.

But this situation is not unique. A growing body of research in critical development studies has called attention to enduring structural unemployment and underemployment across the Global South, and increasingly in the Global North, ensuing from industrial relocation, automation, and the casualization of labor.[3] It is telling that, in Myanmar, antidispossession struggles by small-holder farmers and independent fishers remain widespread, suggesting that many of the country's rural dwellers remain unpersuaded by the promise of good jobs in the urban economy. Meanwhile, what often informs the desire to take up informal self-employment is a refusal of the managerial harassment and workplace discipline encountered in existing forms of waged labor.

Yet nonnormative labor arrangements in the urban informal economy are not by definition outside of capitalist relations or outside the liberal political order. Such has been a central argument of this book, informed by the experiences of individuals residing at the Yadana squatter settlement. At Yadana and other such sites in Myanmar, a lack of wage labor, formal or otherwise, cannot be read as indicating an individual's redundancy to the country's new economy. Nor do such conditions, destitute though they may be, suggest that persons affected are in some way not yet transitioned, not yet modern. Although informal settlements like Yadana have been construed as external to the capitalist norm, the labor of their residents remains critical to Myanmar's new urban political economy. Stated otherwise, marginal labor is here integral; nonnormative, the enduring norm. The Standard Employment Relationship remains stubbornly nonstandard, while illiberalism serves as the constitutive ground for a narrowly hegemonic liberal order. This means, as well, that the illiberal practices so often encountered in nonnormative labor arrangements cannot be sustainably remedied so long as workers and their families remain so radically dependent on the market.

Capitalist Heterogeneity and Proletarian Politics

Historically, progressive political agendas in much of the world were premised on a presumption that an ever-expanding working class would be compelled to enter into full-time wage labor. For liberals, the citizen-worker nexus offered a basis for allocating rights and privileges in capitalist orders. For radicals, an expansion of factory production would establish conditions for communism, as factory employment fostered the working-class solidarity needed for collective struggle while facilitating the socialization of production that makes workers' self-management possible.[4]

Industrial relocation since the late twentieth century has challenged such politics. However, analysis derived from the North Atlantic experience has often erroneously universalized that region's late twentieth-century experience of deindustrialization. The result has been analytical myopia and political parochialism in regards to contemporary industrial production elsewhere, which now dwarfs the Euro-American precedent, even at the height of the latter's post-war Fordist-Keynesian order.[5] It was in response to such parochialism that Ronaldo Munck argued, in a critique of Guy Standing's 2011 nonfiction best-seller, *The Precariat*, "If we only focus on precarity (in the North), we miss out on the massive expansion of the global working class in classic Marxist forms."[6] Indeed, in Myanmar, mass factory strikes—militant, courageous, and mostly led by women—have been recurring features of an expanding industrial landscape over the past decade-plus.

At the same time, the manifest heterogeneity of actually existing capitalist orders challenges political projects that would narrowly privilege a classical working-class employed in normative forms of capitalist labor. What we instead find across the world is what the geographers Jamie Peck and Nick Theodore call *variegated capitalism*—a diversity of production arrangements that, in Myanmar, certainly employ legally unionized factory workers, but also casual day laborers, outsourced subcontractors, gig workers, indentured wage laborers, debt-bound self-employed workers, disguised wage workers, incarcerated workers, family members engaged without wages in the labor of social reproduction, children employed without direct wage payments, and trafficked or otherwise violently subjugated workers laboring in unfree employment relations. This is not an assemblage of autonomous economic forms; it is a social formation comprised of heterogeneous interconnected labor arrangements.

The social basis for political action that emerges here is, accordingly, not a unitary working class whose divisions are merely ideological, nor a classless multitude engaged in an assortment of disconnected livelihoods, but rather a segmented proletariat differently embedded in capitalist relations. It is a social formation at once singular and multiple—a social formation reminiscent of the metaphorical many-headed hydra, which Peter Linebaugh and Marcus Rediker employ to denote the motley crowd of expropriated sailors, slaves, soldiers, laborers, indentured servants, bonded apprentices, and market women whose mutinous refusals revolutionized the trans-Atlantic world over the seventeenth to nineteenth centuries.[7]

Amid such capitalist variegation, disparate struggles for liberation are interconnected, but this heterogeneity poses challenges to an otherwise expansive proletarian solidarity. Spontaneity is here insufficient, as difference demands that coalitions are built. The situation recalls Marx's critique of the movement for a limited workday in the antebellum United States, where industrial workers in the North railed against the injustices of wage labor but, hamstrung by white supremacy, staunchly opposed the abolition of Southern slavery. "In the United States of America," wrote Marx, "every independent movement of the workers was paralyzed so long as slavery disfigured a part of the Republic. Labor cannot emancipate itself in the white skin when in the black it is branded."[8] It was a critique that W.E.B. Du Bois went on to revisit in his monumental history, *Black Reconstruction in America*, wherein he lamented that, regarding a potential coalition of Northern industrial workers, poor Southern whites, and ex-slaves, such a "union of democratic forces never took place."[9] Or as Angela Davis would later critique in her history of the US women's liberation movement: "The leaders of the women's rights movement did not suspect that the enslavement of Black people in the South, the economic exploitation of Northern workers, and the social oppression of women might be systematically related."[10] Simply put, disparate forms of subjugation in capitalist orders are mutually constituted; emancipatory struggles must thus of necessity be relational.

An Anthropology of Relational Difference

Throughout this book I have pursued what can be called an anthropology of relational difference. By this I mean an ethnographic inquiry that approaches divergent socio-cultural formations, not as ontologically autonomous, but as coconstituted through the reciprocal relations in which they are embedded.[11] Understood in this way, objects of anthropological investigation cannot be adequately apprehended in themselves—that is, disembedded from their historical, social, and political milieus.

For this reason, dichotomies are best grasped not as pairs of putatively distinct elements but as a unity of opposites, whose apparent differences are not inherent properties but instead relationally constituted by their very opposition. The urban, for example, cannot be understood apart from the rural, with urban capitalism, in the case at hand, constituted by rural dispossession. Similarly, the formal is made possible by the informal, and the informal, in turn, by the formal. It was likewise the very illiberalism of colonial rule that made possible the establishment of liberal labor regimes in the colonial metropole. More broadly, the colonized and colonizer were mutually formed by the colonial relation. And within legally plural colonial orders, direct and indirect rule were not distinct regulatory modalities but rather "complementary forms of native control."[12] And then poverty, of course, is not an independent condition, but instead a relationship to wealth. Meanwhile, the so-called slum is not a site outside of the modern liberal capitalist order but rather a space constituted by, and in turn constitutive of, the wider social geography in which it is embedded. It was an understanding of this sort that lay behind an earlier critique of classical anthropological village studies, which had conventionally abstracted such rural habitations from the wider social networks in which they were constitutively embedded.[13]

Crucially, however, a relational anthropology equates not with a deterministic analysis—structural or otherwise. Nor do we arrive at a mechanistic system-logic. For it is contradiction, rather than structure, which emerges as a catalyst in such a relational approach. The alternative, therefore, to conceiving nonnormative labor arrangements as ontologically noncapitalist (in the spirit of J. K. Gibson-Graham) is certainly not any sort of economistic determinism. This is because a relational anthropology is at heart a dialectical analysis that refuses to choose between such simplistic alternatives. What we instead arrive at anthropologically here is an analytical appreciation of the ambiguities inherent in any difficult moral decision. We see, for instance, the complicated trade-offs in choosing to subordinate oneself to managerial despotism on the factory floor rather than taking up the more flexible but economically uncertain option of informal waste collection under historical conditions of propertyless-ness. We also see the contradictions of a chauvinistic Burman Buddhist nationalism, which establishes an ideological scaffolding for the enduring subjugation of, among others, the

Burman Buddhist working class, despite claiming for the latter an ambiguously privileged position in an ethnoreligious polity. What we gain when we analytically embrace such contradictions is a better sense of the tensions informing the ethnographic richness of everyday life, which in the end is what anthropologists must take as their empirical point of departure.

Notes

INTRODUCTION

1. The following account is based on two extended interviews conducted with the victim's parents on January 15 and March 12, 2019. The killing of Zaw Lin Oo took place on November 7, 2018. The victim was twenty-one years old at the time.

2. Stephen Campbell, "Reading Myanmar's Inland Fisheries: Postcolonial literature as theoretical lens," *Inter-Asia Cultural Studies* 20, no.1 (2019): 13.

3. On the casualization of construction employment in Myanmar, see Stephen Campbell, "Labour formalization as selective hegemony in reform-era Myanmar," *Asia-Pacific Journal of Anthropology* 20, no. 1 (2019): 7–8.

4. *Myanmar: Ending Poverty and Boosting Shared Prosperity in a Time of Transition* (Yangon: World Bank Group, 2014), 28.

5. International Crisis Group, "Myanmar: The Politics of Economic Reform," (Jakarta/Brussels, July 27, 2012), www.crisisgroup.org/asia/south-east-asia/myanmar/myanmar-politics-economic-reform.

6. See, for example, Sean Turnell, "Myanmar's Fifty-Year Authoritarian Trap," *Journal of International Affairs* 65, no. 1 (2011).

7. Ardeth Maung Thawngmung, *Everyday Economic Survival in Myanmar* (Madison: University of Wisconsin Press, 2019), 3–4.

8. Stephen McCarthy, "Ten Years of Chaos in Burma: Foreign Investment and Economic Liberalization under the SLORC-SPDC, 1988 to 1998," *Pacific Affairs* 73, no. 2 (2000): 233; John Badgley, "The Burmese Way to Capitalism," *Southeast Asian Affairs* (1990); Ikuko Okamoto, *Economic Disparity in Rural Myanmar: Transformation under Market Liberalization* (Singapore: NUS Press, 2008); Kōichi Fujita, Fumiharu Mieno, and Ikuko Okamoto, eds., *The Economic Transition in Myanmar after 1988: Market Economy versus State Control* (Singapore: NUS Press, 2009).

9. Michael Burawoy and Katherine Verdery, eds., *Uncertain Transition: Ethnographies of Change in the Postsocialist World* (Lanham, MD: Rowman & Littlefield, 1999).

10. Elizabeth L. Rhoads and Courtney T. Wittekind, "Rethinking Land and Property in a 'Transitioning' Myanmar: Representations of Isolation, Neglect, and Natural Decline," *Journal of Burma Studies* 22, no. 2 (2018): 181.

11. See, for example, Arthur Lewis, "Economic Development with Unlimited Supplies of Labour," *Manchester School* 22, no. 2 (1954).

12. Dennis Arnold and Stephen Campbell, "Capitalist Trajectories in Mekong Southeast Asia," *European Journal of East Asian Studies* 17 (2018); Patrick Neveling, "The Political Economy of Special Economic Zones: Pasts, Presents, Futures," in *The Oxford Handbook of Industrial Hubs and Economic Development* (Oxford: Oxford University Press, 2020).

13. Walter Rodney, *How Europe Underdeveloped Africa* (London: Bogle-L'Ouverture, 1972); Andre Gunder Frank, *Capitalism and Underdevelopment in Latin America: Historical Studies of Chile and Brazil* (New York: Monthly Review Press, 1967); Immanuel Wallerstein, *The Modern World-System I: Capitalist Agriculture and the Origins of the European World-Economy in the Sixteenth Century* (Cambridge: Academic Press, 1974).

14. Kathleen Gough, "Anthropology and Imperialism," *Monthly Review* 19, no. 11 (1968); Kathleen Gough, "'Anthropology and Imperialism' Revisited," *Economic and Political Weekly* 25, no. 31 (1990).

15. Garry Rodan, Kevin Hewison, and Richard Robinson, "Theorising South-East Asia's Boom, Bust, and Recovery," in *The Political Economy of South-East Asia: Conflict, Crisis, and Change*, ed. Garry Rodan, Kevin Hewison, and Richard Robinson, 2nd ed. (Oxford: Oxford University Press, 2002).

16. James Ferguson, *Expectations of Modernity: Myths and Meanings of Urban Life on the Zambian Copperbelt* (Berkeley: University of California Press, 1999); Tania Murray Li, "To Make Live or Let Die? Rural Dispossession and the Protection of Surplus Populations," *Antipode* 41, no. s1 (2010); Tania Murray Li, "After Development: Surplus Population and the Politics of Entitlement," *Development and Change* 48, no. 6 (2017).

17. Walt Rostow, *The Stages of Economic Growth: A Non-Communist Manifesto* (Cambridge: Cambridge University Press, 1960).

18. Franco Barchiesi, *Precarious Liberation: Workers, the State, and Contested Social Citizenship in Postapartheid South Africa* (Albany: State University of New York Press, 2011).

19. Dennis Arnold and Stephen Campbell, "Labour Regime Transformation in Myanmar: Constitutive Processes of Contestation," *Development and Change* 48, no. 4 (2017).

20. Elliot Prasse-Freeman and Phyo Win Latt, "Class and Inequality in Contemporary Myanmar," in *The Routledge Handbook of Contemporary Myanmar*, ed. Adam Simpson, Nicholas Farrelly, and Ian Holliday (Abingdon: Routledge, 2018), 409.

21. See, for example, Ferguson, *Expectations of Modernity*; Tania Murray Li, "Centering Labor in the Land Grab Debate," *Journal of Peasant Studies* 38, no. 2 (2011); Arnold and Campbell, "Capitalist Trajectories in Mekong Southeast Asia."

22. Stephen Campbell, *Border Capitalism, Disrupted: Precarity and Struggle in a Southeast Asian Industrial Zone* (Ithaca: Cornell University Press).

23. Barchiesi, *Precarious Liberation*; see also James Ferguson, *Give a Man a Fish: Reflections on the New Politics of Distribution* (Durham: Duke University Press, 2015).

24. For an overview of J.K. Gibson-Graham-inspired anthropology, see Laura Bear, Karen Ho, Anna Lowenhaupt Tsing, and Sylvia Yanagisako, "Gens: A Feminist Manifesto for the Study of Capitalism," *Cultural Anthropology*, March 30, 2015, https://culanth.org/fieldsights/gens-a-feminist-manifesto-for-the-study-of-capitalism.

25. J.K. Gibson-Graham, *The End of Capitalism (as We Knew It): A Feminist Critique of Political Economy* (Minneapolis: University of Minnesota Press, 1996), 6.

26. The question of whether noncapitalist modes of production were enduring in postcolonial countries was central to the modes of production debates of the 1970s. For an overview of these debates, see Utsa Patnaik, *Agrarian Relations and Accumulation: The Mode of Production Debate in India* (Oxford: Oxford University Press, 1990).

27. Arthur Lewis, "Economic Development with Unlimited Supplies of Labour," *Manchester School* 22, no. 2 (1954).

28. Keith Hart, "Informal Income Opportunities and Urban Employment in Ghana," *Journal of Modern African Studies* 11, no. 1 (1973).

29. Li, "To Make Live or Let Die?"

30. Kalyan Sanyal, *Rethinking Capitalist Development: Primitive Accumulation, Governmentality and Post-Colonial Capitalism* (Abingdon: Routledge, 2007), 259.

31. Ferguson, *Give a Man a Fish*, 11.

32. Ferguson, *Give a Man a Fish*, 23.

33. Anna Tsing, *The Mushroom at the End of the World: On the Possibility of Life in Capitalist Ruins* (Durham: Duke University Press, 2015), 66.

34. Benno Teschke, for instance, argues that capitalist labor arrangements are to be understood as "civil contracts among politically (though not economically) free and

equal citizens subject to civil law" (Benno Teschke, *The Myth of 1648: Class, Geopolitics and the Making of Modern International Relations* [London: Verso, 2012], 256). The textual precedent for such a conception of capitalism rests in Marx's statements on the free wage worker: "For the transformation of money into capital, therefore, the owner of money must find the free worker available on the commodity-market; and this worker must be free in the double sense that as a free individual he can dispose of his labor-power as his own commodity, and that, on the other hand, he has no other commodity for sale, i.e. he is rid of them, he is free of all the objects needed for the realization of his labor power" (Karl Marx, *Capital: A Critique of Political Economy, Volume 1*, trans. Ben Fowkes [London: Penguin, 1976], 272–272).

35. Marcel van der Linden, *Workers of the World: Essays toward a Global Labor History* (Leiden: Brill, 2013); Marcel van der Linden and Karl Heinz Roth, eds., *Beyond Marx: Theorising the Global Labour Relations of the Twenty-First Century* (Leiden: Brill, 2014); Jairus Banaji, *Theory as History: Essays on Modes of Production and Exploitation* (Leiden: Brill, 2010); Andrea Komlosy, "Work and Labor Relations," in *Capitalism: The Reemergence of a Historical Concept*, ed. Jürgen Kocka and Marcel van der Linden (London: Bloomsbury, 2016).

36. Jairus Banaji, *Theory as History: Essays on Modes of Production and Exploitation* (Leiden: Brill, 2010), 349–350.

37. Mariarosa Della Costa and Selma James, *The Power of Women and the Subversion of the Community* (London: Falling Wall Press, 1972); Silvia Federici, *Revolution at Point Zero: Housework, Reproduction, and Feminist Struggle* (Oakland: PM Press, 2012).

38. Federici, *Revolution at Point Zero*, 28.

39. Silvia Federici, "Undeclared War: Violence against Women," *Artforum* (2017), www.artforum.com/print/201706/undeclared-war-violence-against-women-68680.

40. Tithi Bhattacharya, "Explaining Gender Violence in the Neoliberal Era," *International Viewpoint*, September 28, 2013, www.internationalviewpoint.org/spip.php?article 3212.

41. On this matter, Wallerstein remarked, "Slavery and so-called 'second serfdom' are not to be regarded as anomalies in a capitalist system." See Immanuel Wallerstein, *The Modern World-System I*, 399–400.

42. Sidney Mintz, *Sweetness and Power: The Place of Sugar in Modern History* (London: Penguin Random House, 1985).

43. See, for example, Tania Murray Li, "The Price of Un/Freedom: Indonesia's Colonial and Contemporary Plantation Labor Regimes," *Comparative Studies in Society and History* 59, no. 2 (2017); Khin Myat Myat Wai, "Enslaved Fishery Workers near Pyapon City," trans. Stephen Campbell, *Tea Circle: A Forum for New Perspectives on Burma/Myanmar*, https://teacircleoxford.com/2018/08/22/enslaved-fishery-workers-near-pyapon-city/; Kate Hodal, Chris Kelly, and Felicity Lawrence, "Revealed: Asian Slave Labour Producing Prawns for Supermarkets in US, UK," *Guardian*, June 10, 2014, www.theguardian.com /global-development/2014/jun/10/supermarket-prawns-thailand-produced-slave-labour; Robin McDowell, Margie Mason, and Martha Mendoza "AP Investigation: Slaves May Have Caught the Fish You Bought," AP, March 25, 2015, www.ap.org/explore/seafood -from-slaves/ap-investigation-slaves-may-have-caught-the-fish-you-bought.html.

44. Jan Breman, "A Dualistic Labour System? A Critique of the 'Informal Sector' Concept: I: The Informal Sector," *Economic and Political Weekly* 11, no. 48 (1976); Dae-Oup Chang, "Informalising Labour in Asia's Global Factory," *Journal of Contemporary Asia* 39, no. 2 (2009).

45. Sharryn Kasmir and August Carbonella, "Introduction: Toward a Global Anthropology of Labor," in *Blood and Fire: Toward a Global Anthropology of Labour*, ed. Sharryn Kasmir and August Carbonella (New York: Berghahn Books, 2014), 24.

46. Campbell, "Reading Myanmar's Inland Fisheries," 6–7.

47. Michael Denning, "Wageless Life," *New Left Review* 66 (2010): 81.

48. The argument that capitalism is inherently "uneven" and "combined" comes from Leon Trotsky. However, for a specifically anthropological use of this approach, see Sharryn Kasmir and Lesley Gill, "No Smooth Surfaces: The Anthropology of Unevenness and Combination," *Current Anthropology* 59, no. 4 (2018).

49. See, for example, Eleanor Leacock and Helen I. Safa, eds., *Women's Work: Development and the Division of Labor by Gender* (New York: Bergin and Garvey, 1986); Claude Meillassoux, *Maidens, Meal and Money: Capitalism and the Domestic Community* (Cambridge: Cambridge University Press, 1975); Nancy Fraser, "Behind Marx's Hidden Abode," *New Left Review* 86 (2014); Federici, *Revolution at Point Zero*; Maria Mies, *Patriarchy and Accumulation on a World Scale: Women in the International Division of Labour* (London: Zed Books, 1986).

50. Robert J. Chaskin and Mark L. Joseph, *Integrating the Inner City: The Promise and Perils of Mixed-Income Public Housing Transformation* (Chicago: University of Chicago Press), 21.

51. Leah Vosko, *Managing the Margins: Gender, Citizenship, and the International Regulation of Precarious Employment* (Oxford: Oxford University Press, 2009), 1.

52. Lisa Lowe, *The Intimacies of Four Continents* (Durham: Duke University Press, 2015).

53. Karl Marx, *Economic and Philosophical Manuscripts of 1844*, trans. Martin Milligan (New York: Prometheus Books, 1988), 86. See also Christopher Krupa, "Ghostly Figures Outside the Domain of Political Economy: Class Analysis and the Invisiblized Livelihoods of an Andean Export Zone," in *Confronting Capital: Critique and Engagement in Anthropology*, ed. Belinda Leach, Pauline Barber, and Winnie Lem (New York: Routledge, 2012).

54. Sandro Mezzadra and Brett Neilson, *Border as Method, or, the Multiplication of Labor* (Durham: Duke University Press, 2013).

55. Erik Harms, *Saigon's Edge: On the Margins of Ho Chi Minh City* (Minneapolis: University of Minnesota Press, 2010).

56. Eben I. Forbes, "On the Frontier of Urbanization: Informal Settlements in Yangon, Myanmar," *Independent Journal of Burmese Scholarship* 1, no. 1 (2016), 207.

57. For a discussion of the term *kyu-kyaw yatkwet* and its use in legitimizing the government's evictions and relocations of urban residents in postsocialist Yangon, see Jennifer Leehey, "Open Secrets, Hidden Meanings: Censorship, Esoteric Power, and Contested Authority in Urban Burma in the 1990s" (PhD diss., University of Washington, 2010), 68–69.

58. *The Challenge of Slums: Global Report on Human Settlement 2003* (London: United Nations Human Settlements Programme, 2003), https://www.un.org/ruleoflaw/files/Challenge%20of%20Slums.pdf, xxv.

59. Mike Davis, *Planet of Slums* (London: Verso, 2005).

60. See Anthony Leeds, *Cities, Classes, and the Social Order*, ed. Roger Sanjek (Ithaca: Cornell University Press, 1994). See also Peter Cutt Lloyd, *Slums of Hope? Shanty Towns of the Third World* (Manchester: Manchester University Press, 1979). For a review of the anthropology of slums since the mid-twentieth century, see Atreyee Sen, "Slums and Shanty Towns," in *The International Encyclopedia of Anthropology* (Hoboken: John Wiley & Sons, 2018).

61. More recent ethnographies on shanty towns and urban slums include Nancy Scheper-Hughes, *Death without Weeping: The Violence of Everyday Life in Brazil* (Berkeley: University of California Press, 1993); Donna M. Goldstein, *Laughter out of Place Race, Class, Violence, and Sexuality in a Rio Shantytown* (Berkeley: University of California Press, 2013); Kerry Ryan Chance, *Living Politics in South Africa's Urban Shacklands* (Chi-

cago: University of Chicago Press, 2018); Atreyee Sen, *Shiv Sena Women: Violence and Communalism in a Bombay Slum* (Bloomington: University of Indiana Press, 2007).

62. Sandro Mezzadra, "Bringing Capital Back In: A Materialist Turn in Postcolonial Studies?" *Inter-Asia Cultural Studies* 12, no. 1 (2011).

63. The results of that research were published as Campbell, "Labour Formalisation as Selective Hegemony."

64. Robert Redfield's *Tepoztlán, a Mexican Village* (Chicago: University of Chicago Press, 1930) is an illustrative example of classic anthropological village studies. For a critique of such studies, and of Redfield's work, in particular, see Leeds, *Cities, Classes, and the Social Order*, 57. For a recent reflection on the rise and decline of anthropological village studies in the twentieth century, see Antonio Sorge and Jonathan Padwe, "The Abandoned Village? Introduction to the Special Issue," *Critique of Anthropology* 35, no. 3 (2015).

1. A DEEPER HISTORY OF MYANMAR'S POLITICAL TRANSFORMATION

1. David Price, *Cold War Anthropology: The CIA, the Pentagon, and the Growth of Dual Use Anthropology* (Durham: Duke University Press, 2015), 128–130 and 378.

2. Walt Rostow, *The Stages of Economic Growth: A Non-Communist Manifesto* (Cambridge: Cambridge University Press, 1959).

3. Kyaw Hsu Mon, "Finance Minister Predicts 'Take Off' for Burma Economy," *Irrawaddy*, June 6, 2017, https://www.irrawaddy.com/business/finance-minister-predicts-take-off-burma-economy.html.

4. Aung Shin and Aye Thidar Kyaw, "NLD Finance Minister Admits to Bogus PhD," *Myanmar Times*, March 23, 2016, https://www.mmtimes.com/business/19597-nld-finance-minister-admits-to-bogus-phd.html.

5. "Myanmar—Reengagement and Reform Support Credit: Summary of Discussion (English)," World Bank, 2013, http://documents.worldbank.org/curated/en/202781468053669202/Myanmar-Reengagement-and-Reform-Support-Credit-summary-of-discussion.

6. "International Development Association Program Document for a Proposed Credit in the Amount of Equivalent to SDR 147.8 Million (USD 200 Million Equivalent) to the Republic of the Union of Myanmar for the First Macroeconomic Stability and Fiscal Resilience Development Policy Operation" Washington DC, World Bank, 2017, http://documents.worldbank.org/curated/en/632531493517715510/pdf/113808-REVISED-OUO-9-MM-SRDPO-1-PD-04282017.pdf, p.10 and 26; "Myanmar and World Bank Sign Agreement for Budget Support to Accelerate Economic Changes Needed for Long-Term Peace and Prosperity" World Bank, 2017, www.worldbank.org/en/news/press-release/2017/08/18/myanmar-and-world-bank-sign-agreement-for-budget-support-to-accelerate-economic-changes-needed-for-long-term-peace-and-prosperity; "Myanmar: Ending Poverty and Boosting Shared Prosperity in a Time of Transition" World Bank, 2014, www.themimu.info/sites/themimu.info/files/documents/Report_A_Systematic_Country_Diagnostic_WorldBank_Nov2014.pdf.

7. Ludu Sein Win, "*Thamaingko bethu hpantitalè* [Who makes history?]," *Weekly Eleven News*, September 28, 2010, http://oothandar.blogspot.com/2010/09/blog-post_27.html. An English translation of the article was published shortly thereafter as Ludu U Sein Win, "The Myth of the Makers of History," translated by May Ng, *Mizzima News*, October 5, 2010.

8. As an exemplary anthropological study of the nationalist reconstruction of political history in a different context, see Richard Handler, *Nationalism and the Politics of Culture in Quebec* (Madison: University of Wisconsin Press, 1988).

9. Maitrii Aung-Thwin, *The Return of the Galon King: History, Law, and Rebellion in Colonial Burma* (Singapore: National University of Singapore Press, 2011), 21–22.

10. Stephen Campbell, "Introduction," in Thakin Po Hla Gyi, *The Strike War*, translated by Stephen Campbell (Passau: Myanmar Literature Project, University of Passau, [1938] 2012), 5.

11. Thakin Po Hla Gyi, *The Strike War*, 8.

12. Khin Yi, *The Dobama Movement in Burma (1930–1938)* (Ithaca: Cornell Southeast Asia Program, 1988), 57–83 and 98–132.

13. *Final Report of the Riot Inquiry Committee* (Rangoon: Rangoon Printing And Stationery, 1939), 281, https://archive.org/details/in.ernet.dli.2015.206317/page/n297.

14. Ian Brown, *A Colonial Economy in Crisis: Burma's Rice Cultivators and the World Depression of the 1930s* (London: Routledge, 2005), 47–49.

15. Michael Adas, "Immigrant Asians and the Economic Impact of European Imperialism: The Role of the South Indian Chettiars in British Burma," *Journal of Asian Studies* 33, no. 3 (1974), 388.

16. Thein Pe Myint, *Indo-Burman Conflict*, translated by Tin Htway (Passau: Myanmar Literature Project, University of Passau, [1938] 2008), 23.

17. Yebaw Htun Oo, "The Emergence of the Working class in Burma and the History of Working Class Activism," *Yaung Chi Oo Workers Association Journal*, April 2012, 10.

18. Maurice Collis, *Trials in Burma* (London: Penguin Books, 1945), 149–150.

19. J.S. Furnivall, *Colonial Policy and Practice: A Comparative Study of Burma and Netherlands India* (Cambridge: Cambridge University Press, [1948] 2014), 311.

20. Furnivall, *Colonial Policy and Practice*, 544.

21. On the prominence of Chinese business owners in colonial Burma, see Yi Li, *Chinese in Colonial Burma: A Migrant Community in A Multiethnic State* (New York: Palgrave Macmillan, 2017), chap. 4.

22. Barbara Metcalf and Thomas Metcalf, *A Concise History of Modern India*, 2nd ed. (Cambridge: Cambridge University Press, 2006), 187–189.

23. Khin Yi, *The Dobama Movement in Burma*, 36–37.

24. Geoffrey Aung, "Reworking Bandung Internationalism: Decolonization and Postcolonial Futurism in Burma/Myanmar," *Critical Asian Studies* 51, no. 2 (2019); Matthew Walton, *Buddhism, Politics and Political Thought in Myanmar* (Cambridge: Cambridge University Press, 2016), 126; Emanuel Sarkisyanz, *Buddhist Backgrounds of the Burmese Revolution* (The Hague: Martinus Nijhoff, 1965), 169–170.

25. Thakin Po Hla Gyi, *The Strike War*, 47.

26. Maung Htin, *Ngaba* (Yangon: Myanmar Ministry of Information, [1947] 1991).

27. Bhamo Tin Aung, *Myaing*, translated by Stephen Campbell (Yangon: Nadi-Mingala Publishing House, [1958] 2011), 134–135.

28. Anna Allott, "Continuity and Change in the Burmese Literary Canon," in *The Canon in Southeast Asian Literatures: Literatures of Burma, Cambodia, Indonesia, Laos, Malaysia, the Philippines, Thailand and Vietnam*, edited by David Smyth (Richmond: Curzon Press, 2000), 27.

29. Robert Taylor, "Introduction," in *Soe, Socialism and Chit Hlaing, Memories*, edited by Hans-Bernd Zöllner (Passau: University of Passau, Myanmar Literature Project, 2008), 6.

30. Bertil Lintner, *The Rise and Fall of the Communist Party of Burma* (Ithaca: Cornell Southeast Asia Program, 1990), 13–14.

31. Ian Brown, *Burma's Economy in the Twentieth Century* (Cambridge: Cambridge University Press, 2013), 169.

32. Lintner, *The Rise and Fall of the Communist Party of Burma*, 18.

33. Robert Taylor, *The State in Myanmar* (Honolulu: University of Hawai'i Press, 2009), 280.

34. Mary Callahan, "The Sinking Schooner: Murder and the State in Independent Burma," in *Gangsters, Democracy, and the State in Southeast Asia*, edited by Carl A. Trocki (Ithaca: Cornell Southeast Asia Program, 1998), 22–23; Kyaw Zaw Win, "A History of the Burma Socialist Party" (PhD diss., University of Wollongong, 2008), 70.

35. Thakin Lwin, *Myanma Alokthema Hlokshahmu Thamaing* (Yangon: Bagan Books, 1968), 275–279.

36. Martin Smith, *Burma: Insurgency and the Politics of Ethnicity* (London: Zed Press, 1991), 48.

37. Mary Callahan, *Making Enemies: War and State Building in Burma* (Ithaca: Cornell University Press, 2003), 209. Kyaw Soe Lwin, "Legal Perspectives on Industrial Disputes in Myanmar," in *Law, Society and Transition in Myanmar*, edited by Melissa Crouch and Tim Lindsey (Oxford: Hart Publishing, 2014), 292.

38. "Law Defining the Fundamental Rights and Responsibilities of the People's Workers," Revolutionary Council, Law No. 6 of 1964, Preamble §3.2.

39. Kyaw Soe Lwin, "Legal Perspectives on Industrial Disputes in Myanmar," 293.

40. Allen Fenichel and Azfar Khan, "The Burmese Way to 'Socialism,'" *World Development* 9, no. 9–10 (1981): 815.

41. Sean Turnell, *Fiery Dragons: Banks, Moneylenders and Microfinance in Burma* (Copenhagen: NiAS Press, 2009).

42. Allen Fenichel and Azfar Khan, "The Burmese Way to 'Socialism,'" *World Development* 9, no. 9–10 (1981).

43. Bertil Lintner, *Outrage: Burma's Struggle for Democracy* (Bangkok: White Lotus, 1990), 59.

44. Lintner, *Outrage*, 44.

45. Lintner, *Outrage*, 51.

46. In July 2016, I visited the town of Chauk, where I spoke with an octogenarian oilfield worker who recounted his involvement as an organizer in the 1974 strike. For details on the Thakin Po Hla Gyi monument in Chauk, see Stephen Campbell, "Touring Myanmar's Leftist History," *Focaalblog*, May 14, 2019, http://www.focaalblog.com/2019/05/14/stephen-campbell-touring-myanmars-leftist-history/.

47. Lintner, *Outrage*, 51.

48. For a depiction in popular culture of class inequality during the "socialist" era, see the 1985 Burmese film *Thingyan Moe*, directed by Maung Tin Oo.

49. Christina Fink, *Living Silence: Burma under Military Rule* (London: Zed Books, 2001), 229.

50. For hagiographic liberal accounts in English of Aung San Suu Kyi's involvement in the events of 1988, see Peter Popham, *The Lady and the Peacock: The Life of Aung San Suu Kyi* (New York: Experiment, 2013); Justin Wintle, *Perfect Hostage: A Life of Aung San Suu Kyi, Burma's Prisoner of Conscience* (New York: Skyhorse, 2007); and *The Lady*, directed by Luc Besson (Cohen Media Group, 2012).

51. Philippa Fogarty, "Was Burma's 1988 Uprising Worth It?" *BBC*, August 6, 2008, http://news.bbc.co.uk/2/hi/asia-pacific/7543347.stm.

52. Kyaw Zaw Moe, "70 Years On, the Struggle for Independence Goes On," *Irrawaddy*, January 4, 2018, https://www.irrawaddy.com/opinion/commentary/70-years-struggle-independence-goes.html.

53. Michael Aung-Thwin, *Myth and History in the Historiography of Early Burma: Paradigms, Primary Sources, and Prejudices* (Athens: Ohio University Press, 1998), 158.

54. Gustaaf Houtman, "Sacralizing or Demonizing Democracy?" in *Burma at The Turn of the 21st Century*, edited by Monique Skidmoore (Honolulu: University of Hawai'i Press, 2005).

55. Lintner, *Outrage*, 117.

56. Stephen McCarthy, "Ten Years of Chaos in Burma: Foreign Investment and Economic Liberalization under the SLORC-SPDC, 1988 to 1998," *Pacific Affairs* 73, no. 2 (2000): 233; John Badgley, "The Burmese Way to Capitalism," *Southeast Asian Affairs* (1990); Ikuko Okamoto, *Economic Disparity in Rural Myanmar: Transformation under Market Liberalization* (Singapore: NUS Press, 2008); Fujita, Mieno, and Okamoto, *The Economic Transition in Myanmar.*

57. Siusue Mark, "Are the Odds of Justice 'Stacked' against Them? Challenges and Opportunities for Securing Land Claims by Smallholder Farmers in Myanmar," *Critical Asian Studies* 48, no. 3 (2017); "'Nothing for Our Land': Impact of Land Confiscation on Farmers in Myanmar," *Human Rights Watch*, July 17, 2018, https://www.hrw.org/report/2018/07/17/nothing-our-land/impact-land-confiscation-farmers-myanmar.

58. Simon Montlake, "Burma's Showy Crony," *Forbes*, September 18, 2011, https://www.forbes.com/global/2011/1010/feature-people-burma-showy-crony-capitalism-luxury-za-montlake.html#1d61d3627e62.

59. Lee Jones, "The Political Economy of Myanmar's Transition," *Journal of Contemporary Asia*, 44, no. 1 (2014); Michele Ford, Michael Gillan, and Htwe Htwe Thein, "From Cronyism to Oligarchy? Privatisation and Business Elites in Myanmar," *Journal of Contemporary Asia* 46, no. 1 (2016); Soe Lin Aung and Stephen Campbell, "The Lady and the Generals," *Jacobin*, January 13, 2016, https://www.jacobinmag.com/2016/01/aung-san-suu-kyi-myanmar-burma-elections-military-generals/.

60. Kang Wan Chern, "South Korea Eyes Myanmar Investments in Manufacturing, Infrastructure," *Myanmar Times*, February 9, 2018, https://www.mmtimes.com/news/south-korea-eyes-myanmar-investments-manufacturing-infrastructure.html.

61. Kyaw Soe Lwin, "Legal Perspectives on Industrial Disputes in Myanmar," 296.

62. Gerard McCarthy, "Regressive Democracy: Explaining Distributive Politics in Myanmar's Political Transition" (PhD Diss., Australian National University, 2018).

63. Campbell, "Labour Formalisation as Selective Hegemony."

64. Fujita, "Agricultural Labourers"; Ikuko Okamoto, *Economic Disparity in Rural Myanmar: Transformation under Market Liberalization* (Singapore: NUS Press, 2008).

65. Ranajit Guha, *Dominance without Hegemony: History and Power in Colonial India* (Cambridge: Harvard University Press, 1997). Several scholars have employed Guha's characterization (or a variant of it) in reference to Myanmar during the 1988–2011 period. See Elliott Prasse-Freeman, "Of Punishment, Protest, and Press Conferences: Contentious Politics amid Despotic Decision in Contemporary Burmese Courtrooms," in *Criminal Legalities in the Global South: Cultural Dynamics, Political Tensions, and Institutional Practices*, edited by Pablo Ciocchini and George Radics (New York: Routledge, 2019), 126; Stephen Campbell, "Labour Formalisation as Selective Hegemony in Reform-era Myanmar," *Asia-Pacific Journal of Anthropology* 20, no. 1 (2019), 65; Nick Cheesman, *Opposing the Rule of Law: How Myanmar's Courts Make Law and Order* (Cambridge: Cambridge University Press, 2015), 101.

66. Toshihiro Kudo, "The Impact of United States Sanctions on the Myanmar Garment Industry," *Asian Survey* 48, no. 6 (2008).

67. Delphine Schrank, *A Tale of Defiance and Deliverance in Burma: The Rebel of Rangoon* (New York: Nation Books, 2015), 59–60.

68. "Burma 'Approves New Constitution,'" BBC, May 15, 2008, http://news.bbc.co.uk/2/hi/asia-pacific/7402105.stm.

69. Zaw Zaw Htwe and Laingnee Barron, "Factory Workers Wary of the Arbitration Council," *Myanmar Times*, September 25, 2015, www.mmtimes.com/index.php/national-news/16690-factory-workers-weary-of-the-arbitration-council.html.

70. Stephen Campbell, "On Labour Organisations in Myanmar," *Global Labour Column* 144 (2013), http://column.global-labour-university.org/2013/07/on-labour-organisations-in-myanmar.html.

71. Jit Shankar Banerjee, "Can Myanmar's Minimum Wage Avoid Pitfalls of Bangladesh's Garment Sector?" *Myanmar Times*, November 3, 2019, https://www.mmtimes.com/opinion/16541-can-myanmar-s-minimum-wage-avoid-pitfalls-of-bangladesh-s-garment-sector.html.

72. "'Like a Gold Eush': Investing in Burma 'High-Risk' and Potentially 'High-Reward,'" *National Post*, November 27, 2012, https://nationalpost.com/news/like-a-gold-rush-investing-in-burma-high-risk-and-potentially-high-reward.

73. Justin Kent, "Myanmar, The Last Frontier?" *Forbes*, November 9, 2012, https://www.forbes.com/sites/connorconnect/2012/11/09/myanmar-the-last-frontier/#4b7045245dce.

74. Jeremy Mullins, "Big Western Brands Sew Way Forward," *Myanmar Times*, May 29, 2015, https://www.mmtimes.com/business/14755-big-western-brands-sew-way-forward.html.

75. Nicholas Farrelly and Giuseppe Gabusi, "Explaining Myanmar's Tentative Renaissance," *European Journal of East Asian Studies* 14, no. 1 (2015).

76. Antonio Gramsci, *Selections from the Prison Notebooks*, edited and translated by Quentin Hoare and Geoffrey Neil Smith (New York: International Publishers, 1971), 59; see also Peter Thomas, *The Gramscian Moment: Philosophy, Hegemony, and Marxism* (Leiden: Brill, 2009), 146–149.

77. Soe Lin Aung and Stephen Campbell, "The Lady and the Generals," *Jacobin*, January 13, 2016, https://www.jacobinmag.com/2016/01/aung-san-suu-kyi-myanmar-burma-elections-military-generals/.

78. Dennis Arnold and Stephen Campbell, "Labour Regime Transformation in Myanmar," 820.

79. The most prominent antidispossession struggles at the time were the protests of villagers evicted to make way for the Letpadaung Copper Mine, jointly owned by the Union of Myanmar Economic Holdings Limited and Wanbao, a subsidiary of China North Industries Group Corp. See Ei Ei Toe Lwin, "Fury over Letpadaung Copper Mine Report," *Myanmar Times*, March 18, 2013, https://www.mmtimes.com/national-news/5175-fury-at-copper-mine-report.html.

80. "Timeline of Student Protests against Education Law," *Irrawaddy*, March 10, 2015, https://www.irrawaddy.com/news/burma/timeline-of-student-protests-against-education-law.html.

81. Elliott Prasse-Freeman and Phyo Win Latt, "Class and Inequality in Contemporary Myanmar," in *The Routledge Handbook of Contemporary Myanmar*, edited by Adam Simpson, Nicholas Farrelly, and Ian Holliday (New York: Routledge, 2018); and Min Zin, "Burma Takes a Big Step Backwards," *Foreign Policy*, March 12, 2015, https://foreignpolicy.com/2015/03/12/burma-takes-a-big-step-backwards/.

82. Thazin Hlaing, "Minimum Wage Fails to Keep Up with Cost of Living, Myanmar Labor Group Says," *Irrawaddy*, November 1, 2019, https://www.irrawaddy.com/news/burma/minimum-wage-fails-keep-cost-living-myanmar-labor-group-says.html?fbclid=IwAR3DYKXoovVR7SoUvI948zMGAgpkACgJXHA_Fl3gFhdYT1K-HDv6f_1ixBA.

83. "The Dark Side of Transition: Violence against Muslims in Myanmar," International Crisis Group, October 1, 2013, www.crisisgroup.org/asia/south-east-asia/myanmar/dark-side-transition-violence-against-muslims-myanmar.

84. "Report of the Independent International Fact-Finding Mission on Myanmar," United Nations Human Rights Council, September 2018, 10–28, https://www.ohchr.org/Documents/HRBodies/HRCouncil/FFM-Myanmar/A_HRC_39_64.pdf.

85. Florence Looi, "Despite Rohingya Crisis, Thousands March in Support of Military," *Al-Jazeera*, October 29, 2017, https://www.aljazeera.com/news/2017/10/thousands-rohingya-march-support-army-crisis-171029163411806.html.

86. Htet Kaung Lin, "Firebrand Monk Calls for Military Parliamentarians to Be 'Worshipped,'" *Irrawaddy*, May 6, 2019, https://www.irrawaddy.com/news/burma/firebrand-monk-calls-military-parliamentarians-worshipped.html.

87. Htet Naing Zaw, "Ma Ba Tha Is a Necessity: Military," *Irrawaddy*, June 19, 2019, https://www.irrawaddy.com/news/burma/ma-ba-tha-necessity-military.html.

88. Thakin Po Hla Gyi, *The Strike War*, 23–24.

89. For an elaboration of this argument, see Stephen Campbell and Elliott Prasse-Freeman, "Revisiting the Wages of Burman-ness: Contradictions of Privilege in Myanmar," *Journal of Contemporary Asia*, https://doi.org/10.1080/00472336.2021.1962390.

2. FROM RURAL DISPOSSESSION TO PRECARIOUS URBANIZATION

1. Hla Hla Htay and Caroline Henshaw, "The Skincare Fad Threatening Myanmar's Elephants," *Myanmar Times*, January 24, 2017, www.mmtimes.com/national-news/24665-the-skincare-fad-threatening-myanmar-s-elephants.html.

2. Myat Thida Win and Aye Mya Thinzar, "Agricultural Mechanization and Structural Transformation in Myanmar's Ayeyarwady Delta," Food Security Policy Project Research Highlights, University of Michigan, 2016, www.ifpri.org/publication/agricultural-mechanization-and-structural-transformation-myanmars-ayeyarwady-delta; Kevin Woods, "Smaller-Scale Land Grabs and Accumulation from Below: Violence, Coercion and Consent in Spatially Uneven Agrarian Change in Shan State, Myanmar," *World Development* 127 (2020); Aye Sapay Phyu, "Myanmar Third-Worst for Deforestation Rate, Says UN," *Myanmar Times*, September 11, 2015, www.mmtimes.com/national-news/16436-myanmar-third-worst-for-deforestation-rate-says-un.html; Kevin Woods, "Rubber out of the Ashes: Locating Chinese Agribusiness Investments in 'Armed Sovereignties' in the Myanmar–China Borderlands," *Territory, Politics, Governance* 7, no. 1 (2019); Salai Thant Zin, "Wild Elephant Poached and Skinned in Myanmar Forest Reserve," *Irrawaddy*, September 12, 2019, www.irrawaddy.com/news/burma/wild-elephant-poached-skinned-myanmar-forest-reserve.html.

3. For an illustrative account by the Myanmar government on internal migration, see "Policy Brief on Migration and Urbanization," Department of Population Ministry of Labour, Immigration and Population, 2017, http://www.dop.gov.mm/sites/dop.gov.mm/files/publication_docs/policy_brief_on_migration_and_unbanization.pdf.

4. Shoon Naing, "Northern Yangon Squatters Notified of Impending Eviction," *Myanmar Times*, August 25, 2016, www.mmtimes.com/national-news/yangon/22138-northern-yangon-squatters-notified-of-impending-eviction.html.

5. *A Country on the Move: Domestic Migration in Two Regions in Myanmar* (Yangon: World Bank Group, 2016), 7.

6. Ardeth Maung Thawngmung, *Everyday Economic Survival in Myanmar* (Madison: University of Wisconsin Press, 2019), 3–4.

7. *A Country on the Move*, 23–25 passim.

8. "Land Grabbing in Dawei (Myanmar/Burma): A (Inter)national Human Rights Concern," Transnational Institute, 2012, www.tni.org/files/download/dawei_land_grab.pdf; "The Origins of Myanmar Migrant Worker Misery," *Human Rights Watch*, January 14, 2016, https://www.hrw.org/news/2016/01/14/origins-myanmar-migrant-worker-misery.

9. Ellen Meiksins Wood, *The Origin of Capitalism: A Longer View* (London: Verso, 2002); Tania Murray Li, *Land's End: Capitalist Relations on an Indigenous Frontier* (Durham: Duke University Press, 2014).

10. Shagun Gupta, "Leveraging Migration for Development: A Review of Literature on Patterns and Movements in Myanmar," in *Migration in Myanmar: Perspectives from Current Research*, edited by Michael Griffiths and Michiko Ito (Yangon: Social Policy and Poverty Research Group, 2016), 19; *Myanmar Population and Housing Census* (Naypyidaw: Department of Population, Ministry of Immigration and Population, May 2015), 127; Michael Griffiths, "Networks of Reciprocity: Precarity and Community Social Organisations in Rural Myanmar," *Journal of Contemporary Asia* 49, no. 4 (2019), 607–609.

11. Michael Griffiths and Michiko Ito, "Introduction," in Griffiths and Ito, *Migration in Myanmar*, 9.

12. Michael Griffiths, "Formal Sector Internal Migration in Myanmar," in Griffiths and Ito, *Migration in Myanmar*, 79.

13. Corey Pattison et al., "A Country on the Move: Migration Networks and Risk Management in Two Regions of Myanmar," in Griffiths and Ito, *Migration in Myanmar*, 49.

14. Vishu Prasan, *Mapping Yangon: The Untapped Communities—A Preliminary Study of Informal Settlements in Yangon* (Yangon: UN-Habitat, 2016), 2.

15. Forbes, "On the Frontier of Urbanization," 207.

16. *Post-Nargis Recovery and Preparedness Plan*, Tripartite Core Group, December 2008, https://themimu.info/sites/themimu.info/files/documents/Ref_Doc_Post-Nargis_Recovery_and_Preparedness_Plan.pdf.

17. The narrative account and the quotations, in translation, that follow are abridged excerpts from two extended interviews that the author conducted with Uncle Hla and Aunty Cho on February 6, 2019, and June 13, 2019.

18. The 2014 census gives a figure of 784,919 internal migrants residing in Yangon who were born in Ayeyarwaddy Region. *Myanmar Population and Housing Census* (Naypyidaw: Department of Population, Ministry of Immigration and Population, May 2015), 124.

19. Brad Adams, "The Lessons of Cyclone Nargis," *Human Rights Watch*, May 3, 2009, www.hrw.org/news/2009/05/03/lessons-cyclone-nargis.

20. "I Want to Help My Own People," State Control and Civil Society in Burma after Cyclone Nargis, *Human Rights Watch*, May 3, 2009, www.hrw.org/report/2010/04/28/i-want-help-my-own-people/state-control-and-civil-society-burma-after-cyclone.

21. "Burma 'Approves New Constitution,'" BBC, May 15, 2008, http://news.bbc.co.uk/2/hi/asia-pacific/7402105.stm.

22. The exchange rate at the time of research was approximately US$1 = 1,500 Myanmar kyat.

23. The quoted text that follows is an abridged translation of an extended interview that the author conducted with Aunty Yu Maw on July 18, 2019.

24. Vandana Shiva, *The Violence of Green Revolution: Third World Agriculture, Ecology and Politics* (London: Zed Books, 1991), 78–102.

25. The quoted text that follows is an abridged translation of an extended interview that the author conducted with Uncle Tin on January 21, 2019.

26. The donations to which Uncle Tin refers are offerings made to Buddhist monks for the annual *waso* and *kathein* festivals, which in this case are organized by his children's school.

27. These amounts are lower than the 50,000 to 60,000 kyat that Uncle Tin cited earlier due to the younger ages of the latter's daughters.

28. In this passage, the informant was responding to my question specifically about his pre-1988 experiences, thus my insertion of "before 1988" in the text as a clarification.

29. Than Than Nwe, "Yangon: The Emergence of a New Spatial Order in Myanmar's Capital City," *Sojourn: Journal of Social Issues in Southeast Asia* 13, no.1 (1998).

30. *The 2014 Myanmar Population and Housing Census: The Union Report, Volume 2* (Naypyitaw: Department of Population, Ministry of Immigration and Population, 2017), 206.

31. Mary Beth-Mills, *Thai Women in the Global Labor Force: Consuming Desires, Contested Selves* (New Brunswick, NJ: Rutgers University Press, 1999), 127–146.

3. SQUATTING AMID CAPITALISM AND THE CONTRADICTIONS THEREOF

1. David Graeber, *Direct Action: An Ethnography* (Oakland: AK Press, 2009), 203.

2. Nancy Postero and Eli Elinoff, "Introduction: A Return to Politics," *Anthropological Theory* 19, no. 1 (2019).

3. Natalia Buier, "The Promise of an Anarchist Anthropology: The Three Burials of the Anarchist Project," *Studia Sociologia* 59, no. 1 (2014).

4. For example, Hakim Bey, *T.A.Z.: The Temporary Autonomous Zone, Ontological Anarchy, Poetic Terrorism* (New York: Autonomedia, 1985).

5. See Benjamin Noys, *Communization and Its Discontents: Contestation, Critique, and Contemporary Struggles* (Brooklyn: Autonomedia, 2012), 9–10.

6. Claudio Cattaneo and Miguel Martínez, *The Squatters' Movement in Europe: Everyday Commons and Autonomy as Alternatives to Capitalism* (London: Pluto Press, 2014), 7.

7. Amy Starecheski, *Ours to Lose: When Squatters Became Homeowners in New York City* (Chicago: University of Chicago Press, 2016), 29.

8. Gilles Deleuze, "Capitalism, Flows, the Decoding of Flows, Capitalism and Schizophrenia, Psychoanalysis, Spinoza," November 16, 1971, www.webdeleuze.com/textes/116.

9. Stephen Campbell, "Rendering Assemblage Dialectical," *Anthropological Theory* 21, no. 2 (2019).

10. The dialogue presented here is a transcription of the telephone conversation in question, at which the author was present and recorded in full.

11. UN Habitat, *Guidance Note on Land Acquisition in Myanmar* (Yangon: UN Habitat, 2010), 3–4.

12. Kyaw Yaw Lynn, "Low-Cost Housing Plan Sends Prices Soaring for Squatters' ID Cards," *Frontier Myanmar*, May 14, 2018, https://frontiermyanmar.net/en/low-cost-housing-plan-sends-prices-soaring-for-squatters-id-cards.

13. Htar Htar Khin, "Land Prices Surge on the City's Outskirts," *Myanmar Times*, June 17, 2013, www.mmtimes.com/business/property-news/7163-prices-surge-on-yangon-s-outskirts.html.

14. Noe Noe Aung, "In Hlaing Tharyar, Illegal Residents Face Tough Decisions," *Myanmar Times*, September 15, 2013, www.mmtimes.com/national-news/yangon/8182-in-hlaing-tharyar-illegal-residents-face-tough-decisions.html.

15. This account is based on an interview conducted on May 15, 2019, with a resident of the squatter settlement who played a leading role in the dispute recounted here.

16. Moe Myint, "Four Arrested as Police, Hired Heavies Clear Squatters in Yangon," *Irrawaddy*, June 12, 2017, www.irrawaddy.com/news/burma/four-arrested-police-hired-heavies-clear-squatters-yangon.html.

17. Wa Lone, "Arrests and Clashes as Police Evicts Hundreds from Myanmar slum," Reuters, June 12, 2017, www.reuters.com/article/us-myanmar-squatters/arrests-and-clashes-as-police-evicts-hundreds-from-myanmar-slum-idUSKBN1931VZ.

18. Regarding the structural relationship whereby low-cost housing facilitates lower wages, see David Harvey, *The Limits to Capital* (Oxford: Blackwell, 1982), 232.

19. For a related argument, see Patrick Neveling, "Three Shades of Embeddedness, State Capitalism as the Informal Economy, Emic Notions of the Anti-Market, and Coun-

terfeit Garments in the Mauritian Export Processing Zone," *Research in Economic Anthropology* 34, no. 1 (2014).

20. Myat Moe Aung, "Sucker Fish Terrorise Fishing in Twante," *Myanmar Times*, January 9, 2018, www.mmtimes.com/news/sucker-fish-terrorise-fishing-twante.html.

21. Elizabeth Rhoads, "Forced Evictions as Urban Planning? Traced of Colonial Land Control Practices in Yangon, Myanmar," *State Crime Journal* 7, no. 2 (2018).

22. An earlier version of this section was published as Stephen Campbell, "Of Squatting amid Capitalism on Myanmar's Industrial Periphery," *Anthropology Today* 35, no. 6 (2019).

23. Government of the Republic of the Union of Myanmar, "National Action Plan for Agriculture, Working Paper 10: Land Tenure and Administration," Yangon, 2015, 7.

24. Sidney W. Mintz, *Caribbean Transformations* (New York: Columbia University Press, 1989), 132; see also Jean Besson, "Sidney W Mintz's 'Peasantry' as a Critique of Capitalism: New Evidence from Jamaica," *Critique of Anthropology* 38, no. 4 (2018).

25. Mintz, *Caribbean Transformations*, 132.

26. Besson, "Sidney W Mintz's 'Peasantry' as a Critique of Capitalism," 244.

27. Eric Wolf, "Types of Latin American Peasantry: A Preliminary Discussion," *American Anthropologist* 57, no. 3 (1955): 458.

28. Andrew Walker, *Thailand's Political Peasants: Power in the Modern Rural Economy* (Madison: University of Wisconsin Press, 2012), 9.

29. World Bank, *A Country on the Move*, 32.

30. Tania Murray Li, *Land's End: Capitalist Relations on an Indigenous Frontier* (Durham: Duke University Press, 2014).

31. Cattaneo and Martínez, *The Squatters' Movement in Europe*, 3–4.

32. James Holston, *Insurgent Citizenship: Disjunctions of Democracy and Modernity in Brazil* (Princeton: Princeton University Press, 2008).

33. Elizabeth Rhoads, "Informal (justice) Brokers: Buying, Selling, and Disputing Property in Yangon," in *Everyday Justice in Myanmar: Informal Resolutions and State Evasion in a Time of Contested Transition*, ed. Helene Maria Kyed (Copenhagen: NIAS Press, 2020).

34. The allusion here is Karl Marx and Frederick Engels, *The German Ideology*, ed. C.J. Arthur (New York: International Publishers, 1970), 56–57.

4. DEBT COLLECTION AS LABOR DISCIPLINE

1. Michael Griffiths "Networks of Reciprocity: Precarity and Community Social Organisations in Rural Myanmar," *Journal of Contemporary Asia* 49, no. 4 (2018), 607–609; Kōichi Fujita, "Agricultural Laborers during the Economic Transition: Views from the Study of Selected Villages," in *The Economic Transition in Myanmar after 1988: Market Economy versus State Control*, ed. Kōichi Fujita, Fumiharu Mieno, and Ikuko Okamoto (Singapore: NUS Press, 2009), 264–265.

2. "101 East: Myanmar's Cycle of Debt," *Al-Jazeera*, August 9, 2018, www.aljazeera.com/programmes/101east/2018/08/myanmar-cycle-debt-180808054425609.html.

3. Isabelle Guérin, Solène Morvant-Roux, and Magdalena Villarreal, *Microfinance, Debt and Over-Indebtedness: Juggling with money* (London: Routledge, 2014), 1–2.

4. Cédric Durand, *Fictitious Capital: How Finance Is Appropriating Our Future* (London: Verso, 2017).

5. Jane Guyer and Federico Neiburg, "The Politics of the Real Economy," *Hau: Journal of Ethnographic Theory* 8, no. 1–2 (2018); Jane Guyer and Federico Neiburg, "The Real in the Real Economy," *Hau: Journal of Ethnographic Theory* 7, no. 3 (2017).

6. Paul Krugman, "Profits without Production," *New York Times*, June 20, 2013. www.nytimes.com/2013/06/21/opinion/krugman-profits-without-production.html; John Wake,

"The Debt Shift Theory of the Global Financial Crisis and the Great Real Estate Bubble," *Forbes*, March 15, 2019, www.forbes.com/sites/johnwake/2019/03/15/the-debt-shift-theory-of-the-great-financial-crisis-and-the-great-real-estate-bubble/#5444f86219d0.

7. Barchiesi, *Precarious Liberation*; Denning "Wageless Life"; Ferguson, *Expectations of Modernity*; Li, *Land's End*.

8. Li, "After Development," 1251.

9. Li, "Centering Labor in the Land Grab Debate," 286.

10. Li, "To Make Live or Let Die?" 70.

11. Sanyal, *Rethinking Capitalist Development*, 259.

12. Ferguson, *Give a Man a Fish*, 23, 90.

13. Mike Davis, *Planet of Slums* (London: Verso), 144–175.

14. Brenda Chalfin, "Waste Work and the Dialectics of Precarity in Urban Ghana: Durable bodies and Disposable Things," *Africa* 89, no. 3 (2019): 505.

15. Deborah James, "Deductions and Counter-Deductions in South Africa," *Hau: Journal of Ethnographic Theory* 7, no. 3 (2017), 274.

16. Antonio Negri, *Marx and Foucault* (London: Polity Press, 2017), 63.

17. Michael Hardt, "The Common in Communism," *Rethinking Marxism* 22, no. 3 (2010), 351.

18. Guyer and Neiburg, "The Real in the Real Economy," 267.

19. Cited in Hardt, "The Common in Communism," 351.

20. Carlo Vercellone, "The New Articulation of Wages, Rent and Profit in Cognitive Capitalism," Queen Mary University School of Business and Management, February 2008, https://halshs.archives-ouvertes.fr/halshs-00265584/document.

21. Veronica Gago and Sandro Mezzadra, "A Critique of the Extractive Operations of Capital: Toward an Expanded Concept of Extractivism," *Rethinking Marxism* 29, no. 4 (2008), 579.

22. On Marx's notion of "formal subsumption," see Karl Marx, *Capital: A Critique of Political Economy, Volume 3* (London: Penguin Books, 1981), 1020–1038. Regarding forms of debt-based extraction in Southeast Asia, see Li, *Land's End*, 201n17.

23. Marx, *Capital*, 3: 599.

24. Durand, *Fictitious Capital.*

25. Tim Di Muzio and Richard M. Robbin, *Debt as Power* (London: Bloomsbury Academic, 2015).

26. All personal names employed herein are pseudonyms.

27. Vosko, *Managing the Margins*, 1.

28. Kathleen Millar, *Reclaiming the Discarded: Life and Labor on Rio's Garbage Dump* (Durham: Duke University Press, 2018), 8.

29. Kaveri Gill, *Of Poverty and Plastic: Scavenging and Scrap Trading Entrepreneurs in India's Urban Informal Economy* (New Delhi: Oxford University Press, 2010).

30. Barbara Harriss-White, "Labor and Petty Production," *Development and Change* 45, no. 5 (2014), 988.

31. Stephen Campbell, "Migrant Waste Collectors in Thailand's Informal Economy: Mapping Class Relations," *European Journal of East Asian Studies* 17 (2018), 275–276; and Millar, *Reclaiming the Discarded*, 144.

32. Bronislaw Malinowski, *Argonauts of the Western Pacific: An Account of Native Enterprises and Adventures in the Archipelagoes of Melanesian New Guinea* (Long Grove: Waveland Press, [1922] 1984), 95–96.

33. E.P. Thompson, "The Moral Economy of the English Crowd in the Eighteenth Century," *Past & Present* 50 (1971); Karl Polanyi, *The Great Transformation: The Political and Economic Origins of Our Time* (Boston: Beacon Press, [1944] 2001); Marcel Mauss, *The Gift: Expanded Edition* (London: Hau Books, [1925] 2016).

34. Chris Gregory, *Savage Money: The Anthropology and Politics of Commodity Exchange* (Amsterdam: Harwood Academic, 1997).

35. James Carrier, "Moral Economy: What's in a Name?" *Anthropological Theory* 18, no. 1 (2018); Jaime Palomera and Theodora Vetta, "Moral Economy: Rethinking a Radical Concept," *Anthropological Theory* 16, no. 4 (2016); Andrea Muehlebach, *The Moral Neoliberal: Welfare and Citizenship in Italy* (Chicago: University of Chicago Press, 2012).

36. Jaime Palomera and Theodora Vetta, "Moral Economy: Rethinking a Radical Concept," *Anthropological Theory* 16, no. 4 (2016), 419.

37. David Graeber, *Debt: The First 5,000 Years* (New York: Melville House, 2011).

38. Thawngmung, *Everyday Economic Survival in Myanmar*, 52.

39. Nyein Nyein, "Ending Debt Bondage Is Key to Eradicating Child Labor, Says ILO," *Irrawaddy*, October 23, 2018, www.irrawaddy.com/news/burma/ending-debt-bondage-key-eradicating-child-labor-says-ilo.html.

40. Hart, "Informal Income Opportunities and Urban Employment in Ghana."

41. Breman, "A Dualistic Labor System."

42. Ellen Meiksens Wood, *The Origins of Capitalism: A Longer View* (London: Verso, 1999); Li, *Land's End*.

43. For example, Jairus Banaji, "The Fictions of Free Labor: Contract, Coercion, and So-called Unfree Labor," *Historical Materialism* 11, no. 3 (2003); Jan Breman, Isabelle Guérin, and Aseem Prakash, eds., *India's Unfree Workforce: Of Bondage Old and New* (Oxford: Oxford University Press, 2009); Tania Murray Li, "The Price of Un/freedom: Indonesia's Colonial and Contemporary Plantation Labor Regimes," *Comparative Studies in Society and History* 59, no. 2 (2017).

44. Gibson-Graham, *The End of Capitalism*, xxiv; Wood, *The Origins of Capitalism*, 175.

45. Tsing, *The Mushroom at the End of the World*, 63.

46. Gibson-Graham, *The End of Capitalism*, xiii and 35.

47. Jairus Banaji, "Globalising the History of Capital: Ways Forward," *Historical Materialism* 26, no. 3 (2018).

48. Stephen Campbell, "Putting-Out's Return: Informalization and Differential Subsumption in Thailand's Garment Sector," *Focaal: Journal of Global and Historical Anthropology* 76 (2016).

49. Alexander Chayanov, *The Theory of Peasant Cooperatives*, trans. D.W. Benn (Columbus: Ohio State University Press, 1991), 6.

50. Barchiesi, *Precarious Liberation*.

51. Kathi Weeks, *The Problem with Work: Feminism, Marxism, Antiwork Politics, and Postwork Imaginaries* (Durham: Duke University Press, 2011).

52. Marx, *Capital*, 1:797.

53. Marx, *Capital*, 1:794.

54. Marx, *Capital*, 1:796.

55. Jan Breman and Marcel van der Linden, "Informalizing the Economy: The Return of the Social Question at a Global Level," *Development and Change* 45, no. 5 (2014).

56. Ranabir Samaddar, *Karl Marx and the Postcolonial Age* (London: Palgrave Macmillan, 2018), 109.

57. Jean Comaroff and John Comaroff, *Theory from the South: Or, How Euro-America Is Evolving toward Africa* (Abingdon: Routledge, 2012), 12.

58. Breman and van der Linden. "Informalizing the Economy."

59. Leslie Hook, "Uber Hitches a Ride with Car Finance Schemes," *Financial Times*, August 11, 2016, https://www.ft.com/content/921289f6-5dd1-11e6-bb77-a121aa8abd95.

60. Sharryn Kasmir and Lesley Gill, "No Smooth Surfaces: The Anthropology of Unevenness and Combination," *Current Anthropology* 59, no. 4 (2018); Peck, Jamie, and Nik

Theodore. "Variegated Capitalism." *Progress in Human Geography* 31, no.6 (2007): 731–772.

5. THE INTEGRAL INFORMALITY OF MARGINALIZED WORKERS

1. The song is *Athenudè. Tawkakoyè*, and the artist who released the cover is Ye Myint Myat. A video of the Ye Myin Myat version is available at https://www.youtube.com/watch?v=irCWf7CkRu4.

2. Ferguson, *Give a Man a Fish.*

3. Sanyal, *Rethinking Capitalist Development*, 259.

4. See especially the articles by Anthony Leeds from the 1960s and 1970s on the political economy of the Brazilian favela in Leeds, *Cities, Classes, and the Social Order.*

5. Chang, "Informalising Labour in Asia's Global Factory."

6. Su Myat Mon, "Another Betel Warning, but Is Anyone Listening?" *Frontier Myanmar*, November 19, 2018, https://frontiermyanmar.net/en/another-betel-warning-but-is-anyone-listening.

7. Kait Bolongaro, "A Bad Seed: The Cancer-Causing Palm Nut Ravaging Myanmar," *Politico*, January 30, 2019, www.politico.eu/article/betel-quid-myanmar-cancer-causing-palm-nut-ravaging/.

8. Alan Smart and Josephine Smart, *Petty Capitalists and Globalization: Flexibility, Entrepreneurship, and Economic Development* (Albany: State University of New York Press, 2006).

9. *Report on Conditions of Work and Promotion of Livelihoods in the Unorganised Sector* (Delhi: National Commission for Enterprises in the Unorganised Sector, 2008), 3.

10. See, for example, Michael Griffiths, "Formal Sector Internal Migration in Myanmar," in *Migration in Myanmar: Perspectives from Current Research*, ed. Michael Griffiths and Michiko Ito (Yangon: Social Policy and Poverty Research Group, 2016), 76n35.

11. Lise Vogel, *Marxism and the Oppression of Women: Toward a Unitary Theory* (Leiden: Brill, 1983); Federici, *Revolution at Point Aero*; Tithi Battacharya, ed., *Social Reproduction Theory: Remapping Class, Recentering Oppression* (London: Pluto Press, 2018).

12. Thus writes Nancy Fraser: "With capitalism, by contrast, reproductive labor is split off, relegated to a separate, 'private' sphere, where its social importance is obscured." See Nancy Fraser and Rahel Jaeggi, *Capitalism: A Conversation in Critical Theory* (Cambridge: Polity Press, 2018), 33.

13. Louis Althusser, *On the Reproduction of Capitalism: Ideology and Ideological State Apparatuses* (London: Verso, 2014), 235.

14. For this definition of "casual" employment, see Vosko, *Managing the Margins*, 95.

15. Walton, *Buddhism, Politics and Political Thought in Myanmar*, 60.

16. See, for example, Jonathan Parry, "Company and Contract Labour in a Central Indian Steel Plant," *Economy and Society* 42, no. 3 (2013); and Stephen Campbell, "Putting-Out's Return."

17. Gerard McCarthy, "Regressive Democracy: Explaining distributive politics in Myanmar's political transition" (PhD diss., Australian National University, 2018).

18. Sohini Kar, *Financializing Poverty: Labor and Risk in Indian Microfinance* (Stanford: Stanford University Press, 2018).

19. Carrier, "Moral Economy: What's in a Name?" 19.

20. On total workforce numbers, see "A Snapshot of Myanmar's Garment Industry," The Union of Myanmar Federation of Chambers of Commerce and Industry, 2018, https://investmyanmar2019.com/garment-industry-cmp/myanmars-garment-industry/. For a demographic breakdown of the garment sector, see *A Baseline Survey of Yangon's*

Garment Sector Workforce, C&A Foundation, 2017, http://themimu.info/sites/themimu.info/files/documents/Report_A_Baseline_Survey_of_Yangons_Garment_Sector_Workforce.pdf.

21. Regarding historical changes to the Burmese term *wundan*, see Campbell, "Labour Formalisation as Selective Hegemony," 5–7.

22. Similar views have been offered by Myanmar migrants laboring as informal waste collectors in Thailand. See Campbell, "Migrant Waste Collectors," 275–276.

23. Kathleen Millar, "The Precarious Present: Wageless Labor and Disrupted Life in Rio de Janeiro, Brazil," *Cultural Anthropology* 29, no. 1 (2014).

24. Minh T. N. Nguyen, *Waste and Wealth: An Ethnography of Labor, Value, and Morality in a Vietnamese Recycling Economy* (Oxford: Oxford University Press, 2019).

25. For details of the strike, see Arnold and Campbell, "Labour Regime Transformation in Myanmar."

26. I draw for this data on my ongoing involvement with the Yangon-based Yaung Chi Oo Workers Association, and on discussions with workers who have sought assistance from Yaung Chi Oo for cases of labor law violations at their workplaces.

27. "World Jin Workers Request Yangon Chief to Solve Labour Issues," *Eleven Myanmar*, December 20, 2019, https://elevenmyanmar.com/news/world-jin-workers-request-yangon-chief-to-solve-labour-issues. I obtained further details about this labor dispute by discussing the matter with the workers employed at the factory, and with staff of the Yaung Chi Oo Workers Association, who were providing the workers with legal aid.

28. Millar, *Reclaiming the Discarded*, 4.

29. Susanna Rosenbaum, *Domestic Economies: Women, Work, and the American Dream in Los Angeles* (Durham: Duke University Press, 2018), 158.

30. Rosenbaum, *Domestic Economies*, 147.

31. Rosenbaum, *Domestic Economies*, 142.

32. *Myanmar: Ending Poverty*, 28.

6. UNFREEDOMS OF CAPITALISM

1. Kōichi Fujita, "Agricultural Labourers"; Okamoto, *Economic Disparity in Rural Myanmar*; Campbell, "Reading Myanmar's Inland Fisheries."

2. International Labour Organisation (ILO), ILO Liaison Officer for Myanmar, "Internal Labour Migration in Myanmar: Building an Evidence-Base on Patterns in Migration, Human Trafficking and Forced Labour" (Yangon: ILO, 2015), 6.

3. Nyein Nyein, "Ending Debt Bondage is Key."

4. Ye Naing, "Yangon Family Jailed for Severe Abuse of Child Servants," *Mizzima*, December 16, 2017, www.mizzima.com/news-domestic/yangon-family-jailed-severe-abuse-child-servants; Hla Hla Htay "'There Was a Lot of Blood': Domestic Servant Sisters Scarred by Abuse," *Frontier Myanmar*, February 15, 2017, https://frontiermyanmar.net/en/there-was-a-lot-of-blood-domestic-servant-sisters-scarred-by-abuse.

5. See, for example, Nicolas Lainez, "Commodified Sexuality and Mother-Daughter Power Dynamics in the Mekong Delta," *Journal of Vietnamese Studies* 7, no. 1 (2012).

6. Rosenbaum, *Domestic Economies*.

7. Teschke, *The Myth of 1648*, 141.

8. Teschke, *The Myth of 1648*, 256.

9. Graeber, *Debt*, 351.

10. John Stuart Mill, *Principles of Political Economy*, vol. 1 (New York: Cosimo, [1885] 2009).

11. John Stuart Mill, *On Liberty* (Peterborough: Broadview Literary Texts, [1859] 1999), 52.

12. Domenico Losurdo, *Liberalism: A Counter-History*, trans. Gregory Elliott (London: Verso, 2011), 73; Mill, *Principles of Political Economy*, 201.

13. For a summary of debates surrounding John Stuart Mill's racism and eurocentrism, see Bart Schultz, "Mill and Sidgwick, Imperialism and Racism," *Utilitas* 19, no. 1 (2007).

14. Mintz, *Sweetness and Power*; Lowe, *Intimacies of Four Continents*.

15. Immanuel Wallerstein, *The Capitalist World Economy* (Cambridge: Cambridge University Press, 1979), 16–17.

16. W.E.B. Du Bois, *Black Reconstruction in America: Toward a History of the Part which Black Folk Played in the Attempt to Reconstruct Democracy in America, 1860–1880* (New Brunswick, NJ: Transaction Publishers, [1935] 2013); C.L.R. James, *The Black Jacobins: Toussaint L'Ouverture and the San Domingo Revolution* (New York: Penguin Random House, [1939] 1989); Eric Williams, *Capitalism and Slavery* (Chapel Hill: University of North Carolina Press [1944] 1994); Cedric Robinson, *Black Marxism: The Making of the Black Radical Tradition* (Chapel Hill: University of North Carolina Press, 1983).

17. Della Costa and James, *The Power of Women and the Subversion of the Community*; Federici, *Revolution at Point*.

18. Federici, "Undeclared War."

19. Marx, *Capital*, 1:899.

20. Banaji, "The Fictions of Free Labour," 70.

21. Peter Vandergeest and Melissa Marschke, "Modern Slavery and Freedom: Exploring Contradictions through Labour Scandals in the Thai Fisheries," *Antipode* 52, no. 1 (2019): 293.

22. Tania Murray Li, "The Price of Un/Freedom: Indonesia's Colonial and Contemporary Plantation Labor Regimes," *Comparative Studies in Society and History* 59, no. 2 (2018): 247.

23. Judy Fudge, "(Re)Conceptualising Unfree Labour: Local Labour Control Regimes and Constraints on Workers' Freedoms," *Global Labour Journal* 10, no. 2 (2019).

24. For a critique of conventional logic's opposition between qualitative and quantitative forms of difference, see Georg Wilhelm Friedrich Hegel, *The Science of Logic*, trans. George di Giovanni (Cambridge: Cambridge University Press), 56–57, 145, 282 passim.

25. Yin Nyein and Sebastian Mathew, "The Tiger's Mouth: Myanmar Kyarr Phong Fishery," *Samudra Report* 75 (2017), www.icsf.net/es/samudra/detail/EN/4245.html; Sandar Lwin, "In Pyapon, Many Face an Uncertain Future after Storm," *Myanmar Times*, April 11, 2011, www.mmtimes.com/national-news/3060-in-pyapon-many-face-an-uncertain-future-after-storm.html.

26. Khin Myat Myat Wai, "Enslaved Fishery Workers Near Pyapon," *Tea Circle*, trans. Stephen Campbell, August 22, 2018, https://teacircleoxford.com/2018/08/22/enslaved-fishery-workers-near-pyapon-city/.

27. Yin Nyein and Mathew, "The Tiger's Mouth," 1.

28. Sandar Lwin, "In Pyapon, many face an uncertain future after storm," *Myanmar Times*.

29. Yin Nyein and Mathew, "The Tiger's Mouth," 22

30. Yin Nyein and Mathew, "The Tiger's Mouth," 20.

31. Yin Nyein and Mathew, "The Tiger's Mouth."

32. Radio Free Asia, "*Kyaikami Kyahpaungbaw ngayekan*," January 11, 2018, www.rfa.org/burmese/multimedia/fisherman-mon-state-01112018231927.html; Soe Soe Htun, "*Kyahpaung Myanmarbinletetk laungmyaikse ngayekanmya*," BBC Burmese, October 1, 2018, https://www.bbc.com/burmese/in-depth-45691571; BBC Burmese, "Hell in Myanmar Sea—BBC Burmese's Investigative Report," October 2, 2018, www.youtube.com/watch?v=N3wyn0wjDc4&feature=youtu.be&fbclid=IwAR1nDEA0SCeisrVvvRhPLxuJ

ARjFiep4CP7FO0Z8qmZYy82dVXxEbhOk1kA; Hein Thar, "The Abuse behind Myanmar's Fish Paste Industry," *Frontier Myanmar*, January 20, 2020, www.frontiermyanmar.net/en/the-abuse-behind-myanmars-fish-paste-industry; Salaing Thant Sin, "*Athek tachaung ngwe 6 thein*," *Irrawaddy*, March 11, 2019, https://burma.irrawaddy.com/article/2019/03/11/185976.html.

33. Maryann Bylander, *Debt and the Migration Experience: Insights from South-East Asia*, International Organization of Migration (2019), https://thailand.iom.int/debt-and-migration-experience-insights-south-east-asia.

34. Yin Nyein and Mathew, "The Tiger's Mouth," 23.

35. Yin Nyein and Mathew, "The Tiger's Mouth," 23.

36. Yin Nyein and Mathew, "The Tiger's Mouth," 23.

37. Yin Nyein and Mathew, "The Tiger's Mouth," 22.

38. Khin Myat Myat Wai, "Enslaved Fishery Workers Near Pyapon."

39. Khin Myat Myat Wai, "Enslaved Fishery Workers Near Pyapon."

40. See, for example, Robin McDowell, Margie Mason and Martha Mendoza, "AP Investigation: Slaves May Have Caught the Fish You Bought," Associated Press, March 25, 2015, https://www.ap.org/explore/seafood-from-slaves/ap-investigation-slaves-may-have-caught-the-fish-you-bought.html; Becky Palmstrom, "Forced to Fish: Slavery on Thailand's Trawlers," BBC News, January 23, 2014, https://www.bbc.com/news/magazine-25814718; Kate Hodal and Chris Kelly, "Trafficked into Slavery on Thai Trawlers to Catch Food for Prawns," *Guardian*, June 10, 2014, https://www.theguardian.com/global-development/2014/jun/10/-sp-migrant-workers-new-life-enslaved-thai-fishing; Environmental Justice Foundation, *Thailand's Seafood Slaves. Human Trafficking, Slavery and Murder in Kantang's Fishing Industry*, November 30, 2015, https://ejfoundation.org/reports/thailands-seafood-slaves-human-trafficking-slavery-and-murder-in-kantangs-fishing-industry.

41. Hodal and Kelly, "Trafficked into Slavery."

42. Khin Myat Myat Wai, "Enslaved Fishery Workers Near Pyapon."

43. The term she used was *wa wa phyo phyo*, which literally means "stout" or "stalky," but is here being used to refer to a generally healthy condition.

44. I am not familiar with this location, and the speaker's pronunciation of this name is not entirely clear in the interview.

45. The Burmese terms *yawkye* and *nitnakya* can both refer to a legal indemnity, but here the speaker appears to understand *yawkye* as a financial compensation resulting from a legal obligation, whereas *ninakye* is understood as a voluntary donation to assist someone who has endured a loss.

46. Yin Nyein and Mathew, "The Tiger's Mouth."

47. Salaing Thant Sin, "*Athek tachaung ngwe 6 thein*."

48. Khin Myat Myat Wai, "Enslaved Fishery Workers Near Pyapon."

49. Salaing Thant Sin, "*Athek tachaung ngwe 6 thein*."

50. Khin Myat Myat Wai, "Enslaved Fishery Workers Near Pyapon."

51. Hein Thar, "The Abuse behind Myanmar's Fish Paste Industry."

52. Hein Thar, "The Abuse behind Myanmar's Fish Paste Industry."

7. SQUATTER SELF-ORGANIZATION AND COLLECTIVE STRUGGLE

1. Partha Chatterjee, *The Politics of the Governed: Reflections on Popular Politics in Most of the World* (New York: Columbia University Press, 2006).

2. James Scott, *Weapons of the Weak: Everyday Forms of Peasant Resistance* (New Haven: Yale University Press, 1985).

3. Christopher Krupa and David Nugent, *State Theory and Andean Politics: New Approaches to the Study of Rule* (Philadelphia: University of Pennsylvania Press, 2015).

4. Denning, "Wageless Life," 81.

5. Richard Horsey, *Ending Forced Labour in Myanmar: Engaging a Pariah Regime* (London: Routledge, 2011); Karen Human Rights Group, *Shouldering the Burden of Militarization* (Chiang Mai, 2007), https://khrg.org/2007/08/khrg0702/shouldering-burden-militarisation-spdc-dkba-and-kpf-order-documents-september-2006, p. 16.

6. Peter Kropotkin, *Mutual Aid: A Factor in Evolution* (Scotts Valley: CreateSpace Independent Publishing Platform, [1902] 2017).

7. Maurice Brinton, *For Workers' Power: The Selected Writings of Maurice Brinton* (Oakland: AK Press, 2004).

8. Federici, "Undeclared War"; Bhattacharya, "Explaining Gender Violence.

9. As an example of such dichotomizing, see Ellen Meiksins Wood, *The Ellen Meiksins Wood Reader* (Leiden: Brill, 2012), 245.

10. The 2016 amendment to the 1951 Factory Act prohibits any employment in a factory of children under fourteen years old and prohibits employment in a factory of adolescents between the ages of fourteen and seventeen who do not possess a statement of medical fitness signed by a registered medical practitioner. In the case under consideration here, none of the ten child workers possessed such a medical certificate.

11. According to Article 14.g of the 2013 Minimum Wages Act, employers, if unable to provide employees with a full day's work to do, must nonetheless pay the affected employees the legal daily minimum wage.

12. Marwaan Macan-Markar, "BURMA: ILO Steps into Political Minefield to Help Revive Trade Unions," Inter Press Service, July 13, 2010, www.ipsnews.net/2010/07/burma-ilo-steps-into-political-minefield-to-help-revive-trade-unions/.

13. Zaw Zaw Htwe and Laignee Barron "Factory Workers Wary of the Arbitration Council," *Myanmar Times*, September 25, 2015, www.mmtimes.com/index.php/national-news/16690-factory-workers-weary-of-the-arbitration-council.html.

14. Ye Yint Khant Maung, "A New Way for Workers' Rights beyond the Legal Framework: The All Burma Federation of Trade Unionism," *Tea Circle*, October 14, 2019, https://teacircleoxford.com/2019/10/14/a-new-way-for-workers-rights-beyond-the-legal-framework-the-all-burma-federation-of-trade-unions/?fbclid=IwAR0v0hAqClZzHh56s-61ql6aQ_mj8-cI3sue5dou1onmRHij-SHsw1AQK4g.

15. Max Gluckman, *Rituals of Rebellion in South-East Africa* (Manchester: Manchester University Press, 1954), 3.

16. Ye Yint Khant Maung, "A New Way for Workers' Rights."

17. See, for example, Democratic Voice of Burma, "Hi Mo Workers Strike," May 25, 2012, https://www.youtube.com/watch?v=Ptnsh0QycdY; Soe Line Aung, "Notes on a Factory Uprising in Yangon," *Chuang*, March 30, 2017, http://chuangcn.org/2017/03/yangon-factory-uprising/; Zaw Zaw Htwe, "Over 200 Workers Set Up Barricades around Factory," Myanmar Times, September 5, 2017, https://www.mmtimes.com/news/over-200-workers-set-barricades-around-factory.html.

18. Arnold and Campbell, "Labour Regime Transformation in Myanmar," 20.

19. Soe Line Aung, "Notes on a Factory Uprising in Yangon."

20. "Clashes at Yangon garment factory leave dozens injured," *Frontier Myanmar*, October 16, 2018, https://frontiermyanmar.net/en/clashes-at-yangon-garment-factory-leave-dozens-injured.

CONCLUSION

1. "International Development Association Program Document for a Proposed Credit in the Amount of Equivalent to SDR 147.8 Million (USD 200 Million Equivalent) to the Republic of the Union of Myanmar for the First Macroeconomic Stability and Fiscal Resilience Development Policy Operation," 10 and 26; "Myanmar: Ending Poverty and Boosting Shared Prosperity," 28.

2. See, for example, Campbell, *Border Capitalism, Disrupted.*

3. Ferguson, *Expectations of Modernity*; Li, "To Make Live or Let Die?"; Li, "After Development"; Barchiesi, *Precarious Liberation.*

4. See Marx, *Capital*, 1:929.

5. Stephen Campbell, "Everyday Recomposition: Precarity and Socialization in Thailand's Migrant Workforce," *American Ethnologist* 43, no. 2 (2016).

6. Ronaldo Munck, "The Precariat: A View from the South," *Third World Quarterly* 34, no. 5 (2013), 754.

7. Peter Linebaugh and Marcus Rediker, *The Many-Headed Hydra: The Hidden History of the Revolutionary Atlantic* (London: Verso, 2010), 20.

8. Marx, *Capital*, 1:414.

9. Du Bois, *Black Reconstruction in America*, 239.

10. Angela Y. Davis, *Women, Race, and Class* (New York: Vintage Books, 1983), 66.

11. For an elaboration of this approach, see Stephen Campbell, "Rendering Assemblage Dialectical," *Anthropological Theory*, https://journals.sagepub.com/doi/full/10.1177/1463499619875904. For an excellent example of a relational anthropology along the lines that I advocate here, see Ognjen Kojanić, "Theory from the Peripheries: What Can the Anthropology of Postsocialism Offer to European Anthropology?" *Anthropological Journal of European Cultures* 29, no. 2 (2020).

12. Mahmoud Mamdani, *Citizen and Subject: Contemporary Africa and the Legacy of Late Colonialism* (Princeton: Princeton University Press, 1996), 18.

13. Leeds, *Cities, Classes, and the Social Order*, 57.

Bibliography

The 2014 Myanmar Population and Housing Census: The Union Report. Vol. 2. Naypyitaw: Department of Population, Ministry of Immigration and Population, 2017.

Adams, Brad. "The Lessons of Cyclone Nargis." *Human Rights Watch*, May 3, 2009, www.hrw.org/news/2009/05/03/lessons-cyclone-nargis.

Badgley Adas, Michael. "Immigrant Asians and the Economic Impact of European Imperialism: The Role of the South Indian Chettiars in British Burma." *Journal of Asian Studies* 33, no. 3 (1974): 385–401.

Al-Jazeera. "101 East: Myanmar's Cycle of Debt." August 9, 2018. www.aljazeera.com/programmes/101east/2018/08/myanmar-cycle-debt-180808054425609.html.

Allott, Anna. "Continuity and Change in the Burmese Literary Canon." In *The Canon in Southeast Asian Literatures: Literatures of Burma, Cambodia, Indonesia, Laos, Malaysia, the Philippines, Thailand and Vietnam*. Edited by David Smyth, 21–40. Richmond: Curzon Press, 2000.

Althusser, Louis. 2014, *On the Reproduction of Capitalism: Ideology and Ideological State Apparatuses*. London: Verso, 2014.

Arnold, Dennis, and Stephen Campbell. "Labour Regime Transformation in Myanmar: Constitutive Processes of Contestation." *Development and Change* 48, no. 4 (2017): 801–824.

Arnold, Dennis, and Stephen Campbell. "Capitalist Trajectories in Mekong Southeast Asia." *European Journal of East Asian Studies* 17 (2018): 181–191.

Aung Shin, and Aye Thidar Kyaw. "NLD Finance Minister Admits to Bogus PhD." *Myanmar Times*, March 23, 2016, https://www.mmtimes.com/business/19597-nld-finance-minister-admits-to-bogus-phd.html.

Aung, Geoffrey. "Reworking Bandung Internationalism: Decolonization and Postcolonial Futurism in Burma/Myanmar." *Critical Asian Studies* 51, no. 2 (2019): 198–209.

Aung-Thwin, Maitrii. *The Return of the Galon King: History, Law, and Rebellion in Colonial Burma*. Singapore: National University of Singapore Press, 2011.

Aung-Thwin, Michael. *Myth and History in the Historiography of Early Burma: Paradigms, Primary Sources, and Prejudices*. Athens: Ohio University Press, 1998.

Aye Sapay Phyu. "Myanmar Third-Worst for Deforestation Rate, Says UN." *Myanmar Times*, September 11, 2015, www.mmtimes.com/national-news/16436-myanmar-third-worst-for-deforestation-rate-says-un.html.

Badgley, John. "The Burmese Way to Capitalism." *Southeast Asian Affairs* (1990): 229–239.

Banaji, Jairus. "The Fictions of Free Labor: Contract, Coercion, and So-called Unfree Labor." *Historical Materialism* 11, no. 3 (2003): 69–95.

Banaji, Jairus. "Globalising the History of Capital: Ways Forward." *Historical Materialism* 26, no. 3 (2018): 143–166.

Banaji, Jairus. *Theory as History: Essays on Modes of Production and Exploitation*. Leiden: Brill, 2010.

Banerjee, Jit Shankar. "Can Myanmar's Minimum Wage Avoid Pitfalls of Bangladesh's Garment Sector?" *Myanmar Times*, November 3, 2019, https://www.mmtimes

.com/opinion/16541-can-myanmar-s-minimum-wage-avoid-pitfalls-of-bangladesh-s-garment-sector.html.
Barchiesi, Franco. *Precarious Liberation: Workers, the State, and Contested Social Citizenship in Postapartheid South Africa*. Albany: State University of New York Press, 2011.
Battacharya, Tithi, ed. *Social Reproduction Theory: Remapping Class, Recentering Oppression*. London: Pluto Press, 2018.
BBC Burmese. "Hell in Myanmar Sea—BBC Burmese's Investigative Report." October 2, 2018, www.youtube.com/watch?v=N3wyn0wjDc4&feature=youtu.be&fbclid=IwAR1nDEA0SCeisrVvvRhPLxuJARjFiep4CP7FO0Z8qmZYy82dVXxEbhOk1kA.
BBC Burmese. "Burma 'Approves New Constitution.'" May 15, 2008. http://news.bbc.co.uk/2/hi/asia-pacific/7402105.stm.
Bear, Laura, Karen Ho, Anna Lowenhaupt Tsing, and Sylvia Yanagisako. "Gens: A Feminist Manifesto for the Study of Capitalism." *Cultural Anthropology*, March 30, 2015. https://culanth.org/fieldsights/gens-a-feminist-manifesto-for-the-study-of-capitalism.
Besson, Jean. "Sidney W Mintz's 'Peasantry' as a Critique of Capitalism: New Evidence from Jamaica," *Critique of Anthropology* 38, no. 4 (2018): 443–460.
Besson, Luc. *The Lady*. New York: Cohen Media Group, 2012.
Bey, Hakim. *T.A.Z.: The Temporary Autonomous Zone, Ontological Anarchy, Poetic Terrorism*. New York: Autonomedia, 1985.
Bhamo Tin Aung. *Myaing*. Yangon: Nadi-Mingala Publishing House, (1958) 2011.
Bhattacharya, Tithi. "Explaining Gender Violence in the Neoliberal Era." *International Viewpoint*, September 28, 2013. www.internationalviewpoint.org/spip.php?article3212.
Bolongaro, Kait. "A Bad Seed: The Cancer-Causing Palm Nut Ravaging Myanmar." *Politico*, January 30, 2019. www.politico.eu/article/betel-quid-myanmar-cancer-causing-palm-nut-ravaging/.
Breman, Jan. "A Dualistic Labour System? A Critique of the 'Informal Sector' Concept: I: The Informal Sector." *Economic and Political Weekly* 11, no. 48 (1976): 1870–1876.
Breman, Jan, Isabelle Guérin, and Aseem Prakash, eds. *India's Unfree Workforce: Of Bondage Old and New*. Oxford: Oxford University Press, 2009.
Breman, Jan, and Marcel van der Linden. "Informalizing the Economy: The Return of the Social Question at a Global Level." *Development and Change* 45, no. 5 (2014): 920–940.
Brinton, Maurice. *For Workers' Power: The Selected Writings of Maurice Brinton*. Oakland: AK Press, 2004.
Brown, Ian. *A Colonial Economy in Crisis: Burma's Rice Cultivators and the World Depression of the 1930s*. London: Routledge, 2005.
Brown, Ian. *Burma's Economy in the Twentieth Century*. Cambridge: Cambridge University Press, 2013.
Buier, Natalia. "The Promise of an Anarchist Anthropology: The Three Burials of the Anarchist Project." *Studia Sociologia* 59, no. 1 (2014): 73–90.
Burawoy, Michael, and Katherine Verdery, eds. *Uncertain Transition: Ethnographies of Change in the Postsocialist World*. Lanham, MD: Rowman & Littlefield.
Bylander, Maryann. *Debt and the Migration Experience: Insights from South-East Asia*. International Organization of Migration, 2019. https://thailand.iom.int/debt-and-migration-experience-insights-south-east-asia.
C&A Foundation. "A Baseline Survey of Yangon's Garment Sector Workforce." Yangon, 2017. https://www.candafoundation.org/en/latest/press/2017/12/mgfpresseng.pdf.

Callahan, Mary. "The Sinking Schooner: Murder and the State in Independent Burma." In *Gangsters, Democracy, and the State in Southeast Asia*. Edited by Carl A. Trocki, 17–38. Ithaca: Cornell Southeast Asia Program, 1998.

Callahan, Mary. *Making Enemies: War and State Building in Burma*. Ithaca: Cornell University Press, 2003.

Campbell, Stephen. *Border Capitalism, Disrupted: Precarity and Struggle in a Southeast Asian Industrial Zone*. Ithaca: Cornell University Press, 2018.

Campbell, Stephen. "Everyday Recomposition: Precarity and Socialization in Thailand's Migrant Workforce." *American Ethnologist* 43, no. 2 (2016): 258–269.

Campbell, Stephen. "Introduction." In Thakin Po Hla Gyi, *The Strike War*. Translated by Stephen Campbell. Passau: Myanmar Literature Project, University of Passau, (1938) 2012.

Campbell, Stephen. "Labour Formalisation as Selective Hegemony in Reform-era Myanmar." *Asia-Pacific Journal of Anthropology* 20, no.1 (2019): 57–73.

Campbell, Stephen. "Migrant Waste Collectors in Thailand's Informal Economy: Mapping Class Relations." *European Journal of East Asian Studies* 17 (2018): 263–288.

Campbell, Stephen. "Of Squatting amid Capitalism on Myanmar's Industrial Periphery." *Anthropology Today* 35, no. 6 (2019): 7–10.

Campbell, Stephen. "On Labour Organisations in Myanmar." *Global Labour Column*, no. 144 (2013). http://column.global-labour-university.org/2013/07/on-labour-organisations-in-myanmar.html.

Campbell, Stephen. "Putting-Out's Return: Informalization and Differential Subsumption in Thailand's Garment Sector." *Focaal: Journal of Global and Historical Anthropology* 76 (2016): 71–84.

Campbell, Stephen. "Reading Myanmar's Inland Fisheries: Postcolonial Literature as Theoretical Lens." *Inter-Asia Cultural Studies* 20, no. 1 (2019): 2–18.

Campbell, Stephen. "Rendering Assemblage Dialectical." *Anthropological Theory*, https://journals.sagepub.com/doi/full/10.1177/1463499619875904.

Campbell, Stephen. "Touring Myanmar's Leftist History." *Focaalblog*, May 14, 2019. http://www.focaalblog.com/2019/05/14/stephen-campbell-touring-myanmars-leftist-history/.

Campbell, Stephen, and Elliott Prasse-Freeman. "Revisiting the Wages of Burmanness: Contradictions of Privilege in Myanmar." *Journal of Contemporary Asia*, https://doi.org/10.1080/00472336.2021.1962390.

Carrier, James. "Moral Economy: What's in a Name?" *Anthropological Theory* 18, no. 1 (2018): 18–35.

Cattaneo, Claudio, and Miguel Martínez, *The Squatters' Movement in Europe: Everyday Commons and Autonomy as Alternatives to Capitalism*. London: Pluto Press, 2014.

Chalfin, Brenda. "Waste Work and the Dialectics of Precarity in Urban Ghana: Durable Bodies and Disposable Things." *Africa* 89, no. 3 (2019): 499–520.

The Challenge of Slums: Global Report on Human Settlement 2003. London: United Nations Human Settlements Program, 2003. www.un.org/ruleoflaw/files/Challenge%20of%20Slums.pdf.

Chance, Kerry R. *Living Politics in South Africa's Urban Shacklands*. Chicago: University of Chicago Press, 2018.

Chang, Dae-Oup. "Informalising Labour in Asia's Global Factory." *Journal of Contemporary Asia* 39, no. 2 (2009): 161–179.

Chaskin, Robert J., and Mark L. Joseph. *Integrating the Inner City: The Promise and Perils of Mixed-Income Public Housing Transformation*. Chicago: University of Chicago Press, 2015.

Chatterjee, Partha. *The Politics of the Governed: Reflections on Popular Politics in Most of the World.* New York: Columbia University Press, 2006.

Cheesman, Nick. *Opposing the Rule of Law: How Myanmar's Courts Make Law and Order.* Cambridge: Cambridge University Press, 2015.

Chern, Kang Wan. "South Korea Eyes Myanmar Investments in Manufacturing, Infrastructure." *Myanmar Times*, February 9, 2018. https://www.mmtimes.com/news/south-korea-eyes-myanmar-investments-manufacturing-infrastructure.html.

Collis, Maurice. *Trials in Burma.* London: Penguin Books, 1945.

Comaroff, Jean, and John Comaroff. *Theory from the South: Or, How Euro-America Is Evolving toward Africa.* Abingdon: Routledge, 2012.

Davis, Angela Y. *Women, Race, and Class.* New York: Vintage Books, 1983.

Davis, Mike. *Planet of Slums.* London: Verso, 2005.

Deleuze, Gilles. "Capitalism, Flows, the Decoding of Flows, Capitalism and Schizophrenia, Psychoanalysis, Spinoza." November 16, 1971. www.webdeleuze.com/textes/116.

Della Costa, Mariarosa, and Selma James. *The Power of Women and the Subversion of the Community.* London: Falling Wall Press, 1972.

Democratic Voice of Burma. "Hi Mo Workers Strike." May 25, 2012. https://www.youtube.com/watch?v=Ptnsh0QycdY.

Denning, Michael. "Wageless Life." *New Left Review* 66 (2010): 79–97.

Department of Population Ministry of Labour, Immigration and Population. "Policy Brief on Migration and Urbanization." 2017. http://www.dop.gov.mm/sites/dop.gov.mm/files/publication_docs/policy_brief_on_migration_and_unbanization.pdf

Di Muzio, Tim, and Richard M. Robbin. *Debt as Power.* London: Bloomsbury Academic, 2015.

Du Bois, W.E.B. *Black Reconstruction in America: Toward a History of the Part which Black Folk Played in the Attempt to Reconstruct Democracy in America, 1860–1880.* New Brunswick, NJ: Transaction Publishers, (1935) 2013.

Durand, Cédric. *Fictitious Capital: How Finance Is Appropriating our Future.* London: Verso, 2017.

Ei Ei Toe Lwin. "Fury over Letpadaung Copper Mine Report." *Myanmar Times*, March 18, 2013. https://www.mmtimes.com/national-news/5175-fury-at-copper-mine-report.html.

Environmental Justice Foundation. *Thailand's Seafood Slaves: Human Trafficking, Slavery and Murder in Kantang's Fishing Industry.* November 30, 2015. https://ejfoundation.org/reports/thailands-seafood-slaves-human-trafficking-slavery-and-murder-in-kantangs-fishing-industry.

Farrelly, Nicholas, and Giuseppe Gabusi. "Explaining Myanmar's Tentative Renaissance." *European Journal of East Asian Studies* 14, no. 1 (2015): 7–14.

Federici, Silvia. *Revolution at Point Zero: Housework, Reproduction, and Feminist Struggle.* Oakland: PM Press, 2012.

Federici, Silvia. "Undeclared War: Violence against Women." *Artforum*, 2017. https://www.artforum.com/print/201706/undeclared-war-violence-against-women-68680.

Fenichel, Allen, and Azfar Khan. "The Burmese Way to 'Socialism.'" *World Development* 9, no. 9–10 (1981): 813–824.

Ferguson, James. *Expectations of Modernity: Myths and Meanings of Urban Life on the Zambian Copperbelt.* Berkeley: University of California Press, 1999.

Ferguson, James. *Give a Man a Fish: Reflections on the New Politics of Distribution.* Durham: Duke University Press, 2015.

Final Report of the Riot Inquiry Committee. Rangoon: Rangoon Printing and Stationery, 1939. https://archive.org/details/in.ernet.dli.2015.206317/page/n297.

Fink, Christina. *Living Silence: Burma under Military Rule.* London: Zed Books, 2001.

Fogarty, Philippa. "Was Burma's 1988 Uprising Worth It?" BBC, August 6, 2008. http://news.bbc.co.uk/2/hi/asia-pacific/7543347.stm.

Forbes, Eben I. "On the Frontier of Urbanization: Informal Settlements in Yangon, Myanmar." *Independent Journal of Burmese Scholarship* 1, no. 1 (2016): 197–238.

Ford, Michele, Michael Gillan, and Htwe Htwe Thein, "From Cronyism to Oligarchy? Privatisation and Business Elites in Myanmar." *Journal of Contemporary Asia* 46, no.1 (2016): 18–41.

Frank, Andre G. *Capitalism and Underdevelopment in Latin America: Historical Studies of Chile and Brazil*. New York: Monthly Review Press, 1967.

Fraser, Nancy. "Behind Marx's Hidden Abode." *New Left Review* no. 86 (2014): 55–72.

Fraser, Nancy, and Rahel Jaeggi. *Capitalism: A Conversation in Critical Theory*. Cambridge: Polity Press, 2018.

Frontier Myanmar. "Clashes at Yangon Garment Factory Leave Dozens Injured." October 16, 2018. https://frontiermyanmar.net/en/clashes-at-yangon-garment-factory-leave-dozens-injured.

Fudge, Judy. "(Re)Conceptualising Unfree Labour: Local Labour Control Regimes and Constraints on Workers' Freedoms." *Global Labour Journal* 10, no. 2 (2019): 108–122.

Fujita, Kōichi. "Agricultural Laborers during the Economic Transition: Views from the Study of Selected Villages." In *The Economic Transition in Myanmar after 1988: Market Economy versus State Control*. Edited by Kōichi Fujita, Fumiharu Mieno, and Ikuko Okamoto, 246–280. Singapore: NUS Press, 2009.

Fujita, Kōichi, Fumiharu Mieno, and Ikuko Okamoto, eds. *The Economic Transition in Myanmar After 1988: Market Economy Versus State Control*. Singapore: NUS Press, 2009.

Furnivall, J.S. *Colonial Policy and Practice: A Comparative Study of Burma and Netherlands India*. Cambridge: Cambridge University Press, (1948) 2014.

Gago, Veronica, and Sandro Mezzadra. "A Critique of the Extractive Operations of Capital: Toward an Expanded Concept of Extractivism." *Rethinking Marxism* 29, no. 4 (2008): 574–591.

Gibson-Graham, J.K. *The End of Capitalism (as We Knew It): A Feminist Critique of Political Economy*. Minneapolis: University of Minnesota Press, 1996.

Gill, Kaveri. *Of Poverty and Plastic: Scavenging and Scrap Trading Entrepreneurs in India's Urban Informal Economy*. New Delhi: Oxford University Press, 2010.

Gluckman, Max. *Rituals of Rebellion in South-East Africa*. Manchester: Manchester University Press, 1954.

Goldstein, Donna M. *Laughter out of Place Race, Class, Violence, and Sexuality in a Rio Shantytown*. Berkeley: University of California Press, 2013.

Gough, Kathleen. "Anthropology and Imperialism." *Monthly Review* 19, no. 11 (1968): 12–27.

Gough, Kathleen. "'Anthropology and Imperialism' Revisited." *Economic and Political Weekly* 25, no. 31 (1990): 1705–1708.

Government of the Republic of the Union of Myanmar. "National Action Plan for Agriculture, Working Paper 10: Land Tenure and Administration." Yangon, 2015.

Graeber, David. *Debt: The First 5,000 Years*. New York: Melville House Publishing, 2011.

Graeber, David. *Direct Action: An Ethnography*. Oakland: AK Press, 2009.

Gramsci, Antonio. *Selections from the Prison Notebooks*. Edited and translated by Quentin Hoare and Geoffrey Neil Smith. New York: International Publishers, 1971.

Gregory, Chris. *Savage Money: The Anthropology and Politics of Commodity Exchange*. Amsterdam: Harwood Academic Publishers, 1997.

Griffiths, Michael. "Formal Sector Internal Migration in Myanmar." In *Migration in Myanmar: Perspectives from Current Research.* Edited by Michael Griffiths and Michiko Ito, 76–87. Yangon: Social Policy and Poverty Research Group, 2016.

Griffiths, Michael. "Networks of Reciprocity: Precarity and Community Social Organisations in Rural Myanmar." *Journal of Contemporary Asia* 49, no. 4 (2019): 602–625.

Griffiths, Michael, and Michiko Ito. "Introduction." In *Migration in Myanmar: Perspectives from Current Research.* Edited by Michael Griffiths and Michiko Ito, 9–16. Yangon: Social Policy and Poverty Research Group, 2016.

Guérin, Isabelle, Solène Morvant-Roux, and Magdalena Villarreal. "Introduction." In *Microfinance, Debt and Over-Indebtedness: Juggling with Money.* Edited by Isabelle Guérin, Solène Morvant-Roux, and Magdalena Villarreal, 1–23. London: Routledge, 2014.

Guha, Ranajit. *Dominance without Hegemony: History and Power in Colonial India.* Cambridge: Harvard University Press, 1997.

Gupta, Shagun. "Leveraging Migration for Development: A Review of Literature on Patterns and Movements in Myanmar." In *Migration in Myanmar: Perspectives from Current Research.* Edited by Michael Griffiths and Michiko Ito, 17–44. Yangon: Social Policy and Poverty Research Group, 2016.

Guyer, Jane, and Federico Neiburg. "The Politics of the Real Economy." *Hau: Journal of Ethnographic Theory* 8, no. 1–2 (2018): 236–238.

Guyer, Jane, and Federico Neiburg, "The Real in the Real Economy," *Hau: Journal of Ethnographic Theory* 7, no. 3 (2017): 261–279.

Handler, Richard. *Nationalism and the Politics of Culture in Quebec.* Madison: University of Wisconsin Press, 1988.

Hardt, Michael. "The Common in Communism." *Rethinking Marxism* 22, no. 3 (2010): 346–356.

Harms, Erik. *Saigon's Edge: On the Margins of Ho Chi Minh City.* Minneapolis: University of Minnesota Press, 2010.

Harriss-White, Barbara. "Labor and Petty Production." *Development and Change* 45, no. 5 (2014): 981–1000.

Hart, Keith. "Informal Income Opportunities and Urban Employment in Ghana." *Journal of Modern African Studies* 11, no. 1 (1973): 61–89.

Harvey, David. *The Limits to Capital.* Oxford: Blackwell, 1982.

Hegel, Georg W. F. *The Science of Logic.* Translated by George di Giovanni. Cambridge: Cambridge University Press, 2010.

Hein Thar. "The Abuse behind Myanmar's Fish Paste Industry." *Frontier Myanmar,* January 20, 2020. www.frontiermyanmar.net/en/the-abuse-behind-myanmars-fish-paste-industry.

Hla Hla Htay. "'There Was a Lot of Blood': Domestic Servant Sisters Scarred by Abuse." *Frontier Myanmar,* February 15, 2017. https://frontiermyanmar.net/en/there-was-a-lot-of-blood-domestic-servant-sisters-scarred-by-abuse.

Hla Hla Htay, and Caroline Henshaw. "The Skincare Fad Threatening Myanmar's Elephants." *Myanmar Times,* January 24, 2017. www.mmtimes.com/national-news/24665-the-skincare-fad-threatening-myanmar-s-elephants.html.

Hodal, Kate, and Chris Kelly. "Trafficked into Slavery on Thai Trawlers to Catch Food for Prawns." *Guardian,* June 10, 2014. https://www.theguardian.com/global-development/2014/jun/10/-sp-migrant-workers-new-life-enslaved-thai-fishing.

Holston, James. *Insurgent Citizenship: Disjunctions of Democracy and Modernity in Brazil.* Princeton: Princeton University Press, 2008.

Hook, Leslie. "Uber Hitches a Ride with Car Finance Schemes." *Financial Times,* August 11, 2016. https://www.ft.com/content/921289f6-5dd1-11e6-bb77-a121aa8abd95

Horsey, Richard. *Ending Forced Labour in Myanmar: Engaging a Pariah Regime.* London: Routledge, 2011.
Houtman, Gustaaf. "Sacralizing or Demonizing Democracy?" In *Burma at The Turn of the 21st Century.* Edited by Monique Skidmoore, 133–153. Honolulu: University of Hawai'i Press, 2005.
Htar Htar Khin. "Land Prices Surge on the City's Outskirts." *Myanmar Times*, June 17, 2013. www.mmtimes.com/business/property-news/7163-prices-surge-on-yangon-s-outskirts.html.
Htet Kaung Lin. "Firebrand Monk Calls for Military Parliamentarians to be 'Worshipped.'" *Irrawaddy*, May 6, 2019. https://www.irrawaddy.com/news/burma/firebrand-monk-calls-military-parliamentarians-worshipped.html.
Htet Naing Zaw. "Ma Ba Tha Is a Necessity: Military." *Irrawaddy*, June 19, 2019. https://www.irrawaddy.com/news/burma/ma-ba-tha-necessity-military.html.
Human Rights Watch. *"I Want to Help My Own People" State Control and Civil Society in Burma after Cyclone Nargis.* May 3, 2009. www.hrw.org/report/2010/04/28/i-want-help-my-own-people/state-control-and-civil-society-burma-after-cyclone.
Human Rights Watch. *"Nothing for Our Land": Impact of Land Confiscation on Farmers in Myanmar.* July 17, 2018. https://www.hrw.org/report/2018/07/17/nothing-our-land/impact-land-confiscation-farmers-myanmar.
Human Rights Watch. "The Origins of Myanmar Migrant Worker Misery." 2016. https://www.hrw.org/news/2016/01/14/origins-myanmar-migrant-worker-misery.
International Crisis Group. "The Dark Side of Transition: Violence against Muslims in Myanmar." October 1, 2013. www.crisisgroup.org/asia/south-east-asia/myanmar/dark-side-transition-violence-against-muslims-myanmar.
International Crisis Group. "Myanmar: The Politics of Economic Reform." Yangon, 2012. www.crisisgroup.org/asia/south-east-asia/myanmar/myanmar-politics-economic-reform.
International Labour Organisation (ILO). ILO Liaison Officer for Myanmar. "Internal Labour Migration in Myanmar: Building an Evidence-Base on Patterns in Migration, Human Trafficking and Forced Labour." Yangon: ILO, 2015.
Irrawaddy. "Timeline of Student Protests against Education Law." March 10, 2015. https://www.irrawaddy.com/news/burma/timeline-of-student-protests-against-education-law.html.
James, C.L.R. *The Black Jacobins: Toussaint L'Ouverture and the San Domingo Revolution.* New York: Penguin Random House, (1939) 1989.
James, Deborah. "Deductions and Counter-Deductions in South Africa," *Hau: Journal of Ethnographic Theory* 7, no. 3 (2017): 281–304.
Jones, Lee. "The Political Economy of Myanmar's Transition." *Journal of Contemporary Asia*, 44, no. 1 (2014): 144–170.
Kar, Sohini. *Financializing Poverty: Labor and Risk in Indian Microfinance.* Stanford: Stanford University Press, 2018.
Karen Human Rights Group. *Shouldering the Burden of Militarization.* Chiang Mai, 2007. https://khrg.org/2007/08/khrg0702/shouldering-burden-militarisation-spdc-dkba-and-kpf-order-documents-september-2006.
Kasmir, Sharryn, and August Carbonella. "Introduction: Toward a Global Anthropology of Labor." In *Blood and Fire: Toward a Global Anthropology of Labour.* Edited by Sharryn Kasmir and August Carbonella, 1–29. New York: Berghahn Books, 2014.
Kasmir, Sharryn, and Lesley Gill. "No Smooth Surfaces: The Anthropology of Unevenness and Combination." *Current Anthropology* 59, no. 4 (2018): 355–377.
Kate Hodal, Chris Kelly, and Felicity Lawrence. "Revealed: Asian Slave Labour Producing Prawns for Supermarkets in US, UK." *Guardian*, June 10, 2014. www.theguardian

.com/global-development/2014/jun/10/supermarket-prawns-thailand-produced-slave-labour.
Kent, Justin. "Myanmar, The Last Frontier?" *Forbes*, November 9, 2012. https://www.forbes.com/sites/connorconnect/2012/11/09/myanmar-the-last-frontier/#4b7045245dce.
Khin Myat Myat Wai. "Enslaved Fishery Workers Near Pyapon City." *Tea Circle: A Forum for New Perspectives on Burma/Myanmar*. Translated by Stephen Campbell. August 22, 2018. https://teacircleoxford.com/2018/08/22/enslaved-fishery-workers-near-pyapon-city/.
Khin Yi. *The Dobama Movement in Burma (1930–1938)*. Ithaca: Cornell Southeast Asia Program, 1988.
Kojanić, Ognjen. "Theory from the Peripheries: What Can the Anthropology of Postsocialism Offer to European Anthropology?" *Anthropological Journal of European Cultures* 29, no. 2 (2020): 49–66.
Komlosy, Andrea. "Work and Labor Relations." In *Capitalism: The Reemergence of a Historical Concept*. Edited by Jürgen Kocka and Marcel van der Linden, 33–70. London: Bloomsbury, 2016.
Kropotkin, Peter. *Mutual Aid: A Factor in Evolution*. Scotts Valley: CreateSpace Independent Publishing Platform, (1902) 2017.
Krugman, Paul. "Profits without Production." *New York Times*, June 20, 2013. www.nytimes.com/2013/06/21/opinion/krugman-profits-without-production.html.
Krupa, Christopher. "Ghostly Figures Outside the Domain of Political Economy: Class Analysis and the Invisiblized Livelihoods of an Andean Export Zone." In *Confronting Capital: Critique and Engagement in Anthropology*. Edited by Belinda Leach, Pauline Barber, and Winnie Lem, 187–207. New York: Routledge, 2012.
Krupa, Christopher, and David Nugent. *State Theory and Andean Politics: New Approaches to the Study of Rule*. Philadelphia: University of Pennsylvania Press, 2015.
Kudo, Toshihiro. "The Impact of United States Sanctions on the Myanmar Garment Industry." *Asian Survey* 48, no.6 (2008): 997–1017.
Kyaw Hsu Mon. "Finance Minister Predicts 'Take Off' for Burma Economy." *Irrawaddy*, June 6, 2017. https://www.irrawaddy.com/business/finance-minister-predicts-take-off-burma-economy.html.
Kyaw Soe Lwin. "Legal Perspectives on Industrial Disputes in Myanmar." In *Law, Society and Transition in Myanmar*. Edited by Melissa Crouch and Tim Lindsey, 289–304. Oxford: Hart, 2014.
Kyaw Yaw Lynn. "Low-Cost Housing Plan Sends Prices Soaring for Squatters' ID Cards." *Frontier Myanmar*, May 14, 2018. https://frontiermyanmar.net/en/low-cost-housing-plan-sends-prices-soaring-for-squatters-id-cards.
Kyaw Zaw Moe. "70 Years On, the Struggle for Independence Goes On." *Irrawaddy*, January 4, 2018. https://www.irrawaddy.com/opinion/commentary/70-years-struggle-independence-goes.html.
Kyaw Zaw Win. "A History of the Burma Socialist Party." PhD diss., University of Wollongong, 2008.
Lainez, Nicolas. "Commodified Sexuality and Mother-Daughter Power Dynamics in the Mekong Delta." *Journal of Vietnamese Studies* 7, no. 1 (2012): 149–180.
Leacock, Eleanor, and Helen I. Safa, eds. *Women's Work: Development and the Division of Labor by Gender*. New York: Bergin and Garvey, 1986.
Leeds, Anthony. *Cities, Classes, and the Social Order*. Edited by Roger Sanjek. Ithaca: Cornell University Press, 1994.

Leehey, Jennifer. "Open Secrets, Hidden Meanings: Censorship, Esoteric Power, and Contested Authority in Urban Burma in the 1990s," PhD diss., University of Washington, 2010.

Lewis, Arthur. "Economic Development with Unlimited Supplies of Labour." *Manchester School* 22, no. 2 (1954): 139–191.

Li, Tania M. "After Development: Surplus Population and the Politics of Entitlement." *Development and Change* 48, no. 6 (2017): 1247–1261.

Li, Tania M. "Centering Labor in the Land Grab Debate," *Journal of Peasant Studies* 38, no. 2 (2011): 281–298.

Li, Yi. *Chinese in Colonial Burma: A Migrant Community in a Multiethnic State*. New York: Palgrave Macmillan, 2017.

Li, Tania M. *Land's End: Capitalist Relations on an Indigenous Frontier*. Durham: Duke University Press, 2014.

Li, Tania M. "To Make Live or Let Die? Rural Dispossession and the Protection of Surplus Populations," *Antipode* 41, no. s1 (2010): 66–93.

Li, Tania M. "The Price of Un/Freedom: Indonesia's Colonial and Contemporary Plantation Labor Regimes." *Comparative Studies in Society and History* 59, no. 2 (2018): 245–276.

Linebaugh, Peter, and Marcus Rediker. *The Many-Headed Hydra: The Hidden History of the Revolutionary Atlantic*. London: Verso, 2010.

Lintner, Bertil. *Outrage: Burma's Struggle for Democracy*. Bangkok: White Lotus, 1990.

Lintner, Bertil. *The Rise and Fall of the Communist Party of Burma*. Ithaca: Cornell Southeast Asia Program, 1990.

Lloyd, Peter C. *Slums of Hope? Shanty Towns of the Third World*. Manchester: Manchester University Press, 1979.

Looi, Florence. "Despite Rohingya Crisis, Thousands March in Support of Military." *Al-Jazeera*, October 29, 2017. https://www.aljazeera.com/news/2017/10/thousands-rohingya-march-support-army-crisis-171029163411806.html.

Losurdo, Domenico. *Liberalism: A Counter-History*. Translated by Gregory Elliott. London: Verso, 2011.

Lowe, Lisa. *The Intimacies of Four Continents*. Durham: Duke University Press, 2015.

Ludu Sein Win. "*Thamaingko bethu hpantitalè* [Who makes history?]." *Weekly Eleven News*, September 28, 2010. http://oothandar.blogspot.com/2010/09/blog-post_27.html.

Macan-Markar, Marwaan. "BURMA: ILO Steps into Political Minefield to Help Revive Trade Unions." Inter Press Service, July 13, 2010, www.ipsnews.net/2010/07/burma-ilo-steps-into-political-minefield-to-help-revive-trade-unions/.

Malinowski, Bronislaw. *Argonauts of the Western Pacific: An Account of Native Enterprises and Adventures in the Archipelagoes of Melanesian New Guinea*. Long Grove: Waveland Press, (1922) 1984.

Mamdani, Mahmoud. *Citizen and Subject: Contemporary Africa and the Legacy of Late Colonialism*. Princeton: Princeton University Press, 1996.

Mark, Siusue. "Are the Odds of Justice 'Stacked' against Them? Challenges and Opportunities for Securing Land Claims by Smallholder Farmers in Myanmar." *Critical Asian Studies* 48, no. 3 (2017): 443–460.

Marx, Karl. *Capital: A Critique of Political Economy*. Vol. 1. Translated by Ben Fowkes. London: Penguin, 1976.

Marx, Karl. *Capital: A Critique of Political Economy*. Vol. 3. Translated by David Fernbach. London: Penguin Books, 1981.

Marx, Karl. *Economic and Philosophical Manuscripts of 1844*. Translated by Martin Milligan. New York: Prometheus Books, 1988.

Marx, Karl, and Frederick Engels, *The German Ideology*. Edited by C.J. Arthur. New York: International Publishers, 1970.
Maung Htin. *Ngaba*. Yangon: Myanmar Ministry of Information, (1947) 1991.
Mauss, Marcel. *The Gift: Expanded Edition*. London: Hau Books, (1925) 2016.
McCarthy, Gerard. "Regressive Democracy: Explaining Distributive Politics in Myanmar's Political Transition." PhD diss., Australian National University, 2018.
McCarthy, Stephen. "Ten Years of Chaos in Burma: Foreign Investment and Economic Liberalization under the SLORC-SPDC, 1988 to 1998." *Pacific Affairs* 73, no. 2 (2000): 233–262.
McDowell, Robin, Margie Mason, and Martha Mendoza. "AP Investigation: Slaves May Have Caught the Fish You Bought." *Associated Press*, March 25, 2015. https://www.ap.org/explore/seafood-from-slaves/ap-investigation-slaves-may-have-caught-the-fish-you-bought.html.
Meillassoux, Claude. *Maidens, Meal and Money: Capitalism and the Domestic Community*. Cambridge: Cambridge University Press, 1975.
Metcalf, Barbara, and Thomas Metcalf. *A Concise History of Modern India*. 2nd ed. Cambridge: Cambridge University Press, 2006.
Mezzadra, Sandro. "Bringing Capital Back In: A Materialist Turn in Postcolonial Studies?" *Inter-Asia Cultural Studies* 12, no. 1 (2011): 154–164.
Mezzadra, Sandro, and Brett Neilson. *Border as Method, or, the Multiplication of Labor*. Durham: Duke University Press, 2013.
Mies, Maria. *Patriarchy and Accumulation on a World Scale: Women in the International Division of Labour*. London: Zed Books, 1986.
Mill, John Stuart. *On Liberty*. Peterborough: Broadview Literary Texts, (1859) 1999.
Mill, John Stuart. *Principles of Political Economy*. Vol. 1. New York: Cosimo, (1885) 2009.
Mills, Mary Beth. *Thai Women in the Global Labor Force: Consuming Desires, Contested Selves*. New Brunswick, NJ: Rutgers University Press, 1999.
Millar, Kathleen. "The Precarious Present: Wageless Labor and Disrupted Life in Rio de Janeiro, Brazil." *Cultural Anthropology* 29, no. 1 (2014): 32–53.
Millar, Kathleen. *Reclaiming the Discarded: Life and Labor on Rio's Garbage Dump*. Durham: Duke University Press, 2018.
Min Zin. "Burma Takes a Big Step Backwards." *Foreign Policy*, March 12, 2015. https://foreignpolicy.com/2015/03/12/burma-takes-a-big-step-backwards/.
Mintz, Sidney W. *Caribbean Transformations*. New York: Columbia University Press, 1989.
Mintz, Sidney. *Sweetness and Power: The Place of Sugar in Modern History*. London: Penguin Random House, 1985.
Moe Myint. "Four Arrested as Police, Hired Heavies Clear Squatters in Yangon." *Irrawaddy*, June 12, 2017. www.irrawaddy.com/news/burma/four-arrested-police-hired-heavies-clear-squatters-yangon.html.
Montlake, Simon. "Burma's Showy Crony." *Forbes*, September 18, 2011. https://www.forbes.com/global/2011/1010/feature-people-burma-showy-crony-capitalism-luxury-za-montlake.html#1d61d3627e62.
Muehlebach, Andrea. *The Moral Neoliberal: Welfare and Citizenship in Italy*. Chicago: University of Chicago Press, 2012.
Mullins, Jeremy. "Big Western Brands Sew Way Forward." *Myanmar Times*, May 29, 2015. https://www.mmtimes.com/business/14755-big-western-brands-sew-way-forward.html.
Munck, Ronaldo. "The Precariat: A View from the South." *Third World Quarterly* 34, no. 5 (2013): 747–762.

Myanmar: Ending Poverty and Boosting Shared Prosperity in a Time of Transition. Yangon: World Bank Group, 2014.

Myanmar Population and Housing Census. Naypyidaw: Department of Population, Ministry of Immigration and Population, May 2015.

Myat Moe Aung. "Sucker Fish Terrorise Fishing in Twante." *Myanmar Times*, January 9, 2018. www.mmtimes.com/news/sucker-fish-terrorise-fishing-twante.html.

Myat Thida Win, and Aye Mya Thinzar. "Agricultural Mechanization and Structural Transformation in Myanmar's Ayeyarwady Delta." *Food Security Policy Project Research Highlights*. Ann Arbor: University of Michigan, 2016. www.ifpri.org/publication/agricultural-mechanization-and-structural-transformation-myanmars-ayeyarwady-delta.

National Post. "'Like a Gold Rush': Investing in Burma 'High-Risk' and Potentially 'High-Reward.'" November 27, 2012. https://nationalpost.com/news/like-a-gold-rush-investing-in-burma-high-risk-and-potentially-high-reward.

Negri, Antonio. *Marx and Foucault*. London: Polity Press, 2017.

Neveling, Patrick. "The Political Economy of Special Economic Zones: Pasts, Presents, Futures." In *The Oxford Handbook of Industrial Hubs and Economic Development*. Edited by Arkebe Oqubay and Justin Yifu Lin, 1–23. Oxford: Oxford University Press, 2020.

Neveling, Patrick. "Three Shades of Embeddedness, State Capitalism as the Informal Economy, Emic Notions of the Anti-Market, and Counterfeit Garments in the Mauritian Export Processing Zone." *Research in Economic Anthropology* 34, no. 1 (2014): 65–94.

Nguyen, Minh T. N. *Waste and Wealth: An Ethnography of Labor, Value, and Morality in a Vietnamese Recycling Economy*. Oxford: Oxford University Press, 2019.

Noe Noe Aung. "In Hlaing Tharyar, Illegal Residents Face Tough Decisions." *Myanmar Times*, September 15, 2013. www.mmtimes.com/national-news/yangon/8182-in-hlaing-tharyar-illegal-residents-face-tough-decisions.html.

Noys, Benjamin. *Communization and Its Discontents: Contestation, Critique, and Contemporary Struggles*. Brooklyn: Autonomedia, 2012.

Nyein Nyein. "Ending Debt Bondage is Key to Eradicating Child Labor, Says ILO." *Irrawaddy*, October 23. 2018, www.irrawaddy.com/news/burma/ending-debt-bondage-key-eradicating-child-labor-says-ilo.html.

Okamoto, Ikuko. *Economic Disparity in Rural Myanmar: Transformation under Market Liberalization*. Singapore: NUS Press, 2008.

Palmstrom, Becky. "Forced to Fish: Slavery on Thailand's Trawlers." BBC News, January 23, 2014. https://www.bbc.com/news/magazine-25814718.

Palomera, Jaime, and Theodora Vetta. "Moral Economy: Rethinking a Radical Concept." *Anthropological Theory* 16, no. 4 (2016): 413–432.

Parry, Jonathan. "Company and Contract Labour in a Central Indian Steel Plant." *Economy and Society* 42, no. 3 (2013): 348–374.

Patnaik, Utsa. *Agrarian Relations and Accumulation—The Mode of Production Debate in India*. Oxford: Oxford University Press, 1990.

Pattison, Corey, John Voss, Andrea Woodhouse, and Matt Zurstrassen. "A Country on the Move: Migration Networks and Risk Management in Two Regions of Myanmar." In *Migration in Myanmar: Perspectives from Current Research*. Edited by Michael Griffiths and Michiko Ito, 45–75. Yangon: Social Policy and Poverty Research Group, 2016.

Peck, Jamie, and Nik Theodore. "Variegated Capitalism." *Progress in Human Geography* 31, no. 6 (2007): 731–772.

Polanyi, Karl. *The Great Transformation: The Political and Economic Origins of Our Time*. Boston: Beacon Press, (1944) 2001.

Popham, Peter. *The Lady and the Peacock: The Life of Aung San Suu Kyi*. New York: Experiment, 2013.

Postero, Nancy, and Eli Elinoff. "Introduction: A Return to Politics." *Anthropological Theory* 19, no. 1 (2019): 3–28.

Prasan, Vishu. *Mapping Yangon: The Untapped Communities—A Preliminary Study of Informal Settlements in Yangon*. Yangon: UN-Habitat, 2016.

Prasse-Freeman, Elliott. "Of Punishment, Protest, and Press Conferences: Contentious Politics amid Despotic Decision in Contemporary Burmese Courtrooms." In *Criminal Legalities in the Global South: Cultural Dynamics, Political Tensions, and Institutional Practices*. Edited by Pablo Ciocchini and George Radics, 124–142. New York: Routledge, 2019.

Prasse-Freeman, Elliott, and Phyo Win Latt. "Class and Inequality in Contemporary Myanmar." In *The Routledge Handbook of Contemporary Myanmar*. Edited by Adam Simpson, Nicholas Farrelly, and Ian Holliday, 404–416. New York: Routledge, 2018.

Price, David. *Cold War Anthropology: The CIA, the Pentagon, and the Growth of Dual Use Anthropology*. Durham: Duke University Press, 2015.

Radio Free Asia. "*Kyaikami Kyahpaungbaw ngayekan*." January 11, 2018. www.rfa.org/burmese/multimedia/fisherman-mon-state-01112018231927.html.

Redfield, Robert. *Tepoztlán, a Mexican Village*. Chicago: University of Chicago Press, 1930.

Report on Conditions of Work and Promotion of Livelihoods in the Unorganised Sector. Delhi: National Commission for Enterprises in the Unorganised Sector, 2008.

Revolutionary Council. "Law Defining the Fundamental Rights and Responsibilities of the People's Workers." Law No. 6 of 1964, Preamble §3.2.

Rhoads, Elizabeth. "Forced Evictions as Urban Planning? Traced of Colonial Land Control Practices in Yangon, Myanmar." *State Crime Journal* 7, no. 2 (2018): 278–305.

Rhoads, Elizabeth. "Informal (Justice) Brokers: Buying, Selling, and Disputing Property in Yangon." In *Everyday Justice in Myanmar: Informal Resolutions and State Evasion in a Time of Contested Transition*, ed. Helene Maria Kyed, 283–313. Copenhagen: NIAS Press, 2020.

Rhoads, Elizabeth L., and Courtney T. Wittekind. "Rethinking Land and Property in a 'Transitioning' Myanmar: Representations of Isolation, Neglect, and Natural Decline." *Journal of Burma Studies* 22, no. 2 (2018): 171–213.

Robinson, Cedric. *Black Marxism: The Making of the Black Radical Tradition*. Chapel Hill: University of North Carolina Press, 1983.

Rodan, Garry, Kevin Hewison, and Richard Robinson. "Theorising South-East Asia's Boom, Bust, and Recovery." In *The Political Economy of South-East Asia: Conflict, Crisis, and Change*. Edited by Garry Rodan, Kevin Hewison, and Richard Robinson, 1–41. 2nd ed. Oxford: Oxford University Press, 2002.

Rodney, Walter. *How Europe Underdeveloped Africa*. London: Bogle-L'Ouverture, 1972.

Rosenbaum, Susanna. *Domestic Economies: Women, Work, and the American Dream in Los Angeles*. Durham: Duke University Press, 2018.

Rostow, Walt. *The Stages of Economic Growth: A Non-Communist Manifesto*. Cambridge: Cambridge University Press, 1960.

Salai Thant Zin. "Wild Elephant Poached and Skinned in Myanmar Forest Reserve." *Irrawaddy*, September 12, 2019. www.irrawaddy.com/news/burma/wild-elephant-poached-skinned-myanmar-forest-reserve.html.

Salaing Thant Sin. "*Athek tachaung ngwe 6 thein* [600,000 for one life]." *Irrawaddy*, March 11, 2019. https://burma.irrawaddy.com/article/2019/03/11/185976.html.

Samaddar, Ranabir. *Karl Marx and the Postcolonial Age*. London: Palgrave Macmillan, 2018.

Sandar Lwin. "In Pyapon, Many Face an Uncertain Future after Storm." *Myanmar Times*, April 11, 2011. www.mmtimes.com/national-news/3060-in-pyapon-many-face-an-uncertain-future-after-storm.html.

Sanyal, Kalyan. *Rethinking Capitalist Development: Primitive Accumulation, Governmentality and Post-Colonial Capitalism*. Abingdon: Routledge, 2007.

Sarkisyanz, Emanuel. *Buddhist Backgrounds of the Burmese Revolution*. The Hague: Martinus Nijhoff, 1965.

Scheper-Hughes. Nancy. *Death without Weeping: The Violence of Everyday Life in Brazil*. Berkeley: University of California Press, 1993.

Schrank, Delphine. *A Tale of Defiance and Deliverance in Burma: The Rebel of Rangoon*. New York: Nation Books, 2015.

Schultz, Bart. "Mill and Sidgwick, Imperialism and Racism." *Utilitas* 19, no. 1 (2007): 104–130.

Scott, James. *Weapons of the Weak: Everyday forms of Peasant Resistance*. New Haven: Yale University Press, 1985.

Sen, Atreyee. *Shiv Sena Women: Violence and Communalism in a Bombay Slum*. Bloomington: University of Indiana Press, 2007.

Sen, Atreyee. "Slums and Shanty Towns." In *The International Encyclopedia of Anthropology*. Edited by Hilary Callan. Hoboken: John Wiley & Sons, 2018, https://onlinelibrary.wiley.com/doi/10.1002/9781118924396.wbiea2009.

Shine Lin Aung. "World Jin Workers Request Yangon Chief to Solve Labour Issues." *Eleven Myanmar*, December 20, 2019. https://elevenmyanmar.com/news/world-jin-workers-request-yangon-chief-to-solve-labour-issues.

Shiva, Vandana. *The Violence of Green Revolution: Third World Agriculture, Ecology and Politics*. London: Zed Books, 1991.

Shoon Naing. "Northern Yangon Squatters Notified of Impending Eviction." *Myanmar Times*, August 25, 2016. www.mmtimes.com/national-news/yangon/22138-northern-yangon-squatters-notified-of-impending-eviction.html.

Smart, Alan, and Josephine Smart, eds. *Petty Capitalists and Globalization: Flexibility, Entrepreneurship, and Economic Development*. Albany: State University of New York Press, 2006.

Smith, Martin. *Burma: Insurgency and the Politics of Ethnicity*. London: Zed Press, 1991.

Soe Lin Aung. "Notes on a Factory Uprising in Yangon." *Chuang*, March 30, 2017. http://chuangcn.org/2017/03/yangon-factory-uprising/.

Soe Lin Aung, and Stephen Campbell. "The Lady and the Generals." *Jacobin*, January 13, 2016. https://www.jacobinmag.com/2016/01/aung-san-suu-kyi-myanmar-burma-elections-military-generals/.

Soe Soe Htun. "Kyahpaung Myanmarbinletetk laungmyaikse ngayekanmya [Tiger rafts are burning hells over Myanmar's sea]." BBC Burmese, October 1, 2018. https://www.bbc.com/burmese/in-depth-45691571.

Sorge, Antonio, and Jonathan Padwe. "The Abandoned Village? Introduction to the Special Issue." *Critique of Anthropology* 35, no. 3 (2015): 235–247.

Starecheski, Amy. *Ours to Lose: When Squatters Became Homeowners in New York City*. Chicago: University of Chicago Press, 2016.

Su Myat Mon. "Another Betel Warning, but Is Anyone Listening?" *Frontier Myanmar*, November 19, 2018. https://frontiermyanmar.net/en/another-betel-warning-but-is-anyone-listening.

Taylor, Robert. "Introduction." In *Soe, Socialism and Chit Hlaing, Memories*. Edited by Hans-Bernd Zöllner, 5–13. Passau: University of Passau, Myanmar Literature Project, 2008.

Taylor, Robert. *The State in Myanmar*. Honolulu: University of Hawai'i Press, 2009.

Teschke, Benno. *The Myth of 1648: Class, Geopolitics and the Making of Modern International Relations*. London: Verso, 2012.
Thakin Lwin. *Myanma Alokthema Hlokshahmu Thamaing*. Yangon: Bagan Books, 1968.
Thakin Po Hla Gyi. *The Strike War*. Translated by Stephen Campbell. Passau: Myanmar Literature Project, University of Passau, (1938) 2012.
Than Than Nwe. "Yangon: The Emergence of a New Spatial Order in Myanmar's Capital City." *Sojourn: Journal of Social Issues in Southeast Asia* 13, no.1 (1998): 86–113.
Thawngmung, Ardeth M. *Everyday Economic Survival in Myanmar*. Madison: University of Wisconsin Press, 2019.
Thazin Hlaing. "Minimum Wage Fails to Keep Up with Cost of Living, Myanmar Labor Group Says." *Irrawaddy*, November 1, 2019. www.irrawaddy.com/news/burma/minimum-wage-fails-keep-cost-living-myanmar-labor-group-says.html?fbclid=IwAR3DYKXoovVR7SoUvI948zMGAgpkACgJXHA_Fl3gFhdYT1K-HDv6f_1ixBA.
Thein Pe Myint. *Indo-Burman Conflict*. Translated by Tin Htway. Passau: Myanmar Literature Project, University of Passau, (1938) 2008.
Thomas, Peter. *The Gramscian Moment: Philosophy, Hegemony, and Marxism*. Leiden: Brill, 2009.
Thompson, E.P. "The Moral Economy of the English Crowd in the Eighteenth Century," *Past & Present* 50 (1971): 76–136.
Transnational Institute. "Land Grabbing in Dawei (Myanmar/Burma): A (Inter)national Human Rights Concern." Yangon, 2012, https://www.tni.org/en/publication/land-grabbing-in-dawei.
Tripartite Core Group. *Post-Nargis Recovery and Preparedness Plan*. Yangon, December 2008. https://themimu.info/sites/themimu.info/files/documents/Ref_Doc_Post-Nargis_Recovery_and_Preparedness_Plan.pdf.
Tsing, Anna. *The Mushroom at the End of the World: On the Possibility of Life in Capitalist Ruins*. Durham: Duke University Press, 2015.
Turnell, Sean. *Fiery Dragons: Banks, Moneylenders and Microfinance in Burma*. Copenhagen: NiAS Press, 2009.
Turnell, Sean. "Myanmar's Fifty-Year Authoritarian Trap,. *Journal of International Affairs* 65, no. 1 (2011): 79–92.
UN Habitat, *Guidance Note on Land Acquisition in Myanmar*. Yangon: UN Habitat, 2010.
The Union of Myanmar Federation of Chambers of Commerce and Industry. "A Snapshot of Myanmar's Garment Industry." 2018. https://investmyanmar2019.com/garment-industry-cmp/myanmars-garment-industry/.
United Nations Human Rights Council. "Report of the Independent International Fact-Finding Mission on Myanmar." September 10–28, 2018. https://www.ohchr.org/Documents/HRBodies/HRCouncil/FFM-Myanmar/A_HRC_39_64.pdf.
van der Linden, Marcel. *Workers of the World: Essays toward a Global Labor History*. Leiden: Brill, 2013.
van der Linden, Marcel, and Karl Heinz Roth, eds. *Beyond Marx: Theorising the Global Labour Relations of the Twenty-First Century*. Leiden: Brill, 2014.
Vandergeest, Peter, and Melissa Marschke. "Modern Slavery and Freedom: Exploring Contradictions through Labour Scandals in the Thai Fisheries." *Antipode* 52, no.1 (2019): 291–315.
Vercellone, Carlo. "The New Articulation of Wages, Rent and Profit in Cognitive Capitalism." London: Queen Mary University School of Business and Management, February 2008. https://halshs.archives-ouvertes.fr/halshs-00265584/document.
Vogel, Lise. *Marxism and the Oppression of Women: Toward a Unitary Theory*. Leiden: Brill, 1983.

Vosko, Leah. *Managing the Margins: Gender, Citizenship, and the International Regulation of Precarious Employment.* Oxford: Oxford University Press, 2009.

Wa Lone. "Arrests and Clashes as Police Evicts Hundreds from Myanmar Slum." Reuters, June 12, 2017. www.reuters.com/article/us-myanmar-squatters/arrests-and-clashes-as-police-evicts-hundreds-from-myanmar-slum-idUSKBN1931VZ.

Wake, John. "The Debt Shift Theory of the Global Financial Crisis and the Great Real Estate Bubble." *Forbes*, March 15, 2019. www.forbes.com/sites/johnwake/2019/03/15/the-debt-shift-theory-of-the-great-financial-crisis-and-the-great-real-estate-bubble/#5444f86219d0.

Walker, Andrew. *Thailand's Political Peasants: Power in the Modern Rural Economy.* Madison: University of Wisconsin Press, 2012.

Wallerstein, Immanuel. *The Capitalist World Economy.* Cambridge: Cambridge University Press, 1979.

Wallerstein, Immanuel. *The Modern World-System I: Capitalist Agriculture and the Origins of the European World-Economy in the Sixteenth Century.* Cambridge: Academic Press, 1974.

Walton, Matthew. *Buddhism, Politics and Political Thought in Myanmar.* Cambridge: Cambridge University Press, 2016.

Weeks, Kathi. *The Problem with Work: Feminism, Marxism, Antiwork Politics, and Postwork Imaginaries.* Durham: Duke University Press, 2011.

Williams, Eric. *Capitalism and Slavery.* Chapel Hill: University of North Carolina Press, (1944) 1994.

Wintle, Justin. *Perfect Hostage: A Life of Aung San Suu Kyi, Burma's Prisoner of Conscience.* New York: Skyhorse, 2007.

Wolf, Eric. "Types of Latin American Peasantry: A Preliminary Discussion." *American Anthropologist* 57, no. 3 (1955): 452–471.

Wood, Ellen Meiksins. *The Origin of Capitalism: A Longer View.* London: Verso, 2002.

Wood, Ellen Meiksins. *The Ellen Meiksins Wood Reader.* Leiden: Brill, 2012.

Woods, Kevin. "Rubber Out of the Ashes: Locating Chinese Agribusiness Investments in 'Armed Sovereignties' in the Myanmar–China Borderlands." *Territory, Politics, Governance* 7, no. 1 (2019): 79–95.

Woods, Kevin. "Smaller-Scale Land Grabs and Accumulation from Below: Violence, Coercion and Consent in Spatially Uneven Agrarian Change in Shan State, Myanmar." *World Development* 127 (2020): 1–16.

World Bank Group. *A Country on the Move: Domestic Migration in Two Regions in Myanmar.* Yangon, 2016.

World Bank Group. "International Development Association Program Document for a Proposed Credit in the Amount of Equivalent to SDR 147.8 Million (USD 200 Million Equivalent) to the Republic of the Union of Myanmar for the First Macroeconomic Stability and Fiscal Resilience Development Policy Operation." Washington, DC, March 2017. http://documents.worldbank.org/curated/en/632531493517715510/pdf/113808-REVISED-OUO-9-MM-SRDPO-1-PD-04282017.pdf.

World Bank Group. "Myanmar: Ending Poverty and Boosting Shared Prosperity in a Time of Transition." Yangon, 2014. www.themimu.info/sites/themimu.info/files/documents/Report_A_Systematic_Country_Diagnostic_WorldBank_Nov2014.pdf.

World Bank Group. "Myanmar—Reengagement and Reform Support Credit: Summary of Discussion (English)." Yangon, 2013. http://documents.worldbank.org/curated/en/202781468053669202/Myanmar-Reengagement-and-Reform-Support-Credit-summary-of-discussion.

World Bank Group. "Myanmar and World Bank Sign Agreement for Budget Support to Accelerate Economic Changes Needed for Long-term Peace and Prosperity." 2017.

www.worldbank.org/en/news/press-release/2017/08/18/myanmar-and-world-bank-sign-agreement-for-budget-support-to-accelerate-economic-changes-needed-for-long-term-peace-and-prosperity.

Ye Naing. "Yangon Family Jailed for Severe Abuse of Child Servants." *Mizzima*, December 16, 2017. www.mizzima.com/news-domestic/yangon-family-jailed-severe-abuse-child-servants.

Ye Yint Khant Maung. "A New Way for Workers' Rights beyond the Legal Framework: The All Burma Federation of Trade Unionism." *Tea Circle*, October 14, 2019. https://teacircleoxford.com/2019/10/14/a-new-way-for-workers-rights-beyond-the-legal-framework-the-all-burma-federation-of-trade-unions/?fbclid=IwAR0v0hAqClZzHh56s-61q16aQ_mj8-cI3sue5dou1onmRHij-SHsw1AQK4g.

Yebaw Htun Oo. "The Emergence of the Working Class in Burma and the History of Working Class Activism." *Yaung Chi Oo Workers Association Journal*, April 2012.

Yin Nyein, and Sebastian Mathew. "The Tiger's Mouth: Myanmar Kyarr Phong Fishery." *Samudra Report* 75 (2017). www.icsf.net/es/samudra/detail/EN/4245.html.

Zaw Zaw Htwe. "Over 200 Workers Set Up Barricades around Factory." *Myanmar Times*, September 5, 2017. https://www.mmtimes.com/news/over-200-workers-set-barricades-around-factory.html.

Zaw Zaw Htwe, and Laignee Barron. "Factory Workers Wary of the Arbitration Council." *Myanmar Times*, September 25, 2015. www.mmtimes.com/index.php/national-news/16690-factory-workers-weary-of-the-arbitration-council.html.

Index

CPSIA information can be obtained
at www.ICGtesting.com
Printed in the USA
LVHW030449130722
723317LV00015B/205/J

9 781501 764882